This book explores the relationship between postmodernism and Christianity. Postmodernism regards Christianity as capable of being dismantled and demystified through an uncovering of its strict dualisms between body and soul, the temporal and the transcendental. Professor Ingraffia argues against the version of Christianity constructed by Nietzsche, Heidegger and Derrida. Through an exegesis of the New Testament, and wide reference to philosophers and theologians, Ingraffia argues that biblical theology must be separated from Greek and Modern metaphysics. He demonstrates how any attempted reconciliation between contemporary critical theory and biblical theology is radically misguided. Nietzsche, Heidegger, Derrida and many other representatives of post-modern thought have, he argues, actually absorbed the Judaeo-Christian tradition, thereby demonstrating its priority over secular attempts to displace it. Drawing upon the writings of Luther, Kierkegaard, Barth, Bonhoeffer, Niebuhr and Moltmann, Ingraffia argues that an "either/or" must be articulated between postmodern theory and biblical theology.

POSTMODERN THEORY
AND BIBLICAL THEOLOGY

POSTMODERN THEORY AND BIBLICAL THEOLOGY

Vanquishing God's shadow

BRIAN D. INGRAFFIA

Biola University

CAMBRIDGE
UNIVERSITY PRESS

Published by the Press Syndicate of the University of Cambridge
The Pitt Building, Trumpington Street, Cambridge CB2 1RP
40 West 20th Street, New York, NY 10011–4211, USA
10 Stemford Road, Oakleigh, Melbourne 3166, Australia

First published 1995

A catalogue record for this book is available from the British Library

Library of Congress cataloguing in publication data
Ingraffia, Brian D.
Postmodern theory and biblical theology: vanquishing God's shadow /
Brian D. Ingraffia.
p.   cm.
Includes bibliographical references.
ISBN 0 521 47136 2
1. Theology, Doctrinal – History – 20th century.
2. Postmodernism – Religious aspects – Christianity.
3. Liberalism (Religion) – Protestant churches – Controversial literature.
4. Deconstruction. 5. Bible – Theology.
I. Title.
BT28.I56   1995
230 – dc20   95-7999 CIP

ISBN 0 521 47136 2 hardback
ISBN 0 521 56840 4 paperback

Transferred to digital printing 2000

CE

For Ariella
in thanks for all her unselfish sacrifices
her undying encouragement
her eternal faith and hope
"Many women do noble things, but you surpass them all."

God is dead; but given the way of men, there may still be caves for thousands of years in which his shadow will be shown. – And we – we still have to vanquish his shadow, too.

Nietzsche, *The Gay Science*

What sort of faith is possible after the Freudian and Nietzschean critiques? ... a prophetic preaching that would return to the roots of Judeo-Christian faith and would also be a new beginning for our time ... It would adopt the same attitude in regard to the teleological metaphysics of Western philosophy that Job adopted in regard to the pious words of his friends concerning the god of retribution. It would be a faith that moves forward through the shadows.

Ricoeur, "Religion, Atheism, and Faith"

Contents

Contents

Acknowledgements

I thank my advisors at the University of California, Irvine, John Carlos Rowe, J. Hillis Miller and Stephen Barney; Professor Rowe for his many years of help as a guide through both the intellectual work and bureaucratic maze of graduate school; Professor Miller for his enthusiasm for this project and his help in finding a publisher for it; and Professor Barney for his kindness and graciousness toward me and his careful readings of my manuscript.

I would like to express my great appreciation for my colleague, Virginia Doland, for generously helping me make final revisions. Although I probably should have taken her advice more often, I thank her for helping make this a better book. As a mentor and a friend, she has been a true godsend.

I acknowledge Biola University for awarding me a research grant which provided me part-time release from teaching and research support for this work.

I also acknowledge my undergraduate professor, Walter Reed, who has been a role model for me in his teaching and scholarly writing.

Special thanks to my parents, who sacrificed so much for my education, for their financial and emotional support.

Thanks to my best friends, Wayne Iba and Todd Pickett, for their emotional and spiritual support.

And finally special thanks to my children, Jason, Jesse, and Samara Rose, for their patience as their Daddy worked so many days and nights on this project.

Abbreviations

Nietzsche's works are cited in the body of the text with either section number or page number in parentheses. Abbreviations of titles are followed by the section number in texts where sections are numbered consecutively throughout the translation (*AC, BGE, D, GS, HAH,* and *WP*). Abbreviations of titles are followed by page number if sections are not numbered consecutively throughout the translation (*EH, GM, TI,* and *Z*).

AC	*The Antichrist*
BGE	*Beyond Good and Evil*
D	*Daybreak*
EH	*Ecce Homo*
GM	*On the Genealogy of Morals*
GS	*The Gay Science*
HAH	*Human, All Too Human*
TI	*Twilight of the Idols*
WP	*The Will to Power*
Z	*Thus Spoke Zarathustra*

HEIDEGGER

BT	*Being and Time*
ER	*The Essence of Reasons*
ID	*Identity and Difference*
IM	*An Introduction to Metaphysics*
LH	"Letter on Humanism"
N I	*Nietzsche*, volume I: *The Will to Power as Art*

N II	*Nietzsche*, volume II: *The Eternal Recurrence of the Same*
N III	*Nietzsche*, volume III: *The Will to Power as Knowledge and Metaphysics*
N IV	*Nietzsche*, volume IV: *Nihilism*
OWL	*On the Way to Language*
PLT	*Poetry, Language, Thought*
PT	"Phenomenology and Theology"
QB	*The Question of Being*
QT	*The Question Concerning Technology*
WCT	*What Is Called Thinking?*

DERRIDA

A	*Aporias*
OAT	"Of an Apocalyptic Tone Recently Adopted in Philosophy"
D	"How to Avoid Speaking: Denials"
M	*Margins of Philosophy*
OG	*Of Grammatology*
OS	*Of Spirit*
Pos	*Positions*
SP	*Speech and Phenomenon*
WD	*Writing and Difference*

Note on translations of the Bible

I have used most often the New International Version when quoting from the New Testament. At times I have used the New American Standard Version. All quotations from the Bible were also compared to the original Hebrew or Greek through the use of *The Interlinear Hebrew–Greek–English Bible*.

Introduction: postmodernism, ontotheology, and Christianity

> It is necessary to say whom we consider our antithesis: it is the theologians and whatever has theologians' blood in its veins – and that includes our whole philosophy.
>
> Nietzsche, *The Antichrist*

> Christianity is bereft of the power it had during the Middle Ages *to shape history*. Its historical significance no longer lies in what it is able to fashion for itself, but in the fact that since the beginning of and throughout the modern age it has continued to be that *against which* the new freedom – whether expressly or not – must be distinguished.
>
> Heidegger, *Nietzsche*

> But it would not mean a single step outside of metaphysics if nothing more than a new motif of "return to finitude," of "God's death," etc., were the result of this move. It is that conceptuality and that problematics that must be deconstructed. They belong to the onto-theology they fight against.
>
> Derrida, *Of Grammatology*

THE MODERNIST GROUND OF POSTMODERN THEORY

In this study I seek to analyze critically the antipathy exhibited in postmodern theory toward theology. Whereas modernism tried to elevate man into God's place, postmodern theory seeks to destroy or deconstruct the very place and attributes of God. Heidegger uncovers the originality of postmodern thought in his description of Nietzsche's transvaluation: "With the downfall of the highest values also comes the elimination of the 'above' and the 'high' and the 'beyond,' the former *place* in which values could be posited" (*N* IV 49). Nietzsche calls this place the "shadow" of God which lingers after his death, and I argue in this study that postmodern

1

theory has been intent on completing Nietzsche's project of vanquishing God's shadow. Not only is God seen as a fiction or a
projection of man, as in modernism, but the Christian God is
rejected as a *bad* fiction. This is Nietzsche's claim to originality
against the Enlightenment attacks on Christianity: "That we find no
God – either in history or in nature or behind nature – is not what
differentiates *us*, but that we experience what has been revered as
God, not as 'godlike' but as miserable, as absurd, as harmful, not
merely as an error but as a *crime against life*. We deny God as God"
(*AC* 47).

This denial of God is reflected in postmodern theories of the
nature of language and truth. Lyotard has defined postmodernism
as the rejection of the metanarratives of modernism, "as incredulity
toward metanarratives." Modernism is therefore defined as "science
that legitimates itself with reference to a metadiscourse ... making
an explicit appeal to some grand narrative."[1] But what all these
grand narratives of modernism have in common is the attempt to
replace the grand narrative which had legitimated knowledge in the
Western world for over a millennium: biblical narrative.

Auerbach describes how in the Christian era the Bible was the
foundation for Western society's interpretation of human existence
and history. He argues that the Bible makes claims within itself to be
the grand metanarrative of both history and individual lives. The
biblical text "seeks to overcome our reality: we are to fit our own
reality into its world, feel ourselves to be elements in its structure of
universal history."[2] And during the Christian era the Bible was read
in just this way. "But when, through too great a change in environment and through the awakening of a critical consciousness, this
becomes impossible, the biblical claim to absolute authority is jeop-
ardized; the method of interpretation scorned and rejected, the
biblical stories become ancient legends."[3] Hans Frei, in *The Eclipse
of Biblical Narrative*, describes in detail this loss of belief in the literal
truth and authority of the biblical texts. He describes how the
"breakdown of literal-realistic interpretation of biblical stories"
caused a "reversal in the direction of interpretation that accom-
panied the distancing between the narratively depicted world and
the 'real' world."[4] Instead of the world and individual experience
being interpreted on the basis of Scripture, the biblical texts are
judged and criticized on the basis of the interpreter's own understanding of the world and human experience.

Recall how many major works from the modern, Western philosophical canon perform this reversal, this critique of biblical authority on the basis of modern rationalism and empiricism. Spinoza's *Tractatus Theologico-Politicus* and Hobbes' *Leviathan* both contain long sections which attack the orthodox reading of the Bible. The epistemology of both rationalism and empiricism, as in the writings of Locke and Hume, worked to undermine belief in divine revelation and miracles; consequently, both the authority and content of the biblical gospels were attacked. The German higher criticism, building upon the work of English deism, worked diligently to undermine the belief in the historical validity of the New Testament. Nietzsche may argue that "German philosophy is at bottom ... an *insidious* theology" and castigate "our whole philosophy" for having "theologians' blood in its veins" (*AC* 8), but it would be more true to assert that this whole philosophy, including Nietzsche's own, has had theological *antibodies* in its veins, if we define "theology" as Christian theology. Nietzsche himself asserts that "Modern philosophy, being an epistemological skepticism, is, covertly or overtly, *anti-Christian*" (*BGE* 54). Heidegger echoes this analysis, writing that "since the beginning of and throughout the modern age it [Christianity] has continued to be that *against which* the new freedom – whether expressly or not – must be distinguished" (*N* IV 99). To adapt for a moment the vocabulary of Harold Bloom, Christianity has been the greatest and most enduring source of modern philosophy's anxiety of influence.

Two brief examples will help illustrate my point. Heidegger claims that modern philosophy has defined its freedom, "whether expressly or not," against Christianity. Both Descartes and Feuerbach seek to free modern philosophy from subordination to biblical authority, but Feuerbach seeks this freedom overtly while Descartes seeks this freedom covertly.

René Descartes, often considered the founder of modern philosophy, introduces his *Meditations on First Philosophy* with the following claim: "I have always thought that two questions – that of God and that of the soul – are chief among those that ought to be demonstrated by the aid of philosophy rather than theology."[5] However these questions are answered, whether God's existence is asserted or denied, whether the soul is considered a real unity or a dispersed fiction, these words can stand as an epigraph to both modern philosophy and postmodern theory. In both periods, philosophy stands as judge over the basic questions concerning God and man.

Descartes grounds all knowledge in the certainty of man's subjective existence. The existence of God is proven afterwards and is dependent on this first proof of the existence of the *Cogito*. Heidegger highlights Descartes' break with the "Christian medieval age."

> In the context of man's liberation from the bonds of revelation and church doctrine, the question of first philosophy is "In what way does man, on his own terms and for himself, first arrive at a primary, unshakable truth, and what is that primary truth?" Descartes was the first to ask the question in a clear and decisive way. (*N* iv 89)

Only after demonstrating that man's ego is *res cogitans* does Descartes, in his fourth meditation, attempt to prove the existence of God. But this specious proof of God's existence serves only to ground the validity of the *Cogito*'s reason, the very thing that proves God's existence. It is not the biblical God whose existence is proven, but rather the god of metaphysics, the god of ontotheology.

It is my contention that the god of ontotheology, no matter how descriptions of this god may differ, is always the product of human reason, is always the result of humanity's attempt to formulate an understanding of god rather than the result of God's revelation towards us. In Descartes' ontotheology, God is merely the metaphysical ground for the operation of the independent, autonomous ego.

Feuerbach openly asserts what Descartes only implies, that the "reason is not dependent on God, but God on the reason."[6] As is well known, Feuerbach argues that man has falsely projected his own value upon God. "To enrich God, man must become poor; that God may be all, man must be nothing."[7] Feuerbach calls for the reversal of this projection, for man to take back the values he has given to God. All statements about God are to be translated into statements about man. In this way, the divinity of man is asserted as man is called upon to take God's place.

Feuerbach's opposition to Christian theology, his view of God as an imaginary projection of man, was adopted by the three great masters of the hermeneutics of suspicion at the end of the nineteenth and beginning of the twentieth century.[8] Nietzsche, Marx, and Freud each adapted and made specific Feuerbach's analysis of the essence of religion. But what must be emphasized is that the

God which Feuerbach demystified was the god of ontotheology. His language in *The Essence of Christianity* makes this clear:

God as God, that is, as a being not finite, not human, not materially conditioned, not phenomenal, is only an object of thought. He is the incorporeal, formless, incomprehensible – the abstract, negative being: he is known, *i.e.*, becomes an object, only by abstraction and negation (*via negationis*) ... God, said the schoolmen, the Christian fathers, and long before them the heathen philosophers, – God is immaterial essence, intelligence, spirit, pure understanding.[9]

Although Feuerbach includes the Christian God in this description, it is only the Christian God that has been understood through Greek conceptuality. The God of the Bible may have been confused or even falsely equated with the God of Greek philosophy by many of the Church Fathers and medieval theologians, but only after the advent of modern philosophy does the god of ontotheology replace the God of the Bible.

Although Feuerbach makes no room for this distinction, it is not the God of biblical revelation who is unmasked as a projection of man, but only the god of ontotheology, the god which replaced the biblical God in Descartes.

Thus the understanding is the *ens realissimum*, the most real being of the old ontotheology. "Fundamentally," says onto-theology, "we cannot conceive God otherwise than by attributing to him without limit all the real qualities which we find in ourselves."[10]

Thus says ontotheology, but the Bible asserts that God must be revealed to us. Jürgen Moltmann agrees that "Feuerbach knows only the God of dogmatic philosophy and natural religion, for it is only this God in his abstract identity that can be reduced to man."[11] Karl Barth makes the same argument in his effort to reverse the direction of ontotheology.

That there is no God may perhaps apply to the deity of philosophy, or to a deity that might be regarded as the common denominator of the gods of the different religions, or to a deity that demonstrates its existence by having a place in a world-view of human construction, or even perhaps to the "God" who is in one way or another poorly proclaimed and understood in some Christian tradition or theology. The atheistic negation applies to a "God" who, if he exists, must do so in the same way as the data of other human experience or the contents of other human reflection exist for people. The true and living God, however, is not a "datum" of ours.[12]

All of these gods listed by Barth which are overcome by the atheistic negation belong to ontotheology, since all these gods are projections of human thought and desire, but the modern iconoclasts of ontotheology uncritically extend their destruction of the gods of ontotheology to the biblical God. However, it must be remembered that ontotheology either opposes the God of the Bible as primitive or sublimates the biblical God into an ontotheological god.

Postmodern theory not only continues the modern opposition to Christian theology, but also goes on to criticize the secularization of Christian theology in modern ontotheology. However, postmodern theory relies on the ontotheology it deconstructs for its rejection of biblical Christianity. The rejection of Christianity in both modernism and postmodernism has been for the most part based upon a profound misunderstanding of biblical revelation. Christian faith has all too easily been conflated with ontotheology in modernism and then criticized for being ontotheology in postmodernism.

Theology continues to be that against which postmodernism defines its freedom: the freedom to create one's own values set against submission to an absolute truth, the autonomy of human beings set against obedience to a transcendent God, and the free play of interpretation set against belief in any final, authoritative meaning. Barthes, one of the founders of the post-structuralist movement, articulates the anti-theological thrust of postmodern thought:

> writing ceaselessly posits meaning ceaselessly to evaporate it, carrying out a systematic exemption of meaning. In precisely this way literature (it would be better from now on to say *writing*), by refusing to assign a "secret," an ultimate meaning, to the text (and to the world as text), liberates what might be called an anti-theological activity . . . since to refuse to fix meaning is, in the end, to refuse God.[13]

The death of God, the refusal of God, means that the interpretation of our existence and our world, and even our interpretation of interpretation itself, must be radically changed. If God is that which fixes human meaning, as ontotheology claims, then the absence of a God means that human meaning is unfounded and plays upon an abyss.

Foucault follows Nietzsche and Barthes in seeking an understanding of writing which is released from the problematics of theology. Although Foucault, like Derrida, seeks to go beyond the motifs of man's finitude and God's death, both authors still regard the need to separate postmodern thought from theology as an imperative. As Foucault writes:

In granting a primordial status to writing, do we not, in effect, simply reinscribe in transcendental terms the theological affirmation of its sacred origin or a critical belief in its creative nature? To say that writing, in terms of the particular history it made possible, is subjected to forgetfulness and repression, is this not to reintroduce in transcendental terms the religious principle of hidden meanings (which require interpretation) and the critical assumption of implicit significations, silent purposes, and obscure contents (which give rise to commentary)?[14]

Even though Foucault is seeking to criticize Derrida's deconstructive program for being subconsciously theological, the unspoken and uncritically foundational assumption in both Foucault and Derrida is that the theological is necessarily to be avoided. The theological is that which must not be approximated in any sense.[15] God's shadow must be vanquished.

But what sort of theology are these writers trying to avoid? The uncritical use of the general term "theology" would seem to imply that all theology is meant. Why is all theology bad? Why have postmodern theorists defined theology as their enemy?

NIETZSCHE/HEIDEGGER/DERRIDA ON ONTOTHEOLOGY

All three of the figures focused upon in this study are united in their attack upon metaphysics as ontotheological, though each accounts for the birth and essence of the ontotheological character of Western metaphysics in a distinctive way.

Nietzsche locates the origin of metaphysics in the distinction between two worlds, a true and an apparent world. Following Feuerbach, Nietzsche believes that man has falsely projected his values upon God and upon a true, divine world. According to Nietzsche, this true world is invented by man because he is weak and powerless in this one; therefore, he invents a realm in which the fearful powers of this world are negated. God serves as the negation and indictment of our life and world; therefore, we must kill this God in order to become free to affirm the actual world. Through the death of God and the abolition of the true world, the metaphysical distinction between a true and an apparent world collapses, and along with it collapses all the metaphysical and anthropological dualisms which are dependent upon this distinction. Nietzsche desires to abolish theology's true world because it has served to denigrate the actual world.

Nietzsche focuses his attack upon the "Christian-moral interpretation of the world," or what he derides as "monotonotheism" (*TI* 480). For Nietzsche this is the prime example of a worldview which relies upon the distinction between two worlds. It is Nietzsche's primary example not because the Judaeo-Christian interpretation of the world was the first to negate this world in order to invent another world better suited to human needs, but because it was the first to negate this world in order to take revenge upon the world out of *ressentiment*. Christian theology is considered by Nietzsche to be the strongest opponent to his own affirmation of the actual, natural world because of the virulence of its attack on the natural world and because of the power of its continuing influence on the modern understanding of the world in secular thought systems. Nietzsche believed that he could abolish the distinction between a true and an apparent world only through an overcoming of the Christian-moral interpretation of the world.

While Nietzsche seeks to abolish the distinction between a true and an apparent world, Heidegger seeks to reinscribe a distinction, i.e., the ontological difference between Being and beings. Heidegger wants to destroy the theological character of metaphysics because it forgets this difference in defining Being as a being, as the efficient cause of beings. According to Heidegger, the divinity enters into metaphysics in order to account for the Being of beings.

When metaphysics thinks of beings as such as a whole, that is, with respect to the highest being which accounts for everything, then it is logic as theologic. (*ID* 71)

It is this theo-logic which causes the reliance upon the metaphor of height, the "most high," upon transcendence as the source and guarantor of truth. Like Nietzsche, Heidegger seeks to destroy this theological character of metaphysics which defines God and his transcendence.

In the place of a theological transcendence which defines the position of God, the *ens increatum*, above man, the *ens creatum*, Heidegger formulates the ontological difference, based upon the relationship between human *Dasein* and Being, in which transcendence defines not the place of God above man, but rather designates man's ability, in his essence as *Dasein*, to differentiate between Being and beings.

Transcendence can be understood in a second sense . . . namely, as signifying what is unique to *human Dasein* – unique not as one among other possible, and occasionally actualized, types of behavior but as a *basic constitutive feature of Dasein*. (*ER* 35–37)

Although Heidegger argues vehemently that this is not merely a secularization of theological transcendence, Feuerbach's basic premise remains here in disguised form. It is clear that in Heidegger's redefinition, transcendence has been transferred from a theological to an anthropological term, from a term used to describe God's position above man to one used to describe a "basic constitutive feature" of human Dasein. Therefore the analysis of Dasein, the destruction of the metaphysical definition of man as *animal rationale*, as body and soul, plays a central role in Heidegger's destruction of ontotheology. "Thus an analytic of Dasein must remain our first requirement in the question of Being" (*BT* 37).

Derrida deconstructs ontotheology not through identifying metaphysics as the forgetting of the ontico-ontological difference or as the denigration of the natural world, but rather by defining metaphysics as the debasement of writing. Both Heidegger and Derrida are questioning the privileging of "presence" by ontotheology, but Heidegger looks first to the description of human being while Derrida begins with the description of writing in order to deconstruct the metaphysics of presence. By focusing not upon the metaphysical character of ontology, as Heidegger does in *Being and Time*, but upon the metaphysical character of linguistics, as Derrida does in *Of Grammatology*, Derrida's critique of transcendence in metaphysics takes the form of a deconstruction of philosophy's irrepressible desire for a "transcendental signified," which in exceeding or transcending the play of language serves as the source and guarantor of truth. Like Nietzsche, Derrida questions the belief in a transcendental realm, here a transcendental source of meaning, which seeks to impose a final, true interpretation of the world, or in Derrida's problematic, of the text. In many ways, Derrida's project can be read as an elucidation of Nietzsche's remark that "I am afraid we are not rid of God because we still have faith in grammar" (*TI* 483).

Just as Heidegger reads Nietzsche as the last metaphysician, despite Nietzsche's efforts to abolish metaphysics, so does Derrida place Heidegger within the ontotheological tradition he works to destroy:

The ontico-ontological difference and its ground (*Grund*) in the "transcendence of Dasein" . . . are not absolutely originary. Differance by itself would be more "originary," but one would no longer be able to call it "origin" or "ground," those notions belonging essentially to the history of onto-theology. (*OG* 23)

Not the interpretation of Being, but rather the interpretation of the sign is the source of metaphysics' reliance on divinity, on a transcendent God. "The sign and divinity have the same place and time of birth. The age of the sign is essentially theological" (*OG* 14). Consequently, for Derrida it is not the Christian-moral interpretation of the world or the ontotheological conception of man, but rather the logocentric conception of the sign which must first be deconstructed:

It is thus the idea of the sign that must be deconstructed through a meditation upon writing which would merge, as it must, with the undoing of onto-theology. (*OG* 73)

Derrida therefore begins by deconstructing the metaphysical conception of the sign as signifier and signified in linguistics and as letter and spirit in theology.

To summarize: Nietzsche mocks the "monotono-theism" of Western thought through an attack upon the distinction between a true and apparent world, privileging the example of the Christian-moral interpretation of the world. Heidegger destroys the ontotheological character of metaphysics through a questioning of the ontico-ontological difference, privileging the example of *Dasein*. Derrida deconstructs ontotheology through an attack on the metaphysical conception of writing, privileging the example of the linguistic sign. All three thinkers attack the ontotheological character of Western metaphysics and consider Christian theology an exemplar of ontotheological discourse.

NIETZSCHE/HEIDEGGER/DERRIDA ON CHRISTIANITY

My final purpose in studying these three attacks on ontotheology is to understand better these thinkers' attitude toward Christianity. These philosophers are, in a sense, twice removed from the Christian era. The reinterpretation of biblical theology as ontotheology in modernism has greatly influenced their understanding of Judaeo-Christianity. I seek to define how these thinkers' dismantling of ontotheology is related to, how it affects, Christian or what I will call, in an effort to distinguish it from ontotheology, biblical theology.

Nietzsche's position on the relationship between Christianity and ontotheology is the most unambiguous. Although many critics, including Heidegger, seek to deny this, I argue in the first section of this work that Nietzsche clearly equates Christianity and metaphysical theology by focusing on the distinction between two worlds in each. "Every philosophy ... that knows some *finale*, some final state of some sort, every predominantly aesthetic or religious craving for some Apart, Beyond, Outside, Above" is rejected as a symptom of decadence by Nietzsche (*GS* "Preface" 2). Christianity is included, as is clear when Nietzsche asserts that "Christianity is Platonism for 'the people'" (*BGE* "Preface"). Because Christianity becomes his prime example of the ignoble origins and nihilistic consequences of the distinction between two worlds, it should be acknowledged without any reservations that Nietzsche unequivocally rejects Christian theology in all its forms.

Heidegger, on the other hand, makes a distinction between Christian theology as ontotheology and Christian theology as the expression of Christian faith. Although his rejection of the former is unequivocal, his attitude toward Christian faith is more ambiguous. Heidegger separates his own thinking from Christian faith through a number of rhetorical strategies. In both his early and later writings, he argues that the thought of Being and the faith of Christianity belong to two separate spheres, spheres which cannot be brought into relation because philosophy and faith speak different languages. It is my contention that both before and after his *Kehre*, Heidegger turns his back on the Catholic faith of his childhood and the Christian theology of his education. In the second section of my work I will concentrate upon the early writings of Heidegger, arguing that the theological readings of the early Heidegger in the second half of the twentieth century reached some disastrous conclusions. My rereading of the early Heidegger is in many ways supported by the renewed emphasis upon the young Heidegger's involvement in National Socialism. In my conclusion, I will turn to the later Heidegger, showing that Derrida correctly asserts that Heidegger continues to deny his Christian origins even as he awaits a revelation from the "divine God."

Heidegger's separation of his work from Christian theology leads him to disclaim that:

Someone who has experienced theology in his own roots, both the theology of the Christian faith and that of philosophy, would today rather remain silent about God when he is speaking in the realm of thinking (*ID* 54).

But, while Heidegger may claim to prefer to remain silent about God, in the same essay he claims that his "god-less thinking is more open to Him ['the divine God'] than onto-theo-logic would like to admit" (*ID* 72). And Heidegger is clearly not silent about the possibilities of a Christian philosophy. Through a reading of Paul's formulation of a Christian destruction of philosophy in 1 Corinthians, a reading he repeats in a number of his works, Heidegger concludes that the idea of a Christian philosophy is as foolish as the idea of a "round square" (*IM* 7).

But most persistently Heidegger argues that while his fundamental ontology makes no claims for or against faith, theology, as the thinking elaboration of faith, must adopt his ontological analysis in order to make itself conceptually understood. Heidegger defines theology as an ontic science (PT), and, since his fundamental ontology is supposed to "run ahead of the positive sciences" and lay their foundation (*BT* 30), theology must look to fundamental ontology for the foundation of its concepts. Yet in the same period of his thought, Heidegger claims that biblical revelation "cannot even be brought into relation with our question" (*IM* 7). I will argue, therefore, that the theology for which Heidegger lays the conceptual foundation cannot be biblical; the "divine God" which his later thinking approaches – while distinct in some ways from the god of philosophy, the ontotheological god – cannot be the Living God revealed in the Bible.

Derrida, on the other hand, makes no claims that his work can be used in any theology, whether traditional or new, but in his deconstruction of ontotheology he treats Christian theology as a prime example of logocentric metaphysics. When giving an overview of his project in *Of Grammatology*, he attempts to dismantle the Judaeo-Christian roots of metaphysics through his deconstruction of the Book of books, of truth proceeding from the logos, and of the transcendental signified. It is true that most of the examples through which he deconstructs these concepts are taken from modern, rationalistic ontotheology, but while focusing on the "book of reason," Derrida claims in one of his meditations on writing that the loss of the Jewish God is the source of the disruption caused by the knowledge that "the Book does not exist and that forever there are books."

[To write] is not only to have lost the theological certainty of seeing every page bind itself into the unique text of the truth, the "book of reason" . . . This lost certainty, this absence of divine writing, that is to say, *first of all, the absence of the Jewish God,* does not solely and vaguely define something like "modernity." As the absence and haunting of the divine sign, it regulates all modern criticism and aesthetics. (My emphasis; *WD* 10)

The book of reason is read as a continuing shadow of the Jewish God of the Bible. Both books seek to ground human meaning in the truth of a transcendental signified. I argue in my third section that, although he is less directly hostile to Christianity, Derrida, like Nietzsche, conflates Christian theology and ontotheology.

Nietzsche, Heidegger, and Derrida all tend to confront the "epoch of Christian creationism and infinitism when these appropriate the resources of Greek conceptuality" (*OG* 13). All three condemn Christian theology for its inability to guard against foreign philosophical influences. Heidegger acknowledges Christianity's difference from ontotheology in his separation of Christian theology and Christian faith. Nietzsche begins to specify this difference when he asserts that "the earliest Christianity uses only Jewish-Semitic concepts" (*AC* 32). None of these writers, however, gives any attention to an understanding of this original Judaeo-Christian thought; therefore, when these philosophers claim to have performed a de(con)struction of the whole of Western thought, their projects are severely limited by being blind to one of the most powerful influences on this thought.

It is my contention, and in making this distinction these thinkers would apparently agree with me, that a Christian tradition can be identified which resists the influence of Greek and modern metaphysics. As Derrida responds when Richard Kearney presses him to consider this distinction: "one can argue that these original, heterogeneous elements of Judaism and Christianity were never completely eradicated by Western metaphysics. They perdure throughout the centuries, threatening and unsettling the assured 'identities' of Western philosophy."[16] I will argue that the source of these "original, heterogeneous elements" is the Scriptures of the Judaeo-Christian Bible; therefore, I will compare the attack upon the ontotheological dualisms rejected by each thinker with the related concepts in the Bible. I compare Nietzsche's abolition of the distinction between two worlds with the New Testament distinction between this world (the present age) and the age to come. I compare Heidegger's analysis of *Dasein*, his distinction between inauthenticity and authenticity, with St. Paul's anthropology, his distinction between the flesh and the Spirit. And finally I compare Derrida's deconstruction of the signifier/signified dichotomy with the distinction between the letter and the Spirit in Pauline hermeneutics. Thus, the biblical view of the world, humanity, and language will be compared with the de(con)struction of the metaphysical understanding of these concepts by the three figures I consider to be the founders of postmodern theory.

Most work on postmodernism and theology to date seeks a reconciliation between these two discourses, a postmodern theology of some sort (even if this be an "a/theology"). In Western intellectual thought, this unavoidably means some sort of secularized, "demythologized" or "radical" Christianity. I seek to deny the possibility of such a synthesis, to set up an either/or between postmodern thought and biblical theology. Following in the tradition of Paul, Pascal, Luther, Kierkegaard, Barth, Bonhoeffer, and more recently Jürgen Moltmann, I seek to separate the God of the Bible from the god of the philosophers, for it is the confusion between these two Gods which has caused Christianity to be uncritically equated with ontotheology.[17]

It is undeniable that the early Church Fathers often used Greek conceptuality and philosophy to articulate their faith. While this may have been an effective method of explaining the gospel to a Greco-Roman audience, it often led to the loss of the distinctively Judaeo-Christian tradition articulated in the narratives, poetry and epistles of the Bible. Similarly, the most influential contemporary academic theologians have followed the latest trends in philosophy in order to articulate their faith, as Altizer has done in using Nietzsche to formulate his death of God theology, as Bultmann has used Heidegger to demythologize the New Testament, and as Mark C. Taylor has used Derridean deconstruction to formulate a postmodern a/theology.

It is this synthesis between biblical theology and philosophy, whether this philosophy be ontotheological or anti-ontotheological, which must be teased apart. Although I must confess with Barth that this process can never be complete – "In no case does anyone have the right ... to pride himself ... as though he were completely rid of the Greek influence, as though he did not confuse his Weltanschauung with the New Testament, but rather allowed the text alone to speak for itself"[18] – I believe and hope to demonstrate that the strands can be separated to a large extent.[19] When the original Judaeo-Christian revelation is separated from its synthesis with Greek and modern rationalisms, we are left with a wisdom which can be used to criticize modern ontotheology, but which is separate from and resists the postmodern critique of ontotheology.

PART ONE

Nietzsche's mockery: the rejection of transcendence

The critic of Christianity cannot be spared the task of making Christianity look *contemptible*.

Nietzsche, *The Antichrist*

CHAPTER I

The death of God: loss of belief in the Christian God as the cause of nihilism

> The greatest recent event – that "God is dead," that the belief in the Christian god has become unbelievable – is already beginning to cast its first shadows over Europe ... The event itself is far too great, too distant, too remote from the multitude's capacity for comprehension even for the tidings of it to be thought of as having *arrived* as yet. Much less may one suppose that many people know as yet *what* this event really means.
>
> Nietzsche, *The Gay Science*

This reading of Nietzsche attempts to take seriously his critique and rejection of Christianity. There has been a strong tendency in Nietzsche criticism, especially since Heidegger, to ignore or, at least, to diminish the importance of Nietzsche's indictment of Christianity. There are several strategies and rationales for doing so.

One of the oldest strategies for avoiding an analysis of Nietzsche's denunciation of Christianity illustrates the triumph of his attack. Nietzsche describes in *The Gay Science* how a change in intellectual "taste" is brought about:

What changes the general taste? The fact that some individuals who are powerful and influential announce without any shame, *hoc est ridiculum, hoc est absurdum*, in short, the judgement of their taste and nausea; and then they enforce it tyrannically. (*GS* 39)

Later in this same work he applies this principle to Christianity: "*Against Christianity.* – What is now decisive against Christianity is our taste, no longer our reasons" (*GS* 132).

H. L. Mencken typifies this response to Christianity which sees in Nietzsche an ally in the completed, modern emancipation from religion. "Today a literal faith in the gospel narrative is confined to ecclesiastical reactionaries, pious old ladies and men about to be hanged."[1] Mencken here echoes Nietzsche's remark that "it is indecent to be a Christian today" (*AC* 38). This reading suggests that Nietzsche's "taste" has hardened into an acceptable prejudice. As René Girard describes the situation in Nietzsche scholarship regarding Nietzsche's anti-Christianity (in opposition to the critical response regarding Nietzsche's supposed anti-Semitism): "Why should Nietzsche be exonerated from an attitude that a majority of intellectuals regarded as sound?"[2]

Another way of discounting the seriousness and vehemence of Nietzsche's attack on Christianity is typified by G. Wilson Knight in his book, *Christ and Nietzsche*. Knight sees Nietzsche as attacking only the contemporary Christian church. Nietzsche's doctrines, as presented in *Thus Spoke Zarathustra*, are, according to this reading, not only compatible with Christianity, but are even a call to the original message of the New Testament. Once his criticisms are read as directed against the contemporary church alone, Knight can conclude that "there is little real divergence between *Thus Spake Zarathustra* and the New Testament."[3]

Similar to Knight's interpretation of Zarathustra as a Christian Reformer is the vision conjured up by the "death of God" theology, led by Thomas J. J. Altizer. Altizer does not attempt to reconcile Nietzsche/Zarathustra with a reformed orthodoxy or with the New Testament, but he does see Nietzsche/Zarathustra as a prophet of a new "radical Christian vision" who reveals the true Christ.[4] While appreciating Nietzsche's attack on traditional, ecclesiastical Christianity, Altizer aligns Nietzsche with Hegel and Blake as prophets of a radically unorthodox but nevertheless "uniquely Christian movement of faith." Altizer, like Knight, is misled by the parallels between Zarathustra and Jesus, especially the Jesus presented in *The Antichrist*, whom Nietzsche opposes to the Christ of the New Testament. Ignoring Nietzsche's critique of his Jesus as a decadent type, Altizer interprets "Zarathustra as a radical Christian image of Jesus."[5] Altizer objects that on "every side, scholarly critics and theologians point to Nietzsche's vision of Eternal Recurrence as the antithetical opposite of the Christian gospel ... [and] judge Zarathustra as the Antichrist,"[6] but in reviewing the Nietzsche criticism written after Kaufmann's influential defense of Nietzsche, I have found this statement to be false. On the contrary, viewing Nietzsche as an enemy of Christianity, radical or orthodox, a view which I will show Nietzsche himself endorsed vehemently, has come to be the exception rather than the rule. Even in his own day, Nietzsche could write that "the most serious Christians have always been well disposed toward me" (*EH* 233).

These attempts at noting the positive relation between Nietzsche/ Zarathustra and Jesus were perhaps begun by the influential reading of Karl Jaspers. Jaspers, better informed about Nietzsche's work as a whole than Knight, and a more careful reader of this work than Altizer, writes that he does not want to "blunt" Nietzsche's attacks on Christianity, but his reading has the effect of doing just that. In his preface Jaspers writes that his purpose is "to show how much of a Christian he is, this 'Anti-Christ' Nietzsche," arguing that only "superficial readers blinded by his aggressive extremism can see in him nothing but hostility to all things Christian."[7]

In order to justify his characterization of Nietzsche as "a Christian" in his motives, Jaspers relies on the statements by Nietzsche in which he ties his attack on Christianity with the "honesty" which he was taught by Christian morality. As Jaspers summarizes, "Christian impulses – that is to say, the ultimate moral intensification of truthfulness – have always led to a Christian battle against the realities of Christendom."[8] But this equation between Nietzsche's battle against Christianity and a Kierkegaardian attack upon Christendom does not take into account Nietzsche's curse upon *Christianity*, not just Christendom.

Like the other writers on Nietzsche with Christian sympathies mentioned .above, Jaspers points out the difference between Nietzsche's attack on Christ and his appreciation of Jesus in *The Antichrist*. Jaspers is aware, however, that Nietzsche criticizes even his own picture of Jesus as a decadent, and he criticizes Nietzsche's representation of the "true" Jesus as incomplete, unhistorical, and psychologically improbable; nevertheless, he can write in his preface that "Jesus halts even Nietzsche's attack ... Nietzsche is stirred by the inner consistency of a man whom nothing could sway, and he bows to the truthfulness of Jesus." But it would be more correct to say that Jesus at best diverts Nietzsche's attack. Nietzsche appreciates Jesus only in order to pit him against Christian scripture, theology, and church. He is not stirred by Jesus' inner consistency, but is rather appalled at his naïveté and his weakness. He does not bow to the truthfulness of Jesus, but has Jesus bow to the superior truthfulness of Zarathustra.[9]

Jaspers supports his reading of Nietzsche's admiration for Jesus by pointing out the parallels between Nietzsche's description of the

"real" Jesus in *The Antichrist* and Nietzsche's own self-descriptions in
Ecce Homo. He also points out Nietzsche's identification with "the
Crucified" in the signatures of some of his final letters. But these
parallels, like those between Zarathustra and Jesus, are not intended
in praise of Jesus, but rather in order for Nietzsche to characterize
himself as a *replacement* for Jesus as the most important world-histori-
cal figure. For example, rather than having Jesus be the fixed point
by which time is measured (B.C./A.D.), Nietzsche argues that his
unmasking of the nihilism of Christian morality should be the point
by which time is measured from now on.

The uncovering of Christian morality is an event without parallel, a real
catastrophe. He that is enlightened about that, is a *force majeure*, a destiny –
he breaks the history of mankind in two. One lives before him, or one lives
after him. (*EH* 333)

The same claim is made in *The Antichrist*, in direct opposition to the
Christian reckoning of time:

And time is reckoned from the *dies nefastus* with which this calamity began –
after the *first* day of Christianity! *Why not rather after its last day? After today?*
(*AC* 62)

By not taking Nietzsche's contempt for Christianity seriously
enough, Jaspers misreads his allusions to the Bible and Christian
tradition as pointing to an affinity between Nietzsche's and the
Bible's doctrines.

   One of the few Nietzsche interpreters to understand correctly the
purpose behind Nietzsche's biblical allusions is Karl Löwith. One
example will suffice at this point to show how Löwith identifies
Nietzsche's allusions to Christian, biblical symbols without reading
these allusions as attempts to restore or raise up Christianity. Löwith
sees that Nietzsche *mocks* Christianity and sets his own ideas in direct
opposition to Christian theology. For example, Löwith shows how:

Zarathustra mocks Christ's crown of thorns by crowning himself with a
crown of roses ... Zarathustra's "rosewreath crown" is purely a polemic
contrast to that of the crucified. This perversion is the final end of the
symbol of the cross with roses, which derives from Luther![10]

This reading of Nietzsche's allusions to Christian symbols as part of
a parodic mockery and anti-Christian polemic is the exception
rather than the rule.

More common is Gadamer's judgment of the importance of the anti-Christian polemic of *Zarathustra*:

On a first reading, one will read the book as the announcement of new tables of values that are set up in opposition to the old, Christian values. This reading is certainly not false, but it is somewhat superficial in contrast to the drama whose events are recounted in this book.[11]

This is reminiscent of Jaspers' conclusion that Nietzsche's psychological unmasking of Christian morality and his anti-Christianity as a whole are merely "surface appearances."[12]

Perhaps the most influential Nietzsche scholar who appears to oppose this designation of Nietzsche's anti-Christianity as a mere surface appearance is Walter Kaufmann. In the preface to the first edition of his major work on Nietzsche, Kaufmann writes that the "temptation to eschew any extended treatment of Nietzsche's attack on Christianity had to be resisted because he himself defined his historical significance in terms of this issue, and his philosophy cannot be understood apart from it."[13] (Note that this is a "temptation" which had to be "resisted.") But later, in discussing this attack on Christianity in his reading of *The Antichrist*, Kaufmann denies that this attack should be critically assessed: "Whether Nietzsche's attack on Christianity is tenable need not be discussed here."[14] Against this denial, I believe that Nietzsche's philosophy cannot be understood without a critical appraisal of his attack on Christianity because, as Kaufmann himself asserts: "he himself defined his historical significance in terms of this issue, and his philosophy cannot be understood apart from it."

By not taking Nietzsche's anti-Christianity seriously, Kaufmann is led into misreadings of both the biblical gospels and Nietzschean texts, brought about by an approximation of one to the other, especially in regard to his reading of *Zarathustra*. Kaufmann argues that "the Bible," like Zarathustra, "also considered self-perfection the ideal goal of human effort"[15] – thus ignoring the vast differences between the self-striving of the overman and the Pauline doctrine of salvation by grace. Again, Nietzsche's "polemics" are read as surface phenomena which "obscure his basic contention."[16] Once again, Nietzsche is turned into an underhanded Christian: "In his keen appreciation of suffering and self-sacrifice as indispensable conditions of self-perfection, Nietzsche seems more 'Christian' than most philosophers."[17]

Relying on a comparison with Kierkegaard,[18] Kaufmann reads Nietzsche's polemics as being directed only against Christendom:

What he denounces is not sincere Christianity, but insincere Christianity – those who are unchristian in their practice but nevertheless profess Christianity, as well as those who superficially seem Christian in their practice but whose motivation and state of mind are essentially unchristian.[19]

Kaufmann has unjustifiably softened Nietzsche's critique of Christian morality. Nietzsche is not attacking only hypocritical Christianity; rather, he is attacking Christianity itself as originally and unavoidably hypocritical and "mendacious."

Thus Nietzsche's attack on Christianity has either been uncritically accepted, blunted as a Kierkegaardian attack on Christendom, and/or hailed as a return to or advance towards the true essence of the Christian religion. But in more recent criticism even these inaccurate assessments of Nietzsche's relation to Christianity have been ignored. Analyzing the influential reading of the "new Nietzsche" by French critics, René Girard summarizes their indifference to this problematic:

Different as they are from one another . . . these avatars are all alike in their indifference to the great struggle that obsessed the last lucid years of Nietzsche. Is there some obscure reason why this should be? Is there something inopportune or embarrassing about the theme; is it strategically advisable not to insist on it?[20]

Girard blames the marginalization of this problem, which was central to Nietzsche's work, on the influential reading of Heidegger. "Even those who reject the interpretation of Nietzsche as the last great metaphysician of the West, are dependent on Heidegger for their evacuation of 'Dionysus versus the Crucified.'"[21]

Heidegger, through his work on Nietzsche in the 1930s and 40s, has directed attention away from the question of Nietzsche's relationship to Christianity and toward his relationship to the Western philosophical tradition. Nietzsche is not read as the prophet who claims to have brought about the end of Christianity but rather as the thinker who claims to have brought about the end of metaphysics.

In his essay "Nietzsche's Word: God Is Dead," in which he summarizes much of his work on Nietzsche over the previous decade, Heidegger asserts that "it is clear that Nietzsche's pronouncement concerning the death of God means the Christian god"

(*QT* 61). From this statement it would appear that Heidegger is going to take seriously Nietzsche's own interpretation of the meaning of the madman's assertion that God is dead: "The greatest recent event – that 'God is dead,' *that the belief in the Christian god has become unbelievable* – is already beginning to cast its first shadows over Europe" (my emphasis, *GS* 343). But Heidegger immediately redirects the force of this statement by interpreting the "Christian god" metaphysically: "But it is no less certain, and it is to be considered in advance, that the terms 'God' and 'Christian god' in Nietzsche's thinking are used to designate the suprasensory world in general" (*QT* 61). It is central to my own interpretation of Nietzsche that Heidegger is correct in this statement, *if* it is understood that Nietzsche *misinterprets* Christianity in this way. But Heidegger is not saying that Nietzsche misinterprets Christianity; rather he is asserting that Nietzsche's attack on the "Christian god" is limited to an attack upon this misrepresentation of God in metaphysical ontotheology.

Thus Heidegger directly contradicts Nietzsche's interpretation of "God is dead," of nihilism, as the "recent event . . . that the belief in the Christian god has become unbelievable":

Hence ... nihilism in Nietzsche's sense in no way coincides with the situation conceived merely negatively, that the Christian god of biblical revelation can no longer be believed in. (*QT* 63)

Relying, as we have seen other interpreters do, upon Kierkegaard's terminology, and hence on an implicit comparison between Nietzsche and Kierkegaard, Heidegger turns Nietzsche's attack upon Christianity into an attack upon Christendom only:

Christendom for Nietzsche is the historical, world-political phenomenon of the Church and its claim to power within the shaping of Western humanity and its modern culture. Christendom in this sense and the Christianity of New Testament faith are not the same ... Therefore, a confrontation with Christendom is absolutely not in any way an attack against what is Christian. (*QT* 63–64)[22]

But Nietzsche never attacks "Christendom" as distinct from Christianity. He simply never uses this terminology. Although Heidegger is aware of Nietzsche's attack upon "the missionary propaganda of Paul," the interpretation cited above gives the impression that Nietzsche distinguishes between Christendom, as a corruption, and the original "Christianity of the New Testament," while in fact it is precisely the Christianity of the New Testament which Nietzsche interprets in *The Antichrist* as being motivated by nihilistic *ressentiment*.

Thus Heidegger's conclusion concerning the meaning of Nietzsche's word, God is dead, excludes Christianity from consideration:

The pronouncement "God is dead" means: the suprasensory world is without effective power. It bestows no life. Metaphysics, i.e., for Nietzsche Western philosophy understood as Platonism, is at an end. Nietzsche understands his own philosophy as the countermovement to metaphysics, and that means for him a movement in opposition to Platonism. (*QT* 61)

Heidegger is correct in interpreting the madman's assertion as a prophecy of Western nihilism, both as a revelation of its history and a prediction of its consummation, but he dismisses too quickly the importance of Christianity from this problematic.

Heidegger argues that according to Nietzsche: "Unbelief in the sense of falling away from the Christian doctrine of faith is, therefore, never the essence and ground, but always only a consequence, of nihilism; for it could be that Christendom itself represents one consequence and bodying-forth of nihilism" (*QT* 65). This is true in the sense that Nietzsche would of course reject a return to Christian faith as a way to overcome nihilism, for Christianity is for Nietzsche not *a* but *the* embodiment of nihilism. But in another sense Heidegger is wrong, for, according to Nietzsche, the loss of Christian faith is the cause and not the consequence of nihilism.

In the notes on nihilism presented at the beginning of the writings later assembled as *The Will to Power*, notes which Heidegger relies upon heavily in his interpretation of Nietzsche, Nietzsche makes it clear that he sees the "end of Christianity" as the source and ground of nihilism. Nietzsche asks in the first aphorism of Book One of *The Will to Power* about the source of nihilism: "whence comes this uncanniest of all guests?" (*WP* 1). His answer is direct: "it is in one particular interpretation, the Christian-moral one, that nihilism is rooted." Thus Christianity does not only represent "one consequence and bodying-forth of nihilism," but is rather *the* root and source of nihilism.

Just as loss of belief in the Christian god was presented as the cause of God's death in *The Gay Science*, so also in the second step in his outline on the source of nihilism does Nietzsche assert that it is the end of Christianity which has caused the emergence of nihilism:

The end of Christianity – at the hands of its own morality (which cannot be replaced), which turns against the Christian God (the sense of truthfulness, developed highly by Christianity, is nauseated by the falseness and mendaciousness of all Christian interpretations of the world and of history; rebound from "God is truth" to the fanatical faith "All is false"). (*WP* 1)

This type of note (there are many) is used by Jaspers to soften Nietzsche's critique of Christianity and by Heidegger to argue that Nietzsche's main opponent is Platonism.[23] But Nietzsche is clearly more critical of the falsehood of Christian doctrine than appreciative of the honesty of Christian morality. The irony of these remarks must be heard. Also note that Nietzsche blasts the "falseness and mendaciousness" of "*all* Christian interpretations." He leaves no room for a recovery of some true Christianity, however this be defined, in opposition to Christendom.

The Christian interpretation of the world and history, although nihilistic in its core, held off the manifestation of nihilism by supplying "the great *antidote* against practical and theoretical nihilism" (*WP* 4). The Christian-moral interpretation of the world supplied man with a sense of purpose and meaning. But, when the falsehood of this interpretation is revealed, then man loses all faith and hope in finding any meaning and purpose for life. Once the mendacity of the Christian truth is revealed, one concludes that all is false.

According to Nietzsche, the reason that the rebound from Christianity is so great, the reason that one moves from complete faith to total despair, is the fact that Western society invested so much into this interpretation: "the untenability of one interpretation of the world, upon which a tremendous amount of energy has been lavished, awakens the suspicion that *all* interpretations of the world are false" (*WP* 1). This is the negative response to the loss of faith in Christianity, to the death of the Christian God.

In presenting each of his central prophecies – the death of God and the resultant crisis of nihilism in the coming two centuries, as well as his alternative to the Christian-moral interpretation of the world and history as the eternal recurrence of the same – Nietzsche dramatizes both a negative and positive response to his prophecy. He also presents the unthinking, indifferent response of the last man. The protagonist of Nietzsche's prophecies, the prophet himself, presents and lives through both the negative and positive responses, while the prophet's audience portrays the response of the last man.

This pattern can be seen in the madman's prophecy of God's

death in *The Gay Science*. The madman runs to the "marketplace," the place where the herd gathers, crying " 'I seek God! I seek God!' " (*GS* 125). Isn't it strange that this prophet of God's death and murder should be seeking God? Heidegger objects that interpreters of this passage have passed too quickly over this part of the passage. He interprets the madman as the one who, in contradistinction to the crowd and to metaphysics, seeks the living God. "The madman, on the contrary, is clearly ... for him who can hear, the one who seeks God, since he cries out after God" (*QT* 112). Heidegger is relying on a distinction between the god of ontotheology, invented by metaphysics, and the living God whom Heidegger at times appears to seek, or at least to await, himself. But Nietzsche makes no such distinction in this passage. How then are we to understand the madman's search for God?

As is often the case when he is deriding Christianity, Nietzsche uses a biblical idiom. The Bible, both the Old and New Testaments, is filled with commands and appeals for the listener to "seek God." For example, in Psalm 14 the atheist, the one who says in his heart "There is no God," is described as the "fool." God is described as looking down to see if there are "any who seek God," but, as Paul paraphrases the psalm in Romans, "there is no one who seeks God" (Romans 3:11). Nietzsche mocks this biblical language by having the fool or madman be the one who seeks God, and the one who reveals the fact that no one seeks or believes in God anymore.[24] In Nietzsche's eyes, the madman is "mad" only from the perspective of the herd which fears the opening up of new, endless horizons. "Not truth and certainty are the opposite of the world of the madman, but the universal and binding force of a faith ... precisely the most select spirits bristle at this universal binding force – the explorers of truth above all" (*GS* 76).

Neither can the passage be understood as the exclamation of one genuinely bereft of God, crying out for the God from whom he has been separated, as in Jesus' dying words on the cross: "My God, My God, why have you forsaken me?" (Mark 15:34). Although Nietzsche interprets Jesus' exclamation as "evidence of a general disappointment and enlightenment over the delusion of his life" (*D* 114), in other words, as the realization that his God is an illusion, his hope of heaven a delusion, Jesus clearly cries out to a God he still believes in, "*My* God," but from which he has been separated, as is made clearer from a reading of Psalm 22, the psalm which Jesus is quoting and which contains many prophecies of his crucifixion, such as the mocking and insults of the people, the piercing of his hands and feet, and the casting of lots for his clothes. The psalm concludes with the hope that God "has not despised or disdained the suffering of his afflicted one; he has not hidden his face from him but has listened to his cry for help." Although both the crowd at the foot of the cross and the crowd in Nietzsche's marketplace mock the one who cries out, the madman is devoid of Jesus' hope of being heard by God.

Neither can the madman's cry and his pronouncement of the death of God be read as anything other than a mocking allusion to the death of Jesus in Christian theology. Eric von der Luft, in his Heideggerian reading of this passage, asserts that "far from being only an anti-Christian slogan for Nietzsche, 'God is dead!' involves an intricate and dynamic metaphor which has its roots deep in German religious thought."[25] The idea of the death of God clearly does have deep roots in German theology and idealist philosophy, which are enumerated in von der Luft's essay, but it is wrong not to read this passage from Nietzsche as an "anti-Christian slogan." The many passages following this one which criticize religion, especially Christianity, Jesus and Paul, in addition to the rest of Nietzsche's anti-Christian polemic, should give the reader at least a hint that Nietzsche's madman is not very serious about "seeking God." "Nietzsche denies God – any God, and the Christian God in particular. He does not want subsequently to be appropriated as a 'God-seeker.'"[26] What then does Nietzsche mean by having the madman proclaim "I seek God! I seek God!"?

I would argue that the madman is dramatizing the origin of nihilism as understood by Nietzsche and as presented in his notes collected at the beginning of *The Will to Power*. The madman seeks God as Nietzsche did in his youth (as seen in his youthful poems)[27] and as Western society had done for over two millennia. Nietzsche has the madman proclaim, "I seek God!," in order to dramatize how the origin of God's death and the source of contemporary nihilism are rooted in the Christian-moral interpretation of the world. Because Western culture has sought for all truth in God's transcendent realm, the loss of this God means the loss of all truth to this culture.

The crowd's response to his proclamation reveals that the first stage of nihilism has been reached. The Christian God is no longer believable.

As many of those who did not believe in God were standing around just then, he provoked much laughter. Has he got lost? asked one. Did he lose his way like a child? asked another. Or is he hiding? Is he afraid of us? Has he gone on a voyage? emigrated? – Thus they yelled and laughed. (*GS* 125)

This is the unthinking response of the last man who is unaware of the grave consequences of the loss of belief in this God. This is not the response of an intensified honesty which has become nauseated at the falsehood of the Christian interpretation of the world, but the response of the last man who believes that all remains secure as the Christian God is replaced by secular systems.[28]

The madman's response to their mockery is designed to force them to realize that it is not God who is affected by his death, but rather they themselves, since God is, according to Nietzsche, only a nihilistic projection of man. It is not God who has got lost, who is hiding, who has embarked upon a strange, frightening journey. Rather it is they themselves who will experience these things, for they have lost their ground and orientation in killing this moral-Christian god:

"Whither is God?" he cried; "I will tell you. *We have killed him* – you and I. All of us are his murderers. But how did we do this? How could we drink up the sea? Who gave us the sponge to wipe away the entire horizon? What were we doing when we unchained this earth from its sun? Whither is it moving now? Whither are we moving? Away from all suns? Are we not plunging continually? Backward, sideward, forward, in all directions? Is there still any up or down? Are we not straying as through an infinite nothing? Do we not feel the breath of empty space? Has it not become colder? Is not night continually closing in on us? Do we not need to light lanterns in the morning?" (*GS* 125)

First of all notice that the madman does not say that *they* have killed God, but rather that *we* have killed God. The madman does not continue to seek God but confesses his part in his murder. And Nietzsche writes a few pages later in his own voice that "I myself have now slain all gods" (*GS* 153). Even before he acts out the now in vain search for God, the madman "lit a lantern in the bright morning hours." Yet, after proclaiming the murder of God, the madman states that as a result of this murder, we now "need to light lanterns in the morning." Thus from the beginning the madman knows that God is dead, that nihilism is upon us and that we must now light our own way. He does not hold on to some hope that he can still seek some other God, as Heidegger suggests. Rather, he seeks to bring home to the crowd the most unhomely of guests, nihilism. He wants them to realize that "God remains dead. And we have killed him." As a result, it is not God but we his murderers who are lost and set adrift.

In an attempt to overcome the incomplete nihilism of the herd, the madman must first picture for them the consequences of the loss of God. One must first live through nihilism before overcoming it. As Nietzsche writes of himself in the preface to *The Will to Power*, he is "the first perfect nihilist of Europe who, however, has even now lived through the whole of nihilism, to the end, leaving it behind, outside himself." And the consequences of killing God are apocalyptic according to both the madman and Nietzsche. The madman uses language which evokes the concept of nihilism in describing the event of God's death: "Are we not straying into an infinite nothing? Do we not feel the breath of empty space?" (*GS* 125). Nietzsche uses similar apocalyptic imagery later in *The Gay Science* in describing

how much must collapse now that this faith [in the Christian god] has been undermined because it was built upon this faith, propped up by it, grown into it; for example, the whole of our European morality. This long plenitude and sequence of breakdown, destruction, ruin, and cataclysm that is now impending – who could guess enough of it today to be compelled to play the teacher and advance proclaimer of this monstrous logic of terror, the prophet of a gloom and an eclipse of the sun whose like has probably never yet occurred on earth? (*GS* 343)

The answer, of course, Nietzsche himself who, "as a soothsayer-bird spirit who *looks back* when relating what will come," is "the first perfect nihilist" (*WP* "Preface").

But if this terrified, anguished response to nihilism is the first and necessary response to the murder of the Christian god, it is nevertheless an inadequate and incomplete response. The response of the perfect nihilist, the free spirit, is in many ways the opposite of the fearful response of the incomplete nihilist, though both acknowledge the catastrophic, apocalyptic nature of the event. This second response is,

not at all sad and gloomy but rather like a new and scarcely describable kind of light, happiness, relief, exhilaration, encouragement, dawn.

Indeed, we philosophers and "free spirits" feel, when we hear the news that "the old god is dead," as if a new dawn shone on us; our heart overflows with gratitude, amazement, premonitions, expectation. At long last the horizon appears free to us again, even if it should not be bright; at long last our ships may venture out again, venture out to face any danger; all the daring of the lover of knowledge is permitted again; the sea, *our* sea, lies open again; perhaps there has never yet been such an "open sea" –. (*GS* 343)

The madman's prophecy of the unchaining of the earth from the sun, the wiping away of the horizon, and the drinking up of the sea are here turned into positive images of the brave new world available to free spirits. The sun is replaced by the lantern of the free spirit, which though not as bright is one's own. While the last man will feel himself to be lost on a hopeless journey, the new, free spirit will bravely and gayly chart the new open horizon.

The madman looks forward to this new world and to the new spirit who will inhabit this world: "Must we ourselves not become gods simply to appear worthy of it? There has never been a greater deed; and whoever is born after us – for the sake of this deed he will belong to a higher history than all history hitherto" (*GS* 125). Thus the madman looks forward to the overman who will replace the dead god of Christianity just as Zarathustra does: "*Dead are all gods: now we want the overman to live*" (*Z* 79).

In an interpretation of the history of "the death of God" in German thought, Jürgen Moltmann correctly sees in Nietzsche's parable a philosophy which is most closely aligned with Feuerbach:

Here the death of God is ascribed to man, who has killed him, not to God's expending of his own self. God's death is the exaltation of man above himself ... When the feeling of the modern age that God is dead is thus based on the saying that we have killed him, then this is in very close proximity to Feuerbach's abolition of God through which man is said to come to himself.[29]

But, unlike Feuerbach, Nietzsche urges the free spirits, spirits freed from submission to God and a transcendent truth, not to rest content with the killing of God, "for given the way of men, there may still be caves for thousands of years in which his shadow will be shown." Like the man in Plato's allegory of the cave when he is first freed from the realm of illusion and shadow, Nietzsche's free spirit, though not enlightened by the universal light of the sun but rather by the fire of his own lantern, must also be prevented from returning to the cave, at least until he is able to distinguish between reality and shadows.[30] God's shadow, the continuing influence of the Christian-moral interpretation of the world, must also be vanquished. Nietzsche attempts to accomplish this task by unmasking the nihilism of Christian thought and abolishing its true world.

CHAPTER 2

Vanquishing God's realm: Nietzsche's abolition of the true world

> One has deprived reality of its value to the extent to which one has mendaciously invented an ideal world.
>   The "true world" and the "apparent world" – that means: the mendaciously invented world and reality.
> Nietzsche, Ecce Homo

We have seen how according to Nietzsche the loss of Christian faith is the source and ground of modern nihilism. But how is this Christian faith, which prevented the outbreak of nihilism by giving a meaning and a purpose to the earth and man, at the same time nihilistic in itself?

Nietzsche answers by asserting that the ideals and values posited by the Christian-moral interpretation of the world are fictitious. Although these values served to prevent radical nihilism while they were believed in,[1] now that this belief has been revealed to be illusory, radical nihilism comes upon us. "Now that the shabby origin of these values is becoming clear, the universe seems to have lost value, seems 'meaningless' – but that is only a *transitional stage*" (*WP* 7). This transitional stage of nihilism, this negative interpretation of the loss of religiously based values as the loss of all meaning, purpose, and direction, is necessary in order to overcome the false values by which man has directed his life and society thus far.

For why has the advent of nihilism become *necessary*? Because the values we have had hitherto thus draw their final consequence; because nihilism represents the ultimate logical conclusion of our great values and ideals – because we must experience nihilism before we can find out what value these "values" really had. (*WP* "Preface")

Nietzsche's hermeneutics of suspicion which reveals the falsehood, mendacity, and shabby origins of Christian-moral values is the basis of his most forceful attack on Christianity. "Skepticism regarding

morality is what is decisive. The end of the moral interpretation of
the world, which no longer has any sanction after it has tried to
escape into some beyond, leads to nihilism" (*WP* 1). Christianity is
denounced as propagating values that are harmful to life because
these values are falsely believed to come from a God in an imaginary
realm located beyond this world. Since this God and this realm do
not exist, Christian-moral values are in reality based upon nothing.
Christianity is nihilism. "Nihilism and Christianism: that rhymes,
that does not only rhyme" (*AC* 58).

The attack upon the distinction between two worlds, a real and
an apparent world, as the essence of nihilism is developed
throughout Nietzsche's works. Nietzsche reduces this "antithesis of
the apparent world and the true world ... to the antithesis 'world'
and 'nothing'" (*WP* 567). The "true" world is reduced to an
imaginary, non-existent world, and hence to a lie and nothing
(*nihil*). "This world" is the only world; therefore, one should drop
the designation of the world as "this" world, since there is no
"other" opposed to it. Heidegger correctly identifies this problematic as central to Nietzsche's entire project,[2] but he fails to appreciate how Nietzsche, especially in his later works,[3] came to see
Christianity as the symbol of, and the strongest support for, the
continuation of this moral interpretation of the world.

Nietzsche's first critique of the belief in two worlds is based upon
his unmasking of the psychological origin of this belief. In a critique
reminiscent of the Enlightenment attacks on miracle and revelation,
Nietzsche argues that the scientific *naïveté* of primitive people caused
them to believe in another world.

The man of the ages of barbarous primordial culture believed that in the
dream he was getting to know a *second real world*: here is the origin of all
metaphysics. (*HAH* 5)

He also argues, again as the Enlightenment philosophers did in
attacking the belief in miracles, that primitive man misinterpreted
cause and effect and therefore invented an imaginary realm of
causes which became an other, true world. Nietzsche never drops
this explanation of the primordial origin of the belief in two worlds.
He makes a similar argument in a note written in the final year of his
philosophical thinking:

One was afraid: one postulated a higher world. Sleep and dream, shadows,
the night, natural terrors, have been held responsible for the creation of

two worlds: above all, the symptoms of physiological exhaustion should have been considered in this regard. (*WP* 230)

What Nietzsche has added to his earlier genealogical critique is the emphasis on man's weakness and fear as the cause of his projection of another world. Man dreamed of another world because he was afraid and helpless in this one. Because man was weak he feared and sought to escape the forces of the affects, irrationality and change (*WP* 576).

Thus Nietzsche posits the psychological origin of the belief in another world beyond the physical, of meta-physics, in man's reaction against these feared forces. To protect oneself against the fearful reality of the world, one posits another world which, in antithesis to the real world, is void of these fearful qualities.

Given these two insights, that becoming has no goal and that underneath all becoming there is no grand unity . . . an escape remains: to pass sentence on this whole world of becoming as a deception and to invent a world beyond it, a *true* world. (*WP* 12)

According to Nietzsche, this is the basis for all philosophical, moral and religious denigration of this world or reality.

The places of origin of the notion of "another world":
  the philosopher, who invents a world of reason, where reason and the logical functions are adequate: this is the origin of the "true" world;
  the religious man, who invents a "divine world": this is the origin of the "denaturalized, antinatural" world;
  the moral man, who invents a "free world": this is the origin of the "good, perfect, just holy" world. (*WP* 586)

Nietzsche extends the Enlightenment critique of religion in order to criticize not only religion and faith, but also morality and reason. Although he follows the Enlightenment tradition in defining faith as the belief in an illusion, as an enemy of knowledge, he also criticizes reason as a form of faith, i.e. an illusion, and therefore as another cause of nihilism. It is in this broadening of the hermeneutics of suspicion to include reason and metaphysics that Nietzsche inaugurates postmodern theory.

In addition to this psychological genealogy of the belief in the antithesis of two worlds in prehistorical times, Nietzsche also presents an analysis of the historical development of this belief. The most famous outline of this history is presented in the aphorism from

Twilight of the Idols, "How the True World Became a Fable: The History of An Error" (*TI* 485).

This history begins with Plato's positing of the true world as the "oldest form of the idea." Plato represents for Nietzsche the nihilism caused by faith in the categories of reason. As Bernd Magnus writes in explaining the first stage of Nietzsche's history, "philosophy – which is Platonism at bottom for Nietzsche – employs 'reason' as a weapon to overpower the eternal cycle of genesis, growth, decay, and death – becoming. In so far as reason cannot grasp change without turning it into a static form of being, in so far as reason ossifies, all philosophic systems are grounded in an error."[4] In this same section, immediately prior to "The History of an Error," Nietzsche presents a critique of the logic behind the distinction between a true and an apparent world. His first proposition is the assertion that only "this," "apparent" world is demonstrable. His second proposition asserts that this natural reasoning has been reversed.

The criteria which have been bestowed on the "true being" of things are the criteria of not-being, of *naught*; the "true world" has been constructed out of contradiction to the actual world: indeed an apparent world, insofar as it is merely a moral-optical illusion. (*TI* 484)

This reversal, which denigrates the actual world as a merely apparent world and esteems an illusory world as the "true world," was brought about by Plato.

According to Nietzsche, Plato "reversed the concept 'reality' and said: 'What you take for real is an error, and the nearer we approach the "Idea," the nearer we approach "truth."' – Is this understood? It was the greatest of rebaptisms" (*WP* 572). Whereas Plato argued that the senses do not give true knowledge, using the optical illusion caused by placing a stick in water as an example, Nietzsche calls Plato's realm of ideas an apparent world based upon a moral-optical illusion, thereby utilizing the rhetoric Plato uses to disparage the physical world to criticize Plato's ideal realm. Nietzsche argues in passages such as these that he is simply reversing a previous reversal of natural valuation. He is not standing truth on its head, but returning it to its feet after it has been stood on its head for two millennia. "For truth has been stood on its head when the conscious advocate of nothingness and negation is accepted as the representative of 'truth'" (*AC* 8). According to Nietzsche, we have come to regard the idealist conception of truth as natural only "because it has been adopted by Christianity" (*WP* 572).

It is not Plato but rather Christianity which is seen as the true enemy in Nietzsche's attempt to reverse this original revaluation. Christianity's adoption of this Platonic valuation is worse because the belief in the true world is based not upon the philosopher's assertion of his will to power – "'I, Plato, *am* the truth.'" – but rather upon the weakness and decadence of the "sinner," who accepts this valuation in order to denigrate the actual world in which he is weak and powerless. Magnus argues that in Nietzsche's interpretation, "the Platonic dialectic posed the ascent from defective existence to the plenary mode as a task for the individual, to be accomplished in *this* life," while "Christianity suspends earthly self-overcoming altogether."[5] Consequently, Nietzsche's devaluation of the Christian "true world" is more violent than his revaluation of Plato's "true world." While Plato's true world is rejected, it is nevertheless described in Nietzsche's history as "relatively sensible, simple, and persuasive." Christianity's ideal world, on the contrary, is denigrated as "more subtle, insidious, incomprehensible."

This more dangerous and decadent formulation of the true world is criticized in Nietzsche's "third proposition" regarding the distinction between the true and apparent world.

To invent fables about a world "other" than this one has no meaning at all, unless an instinct of slander, detraction, and suspicion against life has gained the upper hand in us: in that case, we avenge ourselves against life with a phantasmagoria of "another," a "better" life. (*TI* 484)

This is the basis of Nietzsche's central critique of Western thought, and the blame for this "error" is laid on Christianity. Although the psychological and philosophical origins of this idea pre-date Christianity, Christianity is blamed for the continued power and propagation of this mis-valuation of the world and life. Just as Plato's image of the true world is compared favorably to Christianity's, so is the prehistorical projection of the true world out of the dream considered better than Christianity's fiction of the true world as the negation of this world:

This *world of pure fiction* is vastly inferior to the world of dreams insofar as the latter *mirrors* reality, whereas the former falsifies, devalues, and negates reality. Once the concept of "nature" had been invented as the opposite of

"God," "natural" had to become a synonym of "reprehensible": this
whole world of fiction is rooted in *hatred* of the natural (of reality!). (*AC* 15)

The world of pure fiction which Nietzsche attacks here refers
specifically to Christian morality and religion.

Nietzsche's "inverted Platonism" cannot be understood apart
from his anti-Christianity. Heidegger, quoting a note written by
Nietzsche in 1870, interprets Nietzsche's whole philosophy as
"*inverted Platonism*," even asserting that "during the last years of his
creative life, he labors at nothing else than the overturning of
Platonism" (*N* 1 154). Heidegger describes stage two of Nietzsche's
history of an error, which clearly refers to Christianity, by writing
that "In Plato's stead, Platonism now rules" (*N* 1 204). It is, of
course, true that Nietzsche describes Christianity as Platonism for
the people, but to avoid all discussion of Christianity in interpreting
this passage is to oversimplify Nietzsche's target at best. Nietzsche
considers Christianity's fictitious "true world" more dangerous than
the Platonic ideal realm because it is promised to the ignoble herd
rather than to the noble aristocracy.[6]

In addition, it is Christianity and not Platonism which is
responsible for the continuing influence of this nihilistic evaluation
of the world. This is true of the next stage in Nietzsche's history of an
error – represented by Kant. Although Kant's true world is not
only "indemonstrable" and "unattainable for now," but also, unlike
Christianity's true world, "unpromisable," it is still the same ideal,
the same "old sun." This philosophical belief in an unknown world,
the thing-in-itself, results from the loss of belief in Christianity's
divine world. "Under the rule of religious ideas, one has become
accustomed to the notion of 'another world (behind, below, above)'
– and when religious ideas are destroyed one is troubled by an
uncomfortable emptiness and deprivation. From this feeling grows
once again 'another world,' but now merely a metaphysical one that
is no longer religious" (*GS* 151). In fact the "skepticism" through
which the religious ideal is viewed is not intended to weaken the
ideal but rather to protect it from refutation.

The conception of a "*true world*," the conception of morality as the *essence* of
the world (these two most malignant errors of all time!), were once again,
thanks to a wily and shrewd skepticism, if not provable, at least no longer
refutable. Reason, the *right* of reason, does not extend that far. Reality had
been reduced to mere "appearance," and a mendaciously fabricated
world, the world of being, was honored as reality. (*AC* 10)

As always in Nietzsche, Kant is criticized for being an "under-handed Christian" (*TI* 484) just as Nietzsche condemns "our whole philosophy" for having "theologians' blood in its veins" (*AC* 8).

But the next stage in Nietzsche's history of an error takes advantage of the change in the representation of the true world as not only "attainable for now," but also as both "unattainable" and "unpromisable." In attempting to protect the true world from refutation, Kant described this world as "unknown." But positivism, by focusing upon what is known, uses this designation of the true world to refute its importance. According to positivism, because the true world is unknown, it is consequently "not consoling, redeeming, or obligating: how could something unknown obligate us?" (*TI* 485). Nietzsche hails this "cockcrow of positivism" as the "first yawn of reason." Nietzsche uses images of dawn and daybreak ("Gray morning") in order to refer to his own early writings of the late 1870s and early 1880s, often described as Nietzsche's positivist period. In his preface to *Daybreak*, Nietzsche describes himself as working through the night (of nihilism) in order to approach "his own morning, his own redemption, his own *daybreak*" (*D* "Preface" 1). This morning represents the overcoming of the "old sun" still sought by Kant, the sun of the Platonic-Christian-moral ideal, and the positing of a new day lit by one's own sun (or one's own lantern in the imagery of the parable of the madman).

In *Human, All Too Human*, Nietzsche articulates this positivist critique of the true world:

Metaphysical world. – It is true, there could be a metaphysical world; the absolute possibility of it is hardly to be disputed ... Then that possibility still remains over; but one can do absolutely nothing with it, not to speak of letting happiness, salvation and life depend on the gossamer of such a possibility. – For one could assert nothing at all of the metaphysical world except that it was a being-other, an inaccessible, incomprehensible being-other; it would be a thing with negative qualities. Even if the existence of such a world were never so well demonstrated, it is certain that knowledge of it would be the most useless of all knowledge. (*HAH* 9)

Here we see Nietzsche moving from stage four of his history of an error to stage five. Because Kant's unknown world is not consoling, redeeming or obligating, knowledge of such a world is "the most useless of all knowledge." And an idea which is "useless and super-fluous" is "*consequently*, a refuted idea: let us abolish it!" (*TI* 485).[7] Knowledge of the true world as a supersensible, metaphysical realm is useless to us as physical beings who perceive the world through our senses.

But this positivistic critique has its limitations. Maudemarie Clark, in her analysis of the development of Nietzsche's conception of truth, describes Nietzsche's position regarding transcendent truth in *Human, All Too Human* as "agnostic," as opposed to his later "atheistic" rejection of the true world.[8] Nietzsche himself gives a strong critique of the scientific spirit and the positivistic will to truth. In book five of *The Gay Science*, Nietzsche rejects that aspect of the scientific spirit which, although it professes itself "godless," is still based upon faith in the Platonic-Christian-moral ideal. Nietzsche claims that science is based upon the will not to deceive, which is a moral ideal. This moral ideal stands in contradiction to life which, Nietzsche asserts, is "aimed at semblance, meaning error, deception, simulation, delusion, self-delusion" (*GS* 344). Nietzsche therefore interprets the scientific will to truth as a nihilistic will to death, a will to the opposite of life.

No doubt, those who are truthful in that audacious and ultimate sense that is presupposed by the faith in science *thus affirm another world* than the world of life, nature, and history; and insofar as they affirm this "other world" – look must they not by the same token negate its counterpart, this world, *our* world? – But you have gathered what I am driving at, namely, that it is still a *metaphysical faith* upon which our faith in science rests – that even we seekers after knowledge today, we godless anti-metaphysicians still take our fire, too, from the flame lit by a faith that is thousands of years old, that Christian faith which was also the faith of Plato, that God is the truth, that truth is divine. (*GS* 344)

This passage is cited by Jaspers to support his claim that Nietzsche took his "moral impulse," his own "boundless will to truth" from Christianity.[9] But he fails to notice that Nietzsche is *attacking* this Christian-moral will to truth which he formerly shared with other "godless metaphysicians" and positivist scientists because it repeats the error of making a distinction between a true and an apparent world, denigrating our world and our life as only apparent, as deceptive. One must read the closing line of this aphorism, "How we, too, are still pious": "But what if this [belief in truth as divine] should become more and more incredible, if nothing should prove to be divine any more unless it were error, blindness, the lie – if God himself should prove to be our most enduring lie? – " (*GS* 344). Nietzsche builds his entire work on the truth of this "what if."

In *The Genealogy of Morals*, Nietzsche reiterates his critique of science and philosophy which falls short of complete nihilism in that it maintains a faith in truth. In a passage which refers the reader back to section 344 of *The Gay Science* and to the preface of *The Dawn* (both of which I have analyzed above), Nietzsche equates this will to truth with the ascetic ideal. Overcoming this ascetic ideal, accomplished only in stage five of Nietzsche's history of an error, occurs when "faith in the God of the ascetic ideal is denied" (*GM* 153). This is the last "shadow" of God which Nietzsche must vanquish: the place of God, the true world, must be destroyed. Truth must no longer be considered a world separate from us to be discovered. It is this conception of truth as originating in another world which must be abolished.

Heidegger makes a similar argument concerning Nietzsche's reference to his own earlier work:

Nietzsche thinks back on the years of his own metamorphosis . . . Platonism is overcome inasmuch as the supersensuous world, as the true world, is abolished; but by way of compensation the sensuous world remains, and positivism occupies it. (*N* I 207)

However, Heidegger applies this interpretation to stage five of Nietzsche's history, not to stage four. This is a result of his misinterpretation of stage five.

Stage five describes Nietzsche's "no-saying" task, the abolishing of the true world as the only way of affirming our world. In his preface to *Ecce Homo*, in which Nietzsche seeks to sum up his life's work, he again asserts his opposition to any conception of a "true" world opposed to our perspective of the "apparent" world.

No new idols are erected by me . . . *Overthrowing idols* (my word for "ideals") – that comes closer to being part of my craft. One has deprived reality of its value, its meaning, its truthfulness, to precisely the extent to which one has mendaciously invented an ideal world. (*EH* 218)

Nietzsche erects no new idols, no new ideal, true world, but he does recover a meaning of truth which he can affirm. The truth which he affirms is the reversal of the Platonic–Christian, i.e. moral, sense of truth. Nietzsche's Yes-saying is in this sense merely the flip side of his No-saying.

Heidegger, however, interprets stages five and six as separate developments in Nietzsche's thought, arguing that Nietzsche takes the final step of stage six "only in his final creative year (1888)."

Heidegger reads step five as describing Nietzsche's inversion of Platonism without its overcoming.

> If we take the inversion strictly in this sense [sensuous above and non-sensuous below], then the vacant niches of "above and below" are pre-served, suffering only a change of occupancy, as it were. But as long as the "above and below" define the formal structure of Platonism, Platonism in its essence perdures. The inversion does not achieve what it must, as an overcoming of nihilism, namely, an overcoming of Platonism in its very foundation. Such overcoming succeeds only when the "above" in general is set aside as such ... when the true world – in the sense of the ideal – is expunged. (*N* I 201)

Heidegger is incorrect in limiting this insight to the final year of Nietzsche's work. This insight is not the end but the beginning of Nietzsche's thought.

By abolishing the true world, Nietzsche is left not with the merely apparent world. This is the belief of incomplete nihilism, which after realizing that the true world does not exist, must still take the final step of affirming our world.

> Having reached this standpoint, one grants the reality of becoming as the *only* reality, forbids oneself every kind of clandestine access to afterworlds and false divinities – but *cannot endure this world though one does not want to deny it*. (*WP* 12)

Stage five does not describe this incomplete nihilism, as is evident by the reference to the return of "cheerfulness," recalling the first passage of Book Five of *The Gay Science*, "*The meaning of our cheerfulness*" (*GS* 343), in which Nietzsche describes the free spirits who are encouraged and exhilarated by the death of God and the abolition of the true world. Nietzsche can speak of this final stage as both the affirmation of the "apparent" world, with "apparent" in quotation marks referring to the name for our actual world under the old valuation, and also as the realization that with the abolition of the "true" world, our actual world is no longer merely apparent. "*With the true world we have also abolished the apparent one*" (*TI* 486). Nietzsche describes this final stage with images from *Thus Spoke Zarathustra*: "(Noon; moment of the briefest shadow; end of the longest error; high point of humanity; INCIPIT ZARATHUSTRA.)" Stage six cannot be reached by Nietzsche as late as 1888, since Nietzsche refers to the beginning of *Zarathustra* (1883) to represent this stage.

In *Ecce Homo*, Nietzsche reverses the order of the final two stages of his history of an error to assert that the Yes-saying part of his work preceded the No-saying part. "After the Yes-saying part of my task had been solved, the turn had come for the No-saying, *No-doing* part: the revaluation of our values so far, the great war – conjuring up the day of decision" (*EH* 310). Nietzsche is referring to *Thus Spoke Zarathustra* in asserting that the Yes-saying part of his task had been solved. The order between the No-saying task, the abolition of the true world, and the Yes-saying task, the affirmation of our actual world, can be reversed because the two tasks are dependent upon each other, inseparably interrelated. Therefore Nietzsche can describe the "psychological problem in the type of Zarathustra" as the question of "how he that says No and *does* No to an unheard-of degree, to everything to which one has so far said Yes, can nevertheless be the opposite of a No-saying spirit" (*EH* 306).

Because Nietzsche believes the "true" world was invented through a negation of the actual world, it follows that a negation of the "true" world will lead to a restoration of the actual world. Therefore, saying "no" to the Christian-moral "true" world is the same as saying "yes" to the actual world, and affirming the actual world is the same thing as negating the nihilistic denigration of the actual world in religion, morality, and metaphysics.

While Christianity's moral interpretation of the world worked as a temporary antidote to practical nihilism by "conceding to the world, in spite of suffering and evil, the character of perfection" (*WP* 4), the Dionysian affirmation of the world also views the world as "perfect," but not "in spite of" suffering and evil. The Dionysian interpretation of the world affirms the whole of life and existence.

"*The world is perfect*" – thus says the instinct of the most spiritual, the Yes-saying instinct; "imperfection, whatever is beneath us, distance, the pathos of distance – even the chandala still belongs to this perfection." (*AC* 57)

But this similarity between the Christian-moral interpretation of the world and Nietzsche's Dionysian affirmation of the world should not be read as evidence of Nietzsche's "Christian motivations." Rather, Nietzsche is here opposing the Christian view of the world as created, sustained, and guided by a God's sovereign will to the Dionysian view of the world as being without beginning and without end, as a chaos without purpose or goal.

> The total character of the world, however, is in all eternity chaos – in the sense not of a lack of necessity but of a lack of order, arrangement, form, beauty, wisdom, and whatever other names there are for our aesthetic anthropomorphisms. (*GS* 109)

It is this world which the Dionysian must affirm as perfect, not in the sense of being perfectly ordered and arranged, but in the sense of being necessary, fated.

Nietzsche is denying the validity of the etymological origin of the word "world," or *kosmos*, which refers to the "order" of the universe. Nietzsche wants to destroy all the vestiges of this ontotheological interpretation of the world in modern science and philosophy, including the Enlightenment's replacement for the Christian understanding of the world. He does not want to regard the world as a machine, for unlike a machine it was not constructed for one purpose. He also wants to have done with all talk of the "laws" of nature, because this implies that there is a law-giver.

> Let us beware of saying that there are laws in nature. There are only necessities: there is nobody who commands, nobody who obeys, nobody who trespasses. Once you know there are no purposes, you also know that there is no accident; for it is only beside a world of purposes that the word "accident" has meaning. (*GS* 109)

This is another version, published in 1882, of Nietzsche's abolition of the distinction between a true and apparent world. Just as the abolition of the true world means the abolition of an apparent world, so does the description of the world as based on chance or accident lose its meaning once any true world of purpose has been abolished. But, as with the case of the designation of the "apparent" world, Nietzsche can continue to write that the world is based upon "chance" and "accident" in order to oppose the Christian-moral interpretation.

Nietzsche hopes for the overcoming of all the vestiges of the Christian-moral interpretation of the world. "When will all these shadows of God cease to darken our minds?" (*GS* 109). The understanding of the world as ordered or purposeful is another shadow of God which Nietzsche seeks to vanquish. Once again, Nietzsche uses imagery which both recalls and opposes biblical language. In the epistle to the Romans, Paul argues that the "creation of the world" makes plain "God's invisible qualities" (Romans 1:19–20), but because humanity worshipped the creature instead of the creator, God gave humanity over to immorality. Therefore, "their thinking became futile and their foolish hearts were darkened" (Romans 1:21). Paul argues that our thinking has been "darkened" because we have forgotten God and have ceased to glorify him as the creator of the cosmos, while Nietzsche argues that our thinking has been "darkened" by the shadow of God, by our continued deification and de-naturalization of the cosmos. While Paul interprets our desire to understand the *kosmos* apart from God as the work of a darkened mind, Nietzsche believes that our ability and willingness to affirm a godless, purposeless cosmos "might be *a divine way of thinking*" (*WP* 15).

CHAPTER 3

Nietzsche on the Judaeo-Christian denial of the world

We are far from claiming that the world is worth *less*; indeed it would seem laughable to us today if man were to insist on inventing values that were supposed to *excel* the value of the actual world. This is precisely what we have turned our backs on as an extravagant aberration of human vanity and unreason that for a long time was not recognized as such. It found its final expression in modern pessimism, and a more ancient and stronger expression in the teaching of Buddha; but it is part of Christianity also, if more doubtfully and ambiguously so but not for that reason any less seductive.   Nietzsche, *The Gay Science*

We have seen that Nietzsche indicts Christianity for basing its ideals and values upon a fictitious true world. The origin of this critique can be found in the work of Ludwig Feuerbach. Although Nietzsche develops and extends Feuerbach's critique of Christianity, he begins from the same presuppositions as his predecessor. He argues that both God and God's realm are fictitious, imaginative projections of man. And Nietzsche repeats Feuerbach's conclusion that if God is a fiction, then he is in reality nothing. According to Feuerbach, "the Divine essence . . . is only something in the imagination, but in truth and reality nothing."[1]

Nietzsche follows Feuerbach in asserting that man projects his own values onto a transcendent God and a transcendent realm, thereby denying his own value. "To enrich God, man must become poor; that God may be all, man must be nothing."[2] Nietzsche repeats this same argument in analyzing the rudimentary psychology of the religious man, asserting that "in so far as everything great and strong in man has been conceived as superhuman and external, man has belittled himself – he has separated two sides of himself, one very paltry and weak, one very strong and astonishing, into two spheres, and called the former 'man,' the latter 'God'" (*WP* 136). In a masterful use of language, Nietzsche names this an "*altération* of the personality." The French word *altération* captures both the essence and the negative valuation of this process as interpreted by Nietzsche. The word can mean a change (for the worse), an impairing (of health, etc.) and a debasing or falsification of a document or text.[3] The word thus summarizes Nietzsche's critique of man's projection of a god onto an ideal realm as the consequence of the sickliness of the decadent and the result of primitive man's misunderstanding of cause and effect, his poor philology in interpreting the text of the world.

Nietzsche's hope that "perhaps man will rise ever higher as soon as he ceases to *flow out* into a god" is also based upon Feuerbach's analysis of man's projection of God out of himself. Nietzsche calls for the reversal of the projection process described by Feuerbach. Küng concurs that in making these claims, Nietzsche speaks as "a docile student of Ludwig Feuerbach."[4] At times Nietzsche agrees with Feuerbach that man must simply return the values he has projected onto God and the heavenly realm back unto himself:

All the beauty and sublimity we have bestowed upon real and imaginary things I will reclaim as the property and product of man: as his fairest apology. Man as poet, as thinker, as God, as love, as power: with what regal liberality he has lavished gifts upon things so as to impoverish himself and make himself feel wretched! (*WP* 85)

Both Nietzsche and Feuerbach seek to educate man beyond this childlike stage, beyond religion, whose essence is ignorance of the fact that it is man who has created God and projected him onto an illusory divine world.[5]

Both of these theology students turned philosopher can at times appreciate religion's role in the formative period of man's development. Religion served a positive function in educating man, much as fairy tales can be used to teach a child. In the words of Feuerbach, "religion everywhere precedes philosophy, as in the history of the race, so also in that of the individual. Man first of all sees his nature as if *out of* himself, before he finds it in himself."[6] In reference to both Greek and Judaeo-Christian myths, Nietzsche reaches the same conclusion concerning the value of religion for man's childhood:

the whole of *religion* might yet appear as a prelude and exercise to some distant age ... Indeed – one might ask – would man ever have learned without the benefit of such a religious training and prehistory to experience a hunger and thirst for *himself*, and to find satisfaction and fullness in *himself?* Did Prometheus have to *fancy* first he had *stolen* the light and then pay for that – before he finally discovered that he had created the light *by coveting the light* and that not only man but also the *god* was the work of his own hands and had been mere clay in his hands? (*GS* 300)

Here mankind, personified as Prometheus, is given godlike powers; man is deified as in Feuerbach. Instead of man being the work of God's hands, god is the work of man's hands. By describing god as "clay" in man's hands Nietzsche alludes to the narrative of humanity's creation in Genesis, where Adam is described as shaped out of the dust of the ground by YHWH (Genesis 2:7). And, in *Beyond Good and Evil*, Nietzsche argues that it is an ancient, eternal story that as soon as philosophy begins to believe in itself, "It always creates the world in its own image" (9), again reversing the biblical narrative of Genesis where "God created man in His own image" (Genesis 1:27).

As Moltmann argues, this is merely a reversal of the ontotheological projection of God at man's expense. Atheism, in its struggle against theism, "has long been nothing more than a reversed form of theism, especially in modern times. It has not been able to break free from its opponent." Whereas theism thinks of God at man's expense, the atheism of Feuerbach and Nietzsche "thinks of man at God's expense." It "applies all the old theistic divine predicates to man for the purpose of man's incarnation. It is not God who created man in his image but man who creates God in his."[7]

We can now see how the madman's proclamation of the death of God, of man's murder of God, is based upon Feuerbach's assertion that God is only a projection of man. The murder of God means the unmasking of the belief in God as an illusion, the unmasking of religious values as nihilistic. This unmasking is based upon the original presupposition that God is a projection of man. Thus it is correct to assert, as do Heidegger, Biser, and Ricoeur,[8] that the madman proclaims the death of the god of ontotheology, but I must again reiterate that Nietzsche includes all gods, and especially the Christian god, in his prophecy.

Nietzsche extends Feuerbach's insight by analyzing the specific drives which led man to imagine God and a divine realm. Feuerbach believed that self-consciousness about the fact that man has projected God would lead to a new religion of man. This new religion of man is clearly based upon a secularization of *Christian* values and doctrines. Nietzsche denounces the logic of Feuerbach's religion of man in a short poetic aphorism entitled "The Pious Retort:"

> God loves us, *because* we are made *by him.*
> "But man made God!" say the refined.
> Should he not love what he designed?
> Should he, *because* he made him, now *deny him?*
> That inference limps; it has a cloven mind.   (*GS* 38)

Just because man made God does not mean that this creation is worthy of praise. Nietzsche argues that we must differentiate between good projections and bad projections. And the Judaeo-Christian projection of God and heaven are denounced by Nietzsche as not only bad, but as the most corrupt and harmful of lies. Nietzsche finds his originality in going beyond atheism's mere denial of God's existence: "That we find no God – either in history or in nature or behind nature – is not what differentiates *us*, but that we experience what has been revered as God, not as 'godlike' but as miserable, as absurd, as harmful, not merely as an error but as a *crime against life.*"

What has been revered as God and as godlike is denounced by Nietzsche because it has for the most part been the product of the *decadent* or sickly imagination. Nietzsche does not so much reject the creation of gods and ideals – "the conception of gods *in itself* need not lead to the degradation of the imagination" (*GM* 93) – though he does hope to make this process a self-conscious one. What he opposes is the type of god and ideals created by slave morality, by the weak and sick who create these ideals in opposition to the actual world in which they are oppressed: "there are *nobler* uses for the invention of gods than for the self-crucifixion and self-violation of man in which Europe over the past millennia achieved its distinctive mastery" (*GM* 93).

Nietzsche not only extends Feuerbach's insight into the essence of religion, but also criticizes Feuerbach's interpretation of the significance of his insight. The most significant difference can be seen in Nietzsche's parable of the madman. "Feuerbach's relief at the death of God seems to be dangerously innocent and naive compared with the deep horror to which the 'madman' gives expression here."[9] Nietzsche feels that Feuerbach did not appreciate the full consequences of his insight. He did not understand that the loss of belief in the Christian God will mean the collapse of all that had been supported by the Christian faith, including "the whole of our

European morality" (*GS* 343). Feuerbach believed that this morality could be supported by the religion of man. In fact Feuerbach denied he was an atheist because in his view "he alone is the true atheist to whom the predicates of the Divine Being, – for example, love, wisdom, justice, – are nothing; not he to whom merely the subject of these predicates is nothing."[10] But this preservation of the divine attributes and Christian morality after the unmasking of the origin of these values in a nihilistic lie is vehemently opposed by Nietzsche. "When one gives up the Christian faith, one pulls the right to Christian morality out from under one's feet" (*TI* 515).

The basis of morality, the "true" world, the place of God, is also interpreted by Nietzsche as a projection:

> Man projects his drive to truth, his "goal" in a certain sense, outside himself as a world that has being, as a metaphysical world ... as a world already in existence. (*WP* 552)

According to Nietzsche, these creations must be judged according to the will to power which was at work in their creators. Gods are the creation of a people's strength or of a people's weakness; religious ideals are the product of either master or slave morality.

> Indeed, there is no other alternative for gods; *either* they are the will to power, and they remain a people's gods, *or* the incapacity for power, then they necessarily become *good*. (*AC* 16)

It is Judaeo-Christianity which is blamed for the victory of slave morality's conception of God and the true world. The Judaeo-Christian God and divine world are attacked by Nietzsche for being the product of the slave's *ressentiment*. Just as the projection of the Christian God is based upon the impoverishment of man, so is the belief in the Christian heaven based upon a denigration of the natural, actual world.

According to Nietzsche, it is the Jews who were the first to transvalue the natural valuation, which in Nietzsche's opinion is a master or aristocratic evaluation, in order to take revenge upon their enemies. The Jews did not begin with this anti-natural valuation. It is important to Nietzsche's argument that the natural valuation, the valuation of the will to power and of ascending life, precede the anti-natural valuation, the valuation of impotence and decadence. The Jews, during the emergence and growth of their political power, created and worshipped a conception of God which Nietzsche believes was valuable. First consider Nietzsche's general description of the god of a strong and healthy people:

> A people that still believes in itself retains its own god. In him it reveres the conditions which let it prevail, its virtues: it projects its pleasure in itself, its feeling of power, into a being to whom one may offer thanks. (*AC* 16)

This god is clearly a projection, as Feuerbach assured us, but this projection is valuable because it is based upon the natural conditions which allow a people to express its will to power, its will to grow and become stronger. This god is "able to help and to harm," just like Nietzsche's childhood conception of god, as he confesses in the introduction of *The Genealogy of Morals*. This god is beyond good and evil, an "immoral, or at least unmoralistic" god, in that both help and harm can be conditions which cause a people to grow in strength. This conception of god was originally held by the Jews as well.

> Originally, especially at the time of the kings, Israel also stood in the right, that is, natural relationship to all things. Its Yahweh was the expression of a consciousness of power, of joy in oneself, of hope for oneself: through him victory and welfare were expected; through him nature was trusted to give what the people needed – above all, rain. Yahweh is the god of Israel and therefore the god of justice: the logic of every people that is in power and has a good conscience. (*AC* 25)

But the Jews lost this life-promoting conception of god when they suffered political defeat and were led into captivity by their victors. Nietzsche argues that at this point the Jews should have naturally abandoned their god, since he apparently was no longer able to help them. But instead they "changed his concept – they denatured his concept" (*AC* 25). Yahweh was made the god of a justice which was separate from the strength of the people. The Jewish god was "denatured" by being made "moral." This morality was "no longer the expression of the conditions for the life and growth of a people, no longer its most basic instinct for life, but become abstract, become the antithesis of life" (*AC* 25). The conception of morality which the Jews abandoned is the valuation which Nietzsche himself seeks to promote. "The question is to what extent it is life-promoting, life-preserving, species-preserving, perhaps even species-cultivating" (*BGE* 4).

This denaturing of the concept of god and morality was accomplished, according to Nietzsche, by the Jewish priests. Through the

"*lie* of the 'moral world order,'" the priests accomplished the transvaluation which Nietzsche seeks to reverse back to its natural
origins. Nietzsche defines the "moral world order" as the belief that
"there is a will of God, once and for all" as to what man should do
and that the value of a people or an individual is measured according to this absolute, fixed standard (*AC* 26). Instead of values being
relative to the conditions of a people or an individual's conditions of
strength and growth, an absolute value standard is now used to
deprecate life. This absolute standard is then reified as the will of
God issuing from a true, spiritual world which is used to judge and
condemn this world and this life. A distinction is made between a
true and an apparent world, between a divine world of truth and
this world of sin, and the former is used "to imperil life and slander
the world" (*AC* 24). The Jews "were the first to use the term
'world' as an opprobrium ... they mark the beginning of the slave
rebellion in morals" (*BGE* 195).

This rebellion was motivated, according to Nietzsche, by a desire
to take revenge upon Israel's conquerors. But because the leaders of
this rebellion, the priests, were without real, i.e. physical, military
power, they had to take "spiritual" revenge. "It is because of their
impotence that in them hatred grows to monstrous and uncanny
proportions, to the most spiritual and poisonous kind of hatred"
(*GM* 33). This hatred, this *ressentiment*, was expressed in the Jews'
"radical revaluation of their enemies' values."

> All that has been done on earth against "the noble," "the powerful," "the
> masters," "the rulers," fades into nothing compared with what the *Jews*
> have done against them ... It was the Jews who, with awe-inspiring
> consistency, dared to invert the aristocratic value-equation (good = noble =
> powerful = beautiful = happy = beloved of God) ... saying "the wretched
> alone are the good; the poor, impotent, lowly alone are the good; the
> suffering, deprived, sick, ugly alone are pious, alone are blessed by God,
> blessedness is for them alone – and you, the powerful and noble, are on the
> contrary the evil, the cruel, the lustful, the insatiable, the godless to all
> eternity; and you shall be in all eternity the unblessed, accursed, and
> damned!" ... One knows *who* inherited the Jewish revaluation. (*GM* 34)

Although Nazi interpreters could invoke this polemic against "the
Jews" to support their anti-Semitism, at times Nietzsche can appreciate the genius of this revaluation by the Jews, the imagination
which was used to accomplish this revaluation. This morality was
necessary in order for the Jews to survive as a people. It was a

condition for their preservation; it was "life-preserving." But as for those who inherited this valuation, the Christians, Nietzsche has nothing but scorn.

In opposition to German idealism, Nietzsche argues for the continuity between Judaism and Christianity. Judaism is not the dark background upon which the light of Christianity shone; Christianity is not a counter-movement to Judaism, but rather the final consequence of its revaluation, of the degeneration of its god and morals (*AC* 24). Upon the "*false* soil" of Judaism grew up Christianity, which Nietzsche condemns as "a form of mortal enmity against reality that has never yet been surpassed" (*AC* 27). Like the Jews during the Assyrian captivity, the Jews during the occupation by the Roman empire castigated its masters as evil. The first Jewish Christians transvalued the values of the noble aristocracy of the Roman empire in order to seek spiritual revenge. Like Judaism, Christianity "distinguished all other powers on earth from themselves as 'unholy,' as 'world,' as 'sin'" (*AC* 27). Primitive Christianity also directed its *ressentiment* against the Jewish priestly caste, thus setting itself against the last order of rank upheld by this people and eliminating all the pathos of distance which Nietzsche consistently praises as necessary for a strong, healthy society.

Jesus himself is not exempt from this charge of destroying the noble order of rank, although his motivation was not a morality of *ressentiment*, but rather a morality of decadence.

> That holy anarchist ... summoned the people at the bottom, the outcasts and "sinners," the chandalas within Judaism, to opposition against the dominant order. (*AC* 27)

Jesus, unlike the Jewish priestly caste, performed his transvaluation of the dominant order, of the master morality of the Romans, as a result of his decadence.

In formulating his reading of Jesus, Nietzsche argues that the authentic "psychological type of the Redeemer ... could be contained in the Gospels despite the Gospels" (*AC* 29). For Nietzsche, this original type of the Redeemer is epitomized by the "sermonizer on the mount." Nietzsche argues that the transvaluation of noble morality performed in this sermon – in which the poor, meek, and humble rather than the rich, strong, and proud are called blessed – is based upon a decadent sensibility. Jesus finds blessedness in not resisting one's enemy, in meekness and humility, because he was not able to be an enemy. He makes a virtue of necessity. This ethic of non-resistance and passivity was instinct in Jesus. Because Jesus had a pathological resistance to all contact with reality, he created and placed his hope in an inner world in which all struggle is eliminated. Jesus' true world is based upon a negation of reality, "an instinctive hatred of every reality, a flight into 'what cannot be grasped'" (*AC* 29). In opposition to reality Jesus created "a merely 'inner' world, a 'true' world, an 'eternal' world. 'The kingdom of God is *in* you'" (*AC* 29).[11] Although this inner world was not created out of *ressentiment*, it was created out of a decadent physiology which shrinks instinctively away from reality, which avoids at all costs any feelings of struggle and antipathy. Nietzsche considers this inner world envisaged by Jesus a "*world of pure fiction*" which is "rooted in *hatred* of the natural (of reality!)" (*AC* 15), and this fictitious world, this world which is in actuality nothing, was the creation of Jesus. Jesus therefore "provides the very formula for decadence" (*AC* 15).

After the death of Jesus, the disciples misinterpreted the ethic presented by their rabbi by further corrupting Jesus' morality of decadence with their spirit of revenge. Whereas Jesus called upon his disciples to forgive their enemies, including the Jews and Romans who had executed him on the cross, his disciples refused to forgive those responsible for Jesus' death. Just as the Jewish priests sought spiritual revenge for the defeat of the nation, the Christian disciples sought spiritual revenge for the death of their Messiah.

Both Jesus and his disciples created their god and his kingdom in reaction against the world. Jesus created his god of love out of despair of human love (*BGE* 269). Primitive Christianity also "*created* its 'God' according to its needs" (*AC* 31), i.e., its need for revenge. It is this Christian God which Nietzsche considers "the low-water mark in the descending development of divine types." The primitive Christian church takes the *ressentiment* of Jewish slave morality to its highest pitch as "these holy anarchists made it a matter of 'piety' for themselves to destroy 'the world,' *that is*, the *imperium Romanum*" (*AC* 58). It is because they succeeded that Nietzsche cannot forgive the Christian church. Christianity succeeded in making slave morality the only valuation, into the one and only truth. Not only did the Christians express their own decadence and *ressentiment*, but they also succeeded in infecting masters with this anti-natural morality. The early Christians used the death of Jesus on the cross to triumph over their enemies, to infect even the strong with Jewish decadence and *ressentiment*. "What is certain ... is that *sub hoc signo* Israel, with its vengefulness and revaluation of all values, has hitherto triumphed again and again over all other ideals, over all *nobler* ideals" (*GM* 35).[12] Therefore, Nietzsche can take the struggle of "Rome against Judea, Judea against Rome" as the greatest event and the most deadly contradiction (*GM* 52).

Christianity accomplished this victory through the concepts of free will and responsibility. Judaeo-Christian morality holds "no belief more ardently than the belief that *the strong man is free* to be weak and bird of prey to be a lamb – for thus they gain the right to make the bird of prey *accountable* for being a bird of prey" (*GM* 45). Nietzsche's attack upon the belief in a unified subject with a free will is based upon his desire to overcome the Christian-moral evaluation of the world which asserts that man is free in order to hold him responsible, and holds him responsible in order to pronounce him guilty. The master race's will to power was labeled as evil by the impotent slaves. When this slave valuation triumphed, the masters' will to power had to be turned inward. "This *instinct for freedom* [in my language: the will to power] forcibly made latent ... this instinct for freedom pushed back and repressed, incarcerated within and finally able to discharge and vent itself only on itself: that, and that alone, is what the *bad conscience* is in its beginnings" (*GM* 87). Man's instincts must be discharged, and if slave morality denies one the right to discharge these instincts upon others in good conscience, these instincts are turned inward and vented upon oneself. This is the origin of the belief in the "soul" and is "the womb of all ideal and imaginative phenomena" (*GM* 87).

The Christian-moral interpretation of the world, "the concept of guilt and punishment, the whole 'moral world order'" (*AC* 49), is used to rob existence of its innocence. And with the "advent of the Christian God, as the maximum god attained so far," there is also "the maximum feeling of guilty indebtedness on earth" (*GM* 90). According to Nietzsche, Judaeo-Christian morality interprets suffering as the result of man's sin. The concept of "sin" is the most extreme form of bad conscience. Man's guilt is made absolute in being made guilt before the absolute God. Man's feeling of guilt and debt increases "until at last the irredeemable debt gives rise to the conception of irredeemable penance, the idea that it cannot be discharged ('*eternal*' punishment')" (*GM* 91). Whereas for primitive man the ancestors were the ones to whom the descendants owed

their debt, when these ancestors are turned into gods and finally into
the absolute God, the original creditors, the ancestors, are also
charged with guilt.

> Finally ... they are turned back against the "creditor," too: whether we
> think of the *causa prima* of man, the beginning of the human race, its primal
> ancestor who is from now on burdened with a curse ("Adam," "original
> sin," "unfreedom of the will"), or of nature from whose womb mankind
> arose and into whom the principle of evil is projected from now on ("the
> diabolizing of nature"), or of existence in general, which is now considered
> *worthless as such* (nihilistic withdrawal from it, a desire for nothingness or a
> desire for its antithesis, for a different mode of being, Buddhism and the
> like). (*GM* 92)

The concept of God is used to deprecate man, nature, and the
world. In drawing a parallel between Christianity and Buddhism,
Nietzsche evokes the conception of Christianity and religion put
forth by his most immediate predecessor, Arthur Schopenhauer.

Because Nietzsche relied upon Schopenhauer for his understanding of the Christian interpretation of the world, his denunciation
of Christianity is based upon a misunderstanding of Christian
doctrine. Schopenhauer interpreted Christianity through his own
philosophy which "candidly confesses the reprehensible nature of
the world and points to the denial of the will as the road to
redemption from it." Schopenhauer believes that his ethics is "thus
actually in the spirit of the New Testament."[13]

Although Schopenhauer objects to the optimism of the Old Testament story of creation (a point I will return to), he finds in the story
of the Fall the corroboration of his own pessimistic philosophy and
ethic.

> Nothing is more certain than that ... it is the grievous *sin of the world* which
> gives rise to the manifold and great *suffering* of the world ... The story of the
> Fall is consequently the only thing which reconciles me to the Old Testa-
> ment; I even regard it as the sole metaphysical truth contained in that
> book.[14]

Whenever Nietzsche criticizes the Christian-moral interpretation of
the world, he uses Schopenhauer's language. For example, in his
criticism of the priestly conception of sin, Nietzsche writes that the
priest teaches that man "must understand his suffering as a *punishment*" (*GM* 140). Nietzsche seeks to reverse this condemnation of life
and the world which Schopenhauer taught and which he argued
was the essence of both Eastern and Western religion.

In his pessimistic philosophy, Schopenhauer condemned "this world as a place of atonement, a sort of penal colony."[15] Both Schopenhauer and Nietzsche after him believed that the same view of the world was presented in the Bible. According to Schopenhauer,

> this is how the world appears here [in Christianity] as much as it does in Buddhism – and no longer in the light of the Jewish optimism which had found everything "very good": the Devil himself is now styled "Prince of this world" (John xii 31). The world is no longer an end, but a means: the kingdom of joy lies beyond it and beyond death. Renunciation in this world and the direction of hope towards a better world constitutes the spirit of Christianity.[16]

Schopenhauer equates Christianity with Buddhism and all Indian religions in its deprecation of this life as a vale of tears in favor of a divine or true world by which this world is judged and condemned. In the same way Nietzsche can describe the authentic Jesus beneath the corrupt image put forth by his disciples as being "like ... a Buddha on soil that is not at all Indian" (*AC* 31). Both Buddha and Jesus (i.e., Jesus as the psychological type of the redeemer) are described by Nietzsche as decadent and nihilistic, while both are absolved by him of the crime of *ressentiment*. This equation between Buddhism and the teachings of Jesus was certainly suggested by Schopenhauer, and Nietzsche must be criticized for a radically reductive hermeneutic in equating Jesus and Buddha just as Schopenhauer must be criticized for careless scholarship in comparative religion in equating Christianity and Buddhism.

Nietzsche praises Schopenhauer as "the *first* admitted and inexorable atheist among us Germans," for the "ungodliness of existence was for him something given, palpable, indisputable" (*GS* 357). In Nietzsche, as in Schopenhauer, "unconditional and honest atheism is simply the *presupposition* of the way he poses his problem," and Nietzsche, like Schopenhauer, concludes that "the way of this world is anything but divine" (*GS* 346). But Nietzsche condemns Schopenhauer's "Christian-ascetic-moral" conclusion to his pessimistic philosophy. Schopenhauer believed that because the world was not divine, because the world is only the will to live which strives in vain, one must renounce the world and the will to live.

It is in his analysis of the ascetic ideal that Nietzsche equates Schopenhauer's atheistic pessimism and Christianity's theistic nihilism. Both blame man's sin for the suffering of the world, and urge man to escape this world of vanity and suffering through a negation of the instincts, a denial of the will to live. According to Nietzsche, the ascetic ideal, which presents itself as the will to truth, conceals in actuality the nihilistic will, the will to nothingness:

We can no longer conceal from ourselves *what* is expressed by all that willing which has taken its direction from the ascetic ideal: this hatred of the human, and even more of the animal, and more still of the material, the horror of the senses, of reason itself, this fear of happiness and beauty, this longing to get away from all appearance, change, becoming, death, wishing, from longing itself – all this means – let us dare to grasp it – *a will to nothingness*, an aversion to life, a rebellion against the most fundamental presuppositions of life. (*GM* 162–163)

Schopenhauer certainly would not shrink from this conclusion, for he reaches the same one in the final sentence of *The World as Will and Representation*:

On the contrary, we freely acknowledge that what remains after the complete abolition of the will is, for all who are still full of the will, assuredly nothing. But also conversely, to those in whom the will has turned and denied itself, this very real world of ours with all its suns and galaxies, is – nothing.[17]

And if we compare Schopenhauer's conclusion to Nietzsche's condemnation of Christianity, we can see from whence Nietzsche derived his interpretation and the ground of his rejection of Christianity.

The Christian conception of God . . . God as the declaration of war against life, against, nature, against the will to live! God – the formula for every slander against "this world," for every lie about the "beyond"! God – the deification of nothingness, the will to nothingness pronounced holy! (*AC* 18)

Christianity is accused of imagining a God who opposes "the will to live," just as Schopenhauer envisages man's redemption as resulting from the renunciation of this will. Nietzsche rejects both Schopenhauer's nirvana and Christianity's heaven because they are inventions of the weak and suffering. "Who alone has good reason to lie his way out of reality? He who suffers from it" (*AC* 16). Those who suffer from reality "had to invent *another* world from whose point of view this affirmation of life [in noble morality] appeared as evil" (*AC* 24).

Nietzsche thus accepts uncritically Schopenhauer's description of

Christian morality. In a passage which must have greatly influenced Nietzsche, Schopenhauer contrasts the Greek and the Christian interpretation of suffering and death. The Greek "expresses *affirmation* of the will to life, through which life is assured for all time, however swiftly its figures and forms may succeed one another." The Christian, in direct contrast, "expresses *denial* of the will to life and redemption from a world in which death and the Devil reign." Schopenhauer concludes that between "the spirit of Graeco-Roman paganism and the spirit of Christianity the real antithesis is that of affirmation and denial of the will to live – in which regard Christianity is in the last resort fundamentally in the right."[18]

Nietzsche sets up the same antithesis through the comparison of the suffering and death of Dionysus and the Crucified. Although both Dionysus and Christ are martyred, the Greek and Christian interpretation of suffering and death are antithetical. According to the Greek, tragic view, "being is counted *holy enough* to justify even a monstrous amount of suffering. The tragic man is sufficiently strong, rich and capable of deifying to do so." For the Christian, however, suffering "is supposed to be the path to a holy existence . . . The Christian denies even the happiest lot on earth: he is sufficiently weak, poor, disinherited to suffer from life in whatever form he meets it." Nietzsche rejects Christianity for the same reason that Schopenhauer affirms it: "The god on the cross is a curse on life, a signpost to seek redemption from life." And Nietzsche affirms the Greek Dionysus for the same reason that Schopenhauer rejects it: "Dionysus cut to pieces is a *promise* of life: it will be eternally reborn and return from destruction" (*WP* 1052).

Nietzsche uses Schopenhauer's distinctions to reach a conclusion diametrically opposed to his educator, but in complete agreement with his other predecessor, Feuerbach. In the appendix to *The Essence of Christianity*, the part which the author considered the "negative, destructive"[19] part of his book, Feuerbach reaches the same conclusion as Nietzsche regarding the nihilism of Christian supernaturalism.

Where the heavenly life is a truth, the earthly life is a lie; where imagination is all, reality is nothing. To him who believes in an eternal heavenly life, the present life loses its value, – or rather, it has already lost its value: belief in the heavenly life is belief in the worthlessness and nothingness of this life.[20]

Feuerbach, like Nietzsche, rejects this denigration of the earthly world and ascetic morality, which he labels "monachism," because it teaches "separation from the world, the negation of this life."[21]

Feuerbach agrees with both Schopenhauer and Nietzsche that this rejection of the world and earthly life is an essential part of Christianity.

When once Christianity realised itself in a worldly form, it must also necessarily develop the supranaturalistic, supramundane tendency of Christianity into a literal separation from the world. And this disposition to separate from life, from the body, from the world, – this hypercosmic then anti-cosmic tendency, is a genuinely biblical disposition and spirit.[22]

But, while this assertion, accepted fully by Nietzsche, describes ontotheology, this denigration of the world is *not* a "genuinely *biblical* disposition."

Feuerbach continues this passage by contrasting the "heathen" philosophy and the Christian doctrine of the destruction of the world. The Christian doctrine reveals the "anti-cosmic" nature of the Christian faith. "The Christian destruction of the world is ... the triumph of faith over the world, a judgment of God, an anticosmical, supernaturalistic act."[23] The "heathen philosophers," on the other hand, "supposed the world to be destroyed only to arise again renovated as a real world; they granted it eternal life."[24] This "heathen," or in Nietzsche's terms "pagan" view, was to be adopted by Nietzsche in his affirmation of eternal recurrence. But before examining Nietzsche's pagan alternative to the Christian view of the *kosmos*, we must first judge the accuracy of his interpretation and critique of the Judaeo-Christian understanding of the world.

Nietzsche misreads the New Testament because he reads it through the lens of Schopenhauer's pessimistic philosophy. Schopenhauer asserts that Christianity, like Neoplatonic and Eastern religions, denies the reality of the material world in favor of an immaterial divine world. Nietzsche alludes to the source of his misunderstanding of the New Testament in his later works when he groups together "Christianity, the philosophy of Schopenhauer, in a certain sense already the philosophy of Plato" as typical forms of "idealism" (*EH* 272). Nietzsche sets his ideal of Dionysian affirmation against the decadent denial of life and this world by "Plato or Christianity or Schopenhauer" (*EH* 273).

But is this equation between Plato's idealism, Schopenhauer's pessimism, and Christianity's eschatology justified? If we judge by reading the New Testament in its historical context, then we have to answer no. Reinhold Niebuhr gives us a clear explanation of the biblical separation between this world and the world to come. "Salvation lies at the end of history and not in some realm of eternity above history, because Christianity, in common with prophetic thought, does not regard creation as evil."[25] This aspect of the Judaeo-Christian understanding of the earth is rejected by Schopenhauer and subsequently ignored by Nietzsche. Schopenhauer writes, "that a god like *Jehovah* should create this world of want and misery *animi causa* and *de gaieté de cœur* and then go so far as to applaud himself for it, saying it is all very good: that is quite unacceptable."[26] Schopenhauer ignores the New Testament's Semitic background. Instead he falsely argues that it has its origin in Indian religion. He further asserts that the world in the New Testament appears

no longer in the light of Jewish optimism which had found everything "very good" ... This world is no longer an end, but a means: the kingdom of joy lies beyond it and beyond death. Renunciation in this world and the direction of all hope towards a better world constitutes the spirit of Christianity ... Everything true in Christianity is also to be discovered in Brahmanism and Buddhism.[27]

But, while the New Testament (following the Old) does look forward to a "better world" to come, the Bible does not set this new world in opposition to the created world as a separate heavenly realm but rather looks forward in hope to the renewal and redemption of God's created earth. "Salvation [in the Bible] never means flight from the world to God; it means, in effect, God's descent from heaven to bring man in historical experience into fellowship with himself. Therefore the consummation of salvation is eschatological."[28]

CHAPTER 4

The redemptive–eschatological separation between the present world and the world to come in the New Testament

> For God so loved the world that he gave his one and only Son, that whoever believes in him shall not perish but have eternal life. For God did not send his Son into the world to condemn the world, but to save the world through him.   John 3:16–18
>
> Do not love the world or anything in the world. If anyone loves the world, the love of the Father is not in him.   1 John 2:15

Nietzsche makes a mockery of the New Testament. He argues that one must read these writings with gloves on (*AC* 46), but anyone who has read the New Testament with any degree of care must wonder if he read the Bible with something covering his eyes and ears, not his hands.

In an ironic allusion to Jesus' promise that the truth shall set you free, Nietzsche claims that he is the first to be able to interpret correctly the true meaning of Christianity.

Only we, we spirits who have *become free*, have the presuppositions for understanding something that nineteen centuries have misunderstood ... Previous readers were immeasurably removed from our loving and cautious neutrality. (*AC* 36)

Through an investigation of the "presuppositions" which he brings to his criticism of Judeao-Christianity, I want to unmask Nietzsche's "loving and cautious neutrality" as a hostile and resentful slandering of the biblical understanding of the world. Hans Küng articulates a similar critique of Nietzsche's attack on Christianity:

His knowledge of theology and Church history does not come up to the seriousness of his charges. Many passages, especially in the historically and exegetically oriented *Antichrist*, are more like pamphlets than records of cool investigation ... His slips are sometimes embarrassing, generalizations and labels abound, anti-Christian fanaticism clouds his judgment.[1]

62

Nietzsche himself describes how his reading of the Christian scriptures is based upon a hermeneutics of suspicion: "one should always
have one's little fund of reason, mistrust, and malice to hand when
one reads the New Testament" (*WP* 199).[2]

Nietzsche castigates theologians for their "*incapacity for philology,*"
defining philology as "the art of reading well – of reading facts
without falsifying them by interpretation, without losing caution,
patience, delicacy, in the desire to understand" (*AC* 52). This
definition seems doubly ironic in a text which loses all caution and
patience, written by a philosopher who is perhaps most famous
for asserting that there are no facts, only interpretations, but
Nietzsche was willing to contradict himself in his desire to scandalize
and mock Christianity, in order to make Christianity look "contemptible."

But his charges against Christian hermeneutics must be turned
against Nietzsche himself. Most interpreters have followed Kaufmann and Jaspers in mentioning that Nietzsche's interpretations of
the New Testament are unhistorical, unconvincing, and based upon
errors in philology but then excusing Nietzsche because he "sees
vital things and has the power to communicate them vividly" and
because the "errors of great men are more fruitful than the truths of
little men."[3] This sort of vague apology for Nietzsche seems to me to
be special pleading. Nietzsche's critique of Christianity is central to
his philosophical enterprise, and if this interpretation is based upon
prejudice and false generalizations, then his philosophy must be
criticized accordingly.

Nietzsche's misinterpretation of the New Testament is summa-
rized in his assertion that "Christianity is Platonism for the people."
According to Heidegger, "Nietzsche's critique of Christianity has as
its presupposition the interpretation of Christianity as a degenerate
form of Platonism; his critique consists in nothing other than this
interpretation" (*N* III 60). This leads Nietzsche to conclude that
Christian doctrine, including the writings of the New Testament,
teaches that this world is worthless and illusory, and that we must
put our hopes in another ideal realm, i.e. heaven. "As long as
Christianity teaches that our world, as a vale of tears, is merely a
temporal passage to eternal bliss beyond, Nietzsche can regard
Christianity in general as Platonism (the doctrine of two worlds) for
the people" (*N* IV 46). But this is simply not what the Bible teaches
about the world.

The distinction between this world and the world to come in the
Bible is not metaphysical, but rather *eschatological*. Reinhold
Niebuhr defines the eschatology of biblical Christianity and summarizes the resulting differences between the Judaeo-Christian worldview and both naturalism and idealism.

It is this doctrine [eschatology] which distinguishes Christianity both from
naturalistic utopianism and from Hellenistic otherworldliness. In it the
Christian hope of the fulfillment of life is expressed paradoxically and
dialectically, holding fast to its essential conception of the relation of time
and eternity. History is not regarded as meaningless, as in Greek thought,
particularly in later neo-Platonism. For this reason the realm of fulfillment
is not above history, in some heaven in which pure form is abstracted from
the concrete content of historical existence. The realm of fulfillment is at
the end of history. This symbolises that fulfillment both transcends and is
relevant to historical forms.[4]

This interpretation of the Christian view of the world and history
must be elucidated through an analysis of the biblical writings in
order to defend it against Nietzsche's attack on Christian eschatology.

Nietzsche attacks the eschatology of the New Testament as a
·symptom of the original disciples' *ressentiment*, which motivated them
to create a vengeful God as well as "those wholly unevangelical
concepts which now it cannot do without: 'the return,' the 'Last
Judgement,' every kind of temporal expectation and promise"
(*AC* 31). Nietzsche correctly describes these eschatological terms as
temporal symbols, but interprets them as the first Christians' way of
displacing their desire for revenge upon a God who enacts revenge
for them (*AC* 44).

We can perhaps again see the influence of Schopenhauer who
presents a similar critique of the biblical "Last Judgment":

There is finally the further fact that the God who prescribes forbearance
and forgiveness of every sin, even to the point of loving one's enemy, fails to
practise it himself, but rather the opposite: since a punishment which is
introduced at the end of things, when all is over and done with for ever, can
be intended neither to improve nor deter; it is nothing but revenge.[5]

But rather than simply rejecting this Christian doctrine, Schopenhauer interprets it "*sensu allegorico*" to assert that what "this dogma
hypostatizes as eternal damnation is nothing other than this world of
ours: *this* is what devolves upon all the rest. It is a sufficiently evil
place: it is Purgatory, it is Hell."[6] Thus Schopenhauer can conclude

that the New Testament pessimistically denies any value to this world only by allegorizing New Testament doctrine to make it approximate Eastern, Indian religions, just as many of the Church Fathers allegorized the New Testament to make it approximate Hellenic philosophy, subsequently perverting biblical theology into ontotheology.

Nietzsche asserts that Jesus' original conception of the kingdom of heaven, before it was reinterpreted by his disciples after his death, referred to an inner, subjective state. According to Nietzsche, Jesus taught that the "'kingdom of heaven' is a state of the heart – not something that is to come 'above the earth' or 'after death.' ... The 'kingdom of God' is nothing that one expects ... it is an experience of the heart; it is everywhere, it is nowhere" (*AC* 34). Paul is of course criticized most severely for taking Jesus' subjective, existential understanding of the kingdom of God and turning it into the priestly lie about a personal immortality and a coming judgment in order to tyrannize the masses and form herds (*AC* 42). However, a reading of the New Testament which historicizes these writings – by taking into account the worldview of its writers and by investigating the contemporary opposition which the biblical writers were attacking – will expose the weakness of Nietzsche's critique of the biblical division between the kingdom of this world and the kingdom of God taught by Jesus,[7] John, and Paul.

The New Testament understanding of the world is formed and based upon the Old Testament conception of the world as God's creation. One cannot simply reject or ignore this biblical doctrine as do Schopenhauer and Nietzsche. Jewish monotheism holds that God created the world and pronounced it good. The world, "heaven and earth" in the Old Testament and "cosmos" in the New, is not considered the product of a lesser demiurge or an evil god, as in Platonism or Gnosticism. God is separate from the *kosmos*,[8] although he is not the unmoved mover of Aristotelian theology, but is rather related to his creation in love and concern for his creatures.[9]

Because the New Testament holds to both the Old Testament teachings that the world is God's good creation and that this creation was corrupted by the rebellion of humanity against God, the New Testament presents a dialectical and paradoxical understanding of the world, evidenced by the apparently contradictory quotations in my epigraphs to this section. But, when understood in the light of Judaeo-Christian eschatology, the New Testament understanding of the *kosmos* will be revealed as consistent in itself and distinct from both classical and modern understandings of the universe.

Kosmos has three interrelated but distinguishable meanings in the New Testament. *Kosmos* means the world as God's creation, the sum of all created being. The New Testament sometimes uses the terms *ge* (earth), recalling the Hebraic "heaven and earth," and *ktisis* (creation), recalling the Old Testament narrative of creation, in order to designate this positive understanding of the world as the work of God the Creator.

World can also refer in the New Testament to the human world, not only to the earth, but also the people in it. This more restricted meaning of the term *kosmos* leads to the possibility of using the term with a strictly dyslogistic connotation. "World" can be used in this sense to stress the biblical doctrine of humanity's alienation from God.

This use of the term "world" in a negative sense in the New Testament does not contradict the Old Testament doctrine of cre-.ation, but rather presupposes it. "Since the Bible regards the *kosmos* as the object of divine creation, the OT view of God as its Judge necessarily comes to bear upon it once it is regarded as the human world."[10] Thus the world can be used to mean fallen creation and mankind "in its hardened turning from God and his revelation."[11] The world is condemned under God's judgment because it, i.e., humanity, has rebelled against its Creator.

But regarding the world as under God's judgment does not lead to a purely pessimistic view of the world in the New Testament because the world also stands under God's mercy. Thus John can write that Jesus came into "the world," i.e. God's creation and the realm of human existence, because he loved it and wanted to save it, and at the same time assert that Christians should not love "the world," i.e., the attitude of the creature in rebellion against its Creator.

The negative connotation of world as a synecdoche for humanity in its rebellious and alienated condition is used most prominently in the writings of Paul and John; therefore, these two writers are most often cited as providing evidence of a Platonic, metaphysical, or even gnostic dualism in the Bible. Consequently, I will present a close reading of the use of this term in the Pauline epistles and the Johannine writings in order to show that the New Testament does not present a nihilistic denigration of the world.

Paul uses the term *kosmos* in the same three ways which were outlined above. *Kosmos* is used to mean creation as a whole, the world as the place of human existence, and to mean humankind as a whole, humanity as a creature created by God. This final meaning can be used in an ethically neutral sense by Paul to teach that humans are creatures. They are not gods themselves; they are human in distinction from the divine. Therefore they are also, in comparison with the divine, weak and mortal. In biblical anthropology (*contra* Feuerbach and Nietzsche), this does not yet imply a negative determination. But when human beings rebel against their creaturehood, when they forget God and cease to worship Him, when they assert their wills in rebellion against their Creator's and deny Him, they are then designated as "worldly" in the strictly negative sense. In Paul, as in the rest of the New Testament, *kosmos* can have: (1) the positive connotation of God's creation and the place of redemption; (2) the neutral, descriptive meaning of humanity as a creature before God; or (3) the negative connotation of humanity in rebellion against God.

Although Paul can use the term *kosmos* to epitomize unredeemed creation, it is important to note that his writings contain no gnostic dualism in which the physical world or the physical body is inherently evil, a prison for the pure, divine soul.[12] Paul makes it clear that it is humanity's rebellion against God, our sin, which causes "this world" to be evil. C. F. D. Moule calls this a "dualism of the will – a dualism of obedience and disobedience" and distinguishes this Pauline dualism from the philosophical, material dualism which characterizes Platonic and gnostic philosophies.[13] In the New Testament what Moule calls a "moral antithesis" is set in the context of the relationship between the human and the divine, so that Paul is referring to one's status before God, as either guilty of rebellion or forgiven of this sin.

Because *kosmos* is used to designate the sinful existence of humans, Paul uses the term *aion* instead to designate the new life of eschatological hope. The Jewish understanding of the world, both in the Old Testament and in later apocalyptic writings, tends to be conceptualized more in temporal than in spatial terms.[14]

Taking this Hebraic background into account we discover that the division between "two worlds" in the biblical writings does not refer to a spatial, cosmological dualism, but rather to a temporal, eschatological separation between the present age and the age to come. Kosmos "is much more a time concept than a space concept; or, more exactly, it is an *eschatological concept.*"[15]

The eschatological hope of the Bible looks forward to a new age or aeon, in which the world will be purged of evil and suffering. Although this "new age," this new heaven and new earth, is some-times designated as eternal in opposition to "this age," which is transitory, which has a beginning with humanity's rebellion against God and which will end with the advent of the new age, the new age is not represented as a timeless, static heaven without a world in which those present will be pure spirit without bodies. Oscar Cullman in his work on the primitive Christian conception of time explains how the meaning of the contrast between the two ages in the New Testament is opposed to the dualism of time and eternity in Hellenistic thought:

To be sure, there exists a radical contrast between the two ages, of which the one is characterized as "evil" (Gal. 1:4); but this is not meant in the sense that the one is temporal while the other is timeless – in both cases, indeed, the thing meant is called "age."[16]

The eschatological hope of the Bible is designated by a number of terms: the age to come (from Jewish apocalyptic), the new heaven and new earth (from the Old Testament's prophetic eschatology), and also as the kingdom of God (from Jesus' adoption of Jewish eschatology). All of these terms derive from Hebraic, biblical thought.

In the synthesis of biblical thought with Greek philosophy, and consequently in much of the popular understanding of Christianity, the hope of the coming kingdom of God turned into a desire to escape earthly existence, "the world," in favor of an eternal, unchanging realm, "heaven." Everett Ferguson argues that this change in Christian eschatology was a result of (1) battles with Greek thought – "This shift in emphasis from the active sense of kingly power to the static sense of realm illustrates the shift in thinking from the dynamic biblical concepts to the more static concepts of Greco-Roman thought" – and (2) persecutions by the Roman empire – "The church's troubles with the Roman Empire gave it reason to play down the kingdom idea, especially any indication of its present manifestation. Thus in political contexts Christians emphasized that Christ's kingdom is otherworldly and heavenly."[17] Cullman concurs that "very early the Greek conception of time supplanted the biblical one, so that down through the history of doctrine to the present day there can be traced a great misunderstanding, upon the basis of which that is claimed as 'Christian' which in reality is Greek."[18] While Schopenhauer embraces and Nietzsche rejects this ontotheological dualism between the temporal world and an eternal heaven, both thinkers claim to find this philosophy in the New Testament.

But Paul does not teach a purely "otherworldly" hope to the first Christian churches. Rather, he teaches them to hope in the coming of Jesus Christ, his return to this world and the establishment of his reign on earth. The hope of a new heaven and a new earth is made possible in Paul's writings by the faith that Jesus Christ has forgiven the sinful rebellion of humans and made possible their reconciliation with God. "When reconciled and redeemed, the cosmos ceases to be cosmos; it is the kingdom of God, the coming aeon, the new heaven and earth."[19] This biblical antithesis between the world and the kingdom of God I call a *redemptive*–eschatological separation, for it is Jesus' redemption of "the world" which has made possible the reconciliation of humanity with God. But this redemption is not automatic; the biblical *kerygma* sets before human beings the crisis of a decision, a decision to either accept Jesus as God's Son or to reject this revelation. Those who do believe are not taken out of this world, nor do they hope to be taken out of this world into heaven. "Believers live in the cosmos (1 Cor. 5:10), honor its Creator (Acts 17:24) ... and care for the things of the cosmos (1 Cor. 7:32ff.)."[20] In all of these verses, *kosmos* is used in its positive sense to mean God's creation, the realm of human existence.

Yet at the same time Paul tells believers: "Do not conform any longer to the pattern of this world" (Romans 12:2) because through the cross of Christ the world has been crucified to them and they to the world (Galatians 6:14). In these verses Paul is using "world" in the negative sense to mean humanity's sinful rebellion against God. The human world, considered as a whole, does not acknowledge God's reign or his revelation through Jesus Christ. But through the death of Christ, Christians "have crucified the sinful nature" (Galatians 5:24), just as they have "been crucified ... to the world"

(Galatians 6:14). This crucifixion of and to the cosmos refers to the believer's status before God and not to his or her relation to the physical world or corporeal, historical existence. The antithesis between "this" *kosmos* or "this" *aion* and the kingdom of God or the new *aion* is not a metaphysical dualism in which the physical or historical world is denied and denigrated, but rather a redemptive separation between those who have been reconciled with the world's Creator, the spiritual, and those who remain alienated from their Creator, the worldly. This redemptive separation is applied not only to individuals, but also to God's creation as a whole in the eschatological separation between this age and the age to come. A few examples from Paul's letters[21] will illustrate this thesis.

In Romans 8:19–23 Paul looks forward to the redemption of creation (*ktsis*). He celebrates the Christian hope that "the creation itself will be liberated from its bondage to decay and brought into the glorious freedom of the children of God." Note that the passage does not speak at all of the Christian's redemption *from* creation, *from* the bondage of the physical world, but rather looks forward to the redemption *of* both the world and "our bodies" (Romans 8:23) at the *parousia* of Christ. Just as there is no cosmological dualism between an ideal, immaterial heaven and an evil, material world, so is there no anthropological dualism between the person's heavenly soul and his earthly body. Rather, there is a separation between the creation, including humanity, in its current bondage to corruption and evil and the redemption of this creation at the end of the present age.[22] The separation is not based upon a metaphysical, cosmological dualism of the material and immaterial, but rather upon a distinction between creation in sinful alienation from God, the present evil age, and creation in restored fellowship with God, the age to come.

But in addressing Hellenistic audiences and correcting Hellenistic heresies, Paul does at times make use of spatial metaphors for heaven rather than temporal metaphors for the new age. The biblical language of eschatology "involves both vertical and horizontal referents, spatial and temporal categories. In other words eschatology involves heaven as well as the Last Day."[23] Thus far I have concentrated on the temporal determinations of eschatology in the Bible in order to elucidate the Hebraic origins of biblical thought. In turning now to the use of spatial metaphors in biblical eschatology, the Jewish background of the New Testament writers, especially Paul, must not be forgotten.

The *Religionsgeschichtliche* school has interpreted Paul's distinction between heaven and earth as a sign that he, or his followers, began to think in Hellenistic categories of thought.[24] But I want to follow those scholars who focus instead on the continuity of the Bible's *Heilsgeschichte*. Rather than arguing that the Greek language and worldview transformed Paul's thought, I will be arguing that Paul transformed the Greek language and worldview through the eschatological categories of his gospel.

In taking into account Paul's Jewish background, we can see that in Paul "earthly" signifies the order of the present evil age, and "heavenly" characterizes the order of the age to come. Paul has adapted this spatial terminology through the Jewish worldview which is temporal and eschatological.[25]

For example, in Paul's letter to the Philippians, he addresses the danger presented by those he calls "enemies of the cross" (Philippians 3:18). The exact identity of these enemies has been disputed,[26] but it is clear from the context that Paul is warning against the influence of some group which is misusing the doctrine of grace to preach libertinism.[27] Paul calls these people "earthly" – "Their mind is on earthly things" (Philippians 3:19) – not because their "whole attention is fixed on physical and material interests,"[28] but because their conduct is ruled by their own natural self rather than by the Spirit of God. Andrew T. Lincoln further explains that Paul is using the term "earthly" against those who have "prided themselves on being heavenly minded"[29] and therefore have considered themselves free from any moral restraints.

Paul is not distinguishing between those whose focus is fixed on the eternal verities (like Plato's philosopher) and those whose attention is fixed on the material world (like those trapped in Plato's allegory of the cave); rather, he is making a distinction between those who are truly led by the Spirit of God and those who are merely following their own religion and are boasting about being heavenly minded. These enemies of the cross deny any value and meaning to earthly existence, arguing that their conduct on earth does not matter since their true home is in heaven. Thus Paul is attacking the same philosophy which Nietzsche denounces in his crusade against Christianity's nihilism.

Paul asserts that these self-proclaimed heavenly minded people are in actuality earthly minded. The truly heavenly minded are those who follow Paul in teaching godly moral conduct on earth, who teach the imitation of Christ's life.

But our citizenship is in heaven. And we eagerly await a Savior from there, the Lord Jesus Christ, who, by the power that enables him to bring everything under his control, will transform our lowly bodies so that they will be like his glorious body. (Philippians 3:20–21)

Understanding what Paul means when he writes that the Christians' "citizenship" (*politeuma*) is in heaven is crucial. Under the influence of Hellenistic thought, this passage has often been interpreted to mean that our earthly life is meaningless, a vale of tears, and that our true life will begin after we die and go to heaven. The translation of the term *politeuma* as "homeland" gives this impression.[30] This recalls both Plato's teaching on the soul and Philo's use of Plato's philosophy to reinterpret the Jewish scriptures. Plato and Philo taught that we begin as souls in heaven and fall into corporeality and the material world; salvation comes about by practicing Platonic philosophy, by turning away from the material world to contemplate the ideal realm of the forms, and returning to our heavenly home from which we have fallen.[31]

But Paul is not teaching such a doctrine. As he does in Romans 8, Paul counters this cosmological dualism by emphasizing in Philippians 3 the restoration of the world through Jesus Christ who has power to redeem "everything" or "all things" (*pas*), a term used in the New Testament to refer to all of creation, a translation of the Hebraic term for the universe, *'olam.*

And just as in the incarnation God comes "down" to humans to enter the world, so also at the *parousia* does Christ come again to the earth to redeem all things. The spatial metaphors need not be taken literally or as implying that the biblical writers had a simplistic, naive view of the universe as "three-storied" (Bultmann). Rather, the metaphors mean that it is God who comes to us rather than we who think or earn our way to God. Although a large current of Christian theology has for centuries, under the influence of Hellenistic thought, taught Christians to place their hope in the rising or even the return of the soul to a heavenly home from which it has "fallen," the Bible teaches Christians to look forward to the establishment of the kingdom of God on earth and to the redemption and glorification of the human body as well as the soul.

As he does in Romans, Paul emphasizes here in Philippians the redemption of the body: "the Lord Jesus Christ ... will transform our lowly bodies so that they will be like his glorious body." Whereas the King James version mistranslates this passage to refer to the "vile" body, implying a gnostic dualism in which the soul is imprisoned within the corrupt body, the New International Version better translates this passage to read "our lowly bodies."[32] The phrase literally means "our body of humiliation," referring to the suffering and persecution of the Christian in the present age which are imitative of the suffering and humiliation of Jesus Christ in his crucifixion. Rather than constructing metaphysical dualisms, Paul is actually arguing against – "deconstructing" if you prefer – both a cosmological and an anthropological dualism in this passage.

When Paul writes that "our citizenship is in heaven," he is using a "down to earth" metaphor which the Philippians would readily recognize. He is referring to Philippi's status as a colony of Rome which did not make Philippi itself less important, but rather conferred dignity and meaning upon the city.[33] In the same way, the city of God, "Jerusalem that is above" (Galatians 4:26), did not make earthly life meaningless to Christians, but rather bestowed meaning and gave direction to life on earth.[34]

Whereas in Philippians 3 Paul is warning against the influence of libertines who stress freedom from all moral regulations, in my final example from Paul's letter to the Colossians, Paul is warning against ascetic teachings. In his "contextual" reading of Paul's epistles, J. Christiaan Beker has stressed the need to understand Paul's historical opponents,[35] and Lincoln uses a similar hermeneutic method in his work on Paul.[36] Both libertinism and asceticism were characteristic of Paul's opponents, of the syncretism of Jewish apocalyptic and popular Hellenistic religions which led to the development of Gnosticism.[37]

The ascetics felt that they had to free themselves from the influence of matter (the body) by inflicting punishment on their bodies. Those who gave in to license assumed an attitude of indifference to things physical and material, the idea being that only the soul is important and therefore the body may do what it pleases.[38]

Both philosophies are based upon a dualism which teaches that the material world and the physical body are in themselves evil. As in his letter to the Philippians, Paul warns the church in Colossae against such a dualism.

Paul overcomes this dualism through his teaching on Christ, who is the agent of both the creation and redemption of the cosmos. It is by Christ that "all things were created: things in heaven and on earth, visible and invisible . . . all things were created by him and for

him" (Colossians 1:16). Against the proto-gnostics in Colossae, Paul
does not regard Christ as one among a number of emanations of
God, of spiritual intermediaries between God and man. This same
doctrine of emanations was used to disparage the physical world as
far removed from God's heavenly realm. Because of the Jewish
element in this syncretistic philosophy, these proto-gnostics could
not deny that there was a bond between God and creation.

They therefore taught that God put forth from himself a series of "aeons"
or emanations, each a little more distant from him and each having a little
less of deity. At the end of this chain of intermediate beings there is an
emanation possessing enough of deity to make a world but removed far
enough from God that his creative activities could not compromise the
perfect purity of God. The world, they argued, was the creation of this
lesser power, who being so far removed from God was both ignorant of and
hostile to him.[39]

Paul's Christ, by contrast, is not merely a distant emanation of God,
but rather God's only begotten Son. In union with the God of the
Old Testament, Paul's Christ is the creator of "all things," of
"heaven and earth." Thus the Old Testament doctrine of the
goodness of the world as God's creation is maintained in full force.

   Christ is also the "image of the invisible God." Unlike Platonic
dualism which separates the invisible realm of the intellect and the
visible realm of the material world, Paul asserts that God has been
made visible in Jesus Christ. Once again Christ, who created all
things "in heaven and on earth, visible and invisible" (Colossians
1:16), bridges the gap between a philosophical dualism.[40] Paul
further asserts that God was pleased "through him to reconcile to
himself all things, whether things on earth or things in heaven, by
making peace through his blood, shed on the cross" (Colossians
1:20). The dualism between heaven and earth is bridged by Christ,
who brings redemption to all things. Both heaven and earth are
redeemed by the Creator of heaven and earth. The division between
the two is based upon a temporal, eschatological division. Christ
reigns now in heaven and at the *parousia* he will also reign on earth.[41]

   A redemptive separation remains between those who have
accepted the gospel of Jesus Christ and those who have rejected it,
but it is not the material or physical which alienates humanity from
God; rather, it is human sin. "Once you were alienated from God
and were enemies in your minds because of your evil behavior"
(Colossians 1:21). Christ redeems the believer from this alienation

and guilt before God. "But now he has reconciled you by Christ's physical body through death to present you holy in his sight" (Colossians 1:22). Notice Paul's stress upon Christ's "physical body," just as in other passages he stresses the eschatological redemption of the Christian's body as well as soul. The Pauline doctrine of the incarnation teaches that "in Christ all the fullness of the Deity lives in bodily form" (Colossians 2:9); therefore, the body cannot be evil in itself.

Paul's subsequent condemnation of "hollow and deceptive philosophy" should not be read as an anti-intellectual rejection of wisdom and intelligence (*contra* Nietzsche). Rather, Paul is rejecting the dualistic philosophy of the proto-gnostics at Colossae, which is, ironically, a philosophy similar to the nihilistic denigration of the world which Nietzsche condemns in his attack on Christianity. Nietzsche's attack on nihilism cannot be used to condemn biblical theology, for Paul attacks the same type of other-worldly philosophy.

But both Paul's rejection of worldly philosophy and Nietzsche's attack on nihilism can be used to criticize "Christian" ontotheology which distorts the biblical message of redemption through use of the dualistic philosophy of Hellenistic thought, just as the false teachers in the church at Colossae did.

The advocates of the philosophy [at Colosse] take the earthly situation as their starting-point from which by their own efforts and techniques they will ascend into the heavenlies. Paul moves in the reverse direction, since he sees the starting-point and source of the believer's life in the resurrected Christ in heaven, from where it works itself out into earthly life (3:5ff) and from where it will eventually be revealed for what it is (3:4).[42]

Ontotheology makes the same reversal as the Colossian philosophy condemned by Paul by beginning with Greek (or existential or post-structuralist, etc.) philosophy and then using this philosophy to interpret the Bible. By beginning with Being to speak analogously of God (*analogia entis*) or by beginning with Being to speak negatively of God (*via negationis*), ontotheology takes our earthly experience as the starting-point in seeking to reach a concept of God. Paul, in contrast, claims to begin with God's revelation of himself to humanity.

While Greek theology teaches that man achieves salvation through an ascension of the disembodied soul to heaven, Christian eschatology looks forward to the redemption of human existence when God's kingdom descends upon the earth. Therefore when Paul exhorts the Colossians, as he did the Philippians – "Set your minds on things above, not on earthly things" – he is not like Plato's Socrates who in the *Phaedo* exhorts the philosopher to shun the "corporeal element" which "is burdensome and heavy and earthy and visible" in order to contemplate "that which is hidden from the eyes and invisible, to be grasped only by the intelligence and by philosophy."[43] Paul makes it clear that by "earthly things" he is referring to "sexual immorality [not sex], impurity, lust, evil desires [not all desires] and greed, which is idolatry" (Colossians 3:5). The asceticism which Paul argues against in Colossians is condemned as "earthly" because it is based upon human effort alone. Thus when Paul uses "earth" or "world" in a negative sense, he means by these terms the sinful response of unbelievers to God the Creator. This includes attempts, like ontotheology, to reach up to the divine through the human mind or will alone.

John means the same thing when he uses the term "world" in the negative sense. John commands his readers: "Do not love the world or anything in the world. If anyone loves the world, the love of the Father is not in him" (1 John 2:15). Taken out of context this passage seems to support Nietzsche's contention that Christianity is nihilism, a nihilism which denigrates and devalues our earthly existence. But John goes on to delimit what he means by *kosmos* in this passage: "the cravings of sinful man, the lust of his eyes and the boasting of what he has and does" (1 John 2:16). Just as in Paul, John is making a separation not between the ideal and the material, but rather between those who have been redeemed by Christ and those who seek to redeem themselves. This is made clear in John's gospel when Jesus asserts that "God did not send his Son into the world to condemn the world, but to save the world through him. Whoever believes in him is not condemned, but whoever does not believe stands condemned already because he has not believed in the name of God's one and only Son" (John 3:17–18). Like Paul, John is articulating a redemptive separation, not a cosmological dualism.

Even more often than Paul, John has been accused of teaching a gnostic dualism while in fact he is repudiating proto-gnostic teachings in the early church.[44] John, like Paul, uses terminology and symbols familiar to his Greek-speaking audience, but John, again like Paul, reshapes this language to express the thought of the Old

Testament revelation and the new revelation presented by Jesus Christ.

This can be seen in the prologue to John's gospel. John writes that "the world did not know him," that is the *logos*, whom John identifies with Jesus of Nazareth. Karl Barth admits that "we are reminded by [this] verse of the pessimistic judgment on the cosmos that we also find in Hermetic and Mandean writings,"[45] but Barth further notes that this verse is surrounded by passages which keep this judgment from hardening into a dualistic system.

These passages articulate the Judaeo-Christian doctrine of the creation and redemption of the cosmos by God through Jesus which works against any metaphysical dualism. "Through him all things were made" (John 1:3). Through Jesus "all things," both heaven and earth, were created. "He was in the world, and though the world was made through him, the world did not know him" (John 1:10). This, along with John's statement that "the Word became flesh and made his dwelling among us" (John 1:14), is the most well known statement of the Christian doctrine of the incarnation. Jesus, the Word who "was God," became flesh and came into the world. Unlike all gnostic teachings, this doctrine affirms that the human body and the human world are not intrinsically evil. If God himself can enter these they must be capable of good. This is the same emphasis which Paul makes in Colossians when he stresses that in Christ the fullness of the deity lives in "bodily form" and that God reconciled us to him through Christ's "physical body." Both authors are working to correct the proto-gnostic tendencies of their listeners and to attack the proto-gnostic heresies of their enemies.

C. H. Dodd is thus incorrect when he interprets John's prologue as reflecting a Platonic–Philonic dualism of the spiritual and the material.

Here we are in a world of conceptions to which eschatology is strange. Eschatology is cast in a temporal mould. It speaks of this age and that which is to come ... The Prologue on the other hand is based upon the philosophical conception of two orders of being, distinguished not by succession in time, but by the greater or less measure of reality which they possess. There is the order of pure reality, transcendent and eternal, which is the very thought of God, and there is the empirical order, which is real only as it expresses the eternal order.[46]

Although John tends to express the eschatology of Jesus' preaching in "vertical" rather than "horizontal" terms – as does Paul at times,

especially when addressing a Greek audience – the author of the
fourth gospel uses the contrast between two worlds, between the
world above and the world below, to express the same eschatological
message as Paul. We must remember the meaning of "world" in the
New Testament to realize that what John condemns is not the
created, material or empirical world, but rather the human world
which is alienated from God as a result of sin and the rejection of
God's emissary of forgiveness and reconciliation.

John continues his prologue by writing that although the Word
entered into the world which he made, "the world did not know
him." John then describes the redemptive separation between those
who believe in the Word and become sons of God and those who
reject the Word ("the world" in its pejorative sense). "He came to
that which was his own, but his own did not receive him. Yet to all
who received him, to those who believed in his name, he gave the
right to become children of God" (John 1:11–12). John writes that
it is not God who rejected the world, but the world (humanity)
which has rejected God by rejecting his Son. John, while emphasizing different terminology than Paul and the synoptic gospels, continues the New Testament pattern of defining the gospel in terms of
a redemptive–eschatological separation.

John uses not only spatial but also temporal metaphors to describe
the salvation revealed by Jesus.

John has elements of a realistic, futuristic eschatology. While eternal life in
John is usually a present life of "realized eschatology," it is sometimes
future and eschatological (3:36; 5:39). One saying reflects the eschatological dualism of the two ages, even if the distinctive idiom is not used, more
clearly than the parallel saying in the Synoptics: "He who hates his life in
this world will keep it for life eternal" (12:25). Life is the life of the Age to
Come, and in this saying, "this world" is synonymous to the "this age" of
the Synoptics.[47]

Even Dodd admits that John's reference to eternal life "betrays
the Jewish affiliation of its language" and "is used in John with
reference to the Jewish idea of the life of the Age to Come."[48] I agree
fully with Ladd when he concludes that "John does not reflect a
genuinely Greek dualism, either Platonic or Gnostic, but a Jewish–
Synoptic dualism adapted to a Hellenistic audience."[49]

The *Religionsgeschichtliche Schule*, although it recognized the
importance of understanding the historical context of the biblical
writings, minimized the importance of the Hebraic foundation of

the gospel and is responsible for the widespread belief that John's gospel is based upon a Hellenic dualism.[50] Led by the work of Wilhelm Bousset and Richard Reitzenstein, this comparative religions school argued that Gnosticism was a pre-Christian phenomenon which influenced the language and thought of the New Testament writers. This theory was taken up by Bultmann in his interpretation of the fourth gospel.[51]

This theory has been criticized over and over again in subsequent biblical scholarship, largely because all the documents used to discuss a supposedly pre-Christian Gnosticism were written well after the New Testament.[52] Like Nietzsche, the scholars of the *Religionsgeschichtliche Schule* at the turn of this century failed to appreciate the Hebraic context of the New Testament writers and mistook the criticism of proto-gnostic thought for the influence or presence of gnostic thought.

Bultmann has been at the forefront of this work. He has argued in particular that John's prologue and gospel and Paul's image of Christ both derive from the gnostic myth of redemption.[53] His influential essay, "Primitive Christianity as a Syncretistic Phenomenon," asserts that in the New Testament "Jesus is sometimes defined in terms of Jewish and apocalyptic categories, sometimes as the 'Lord' of the cultus, as a mystery deity, sometimes again as a Gnostic redeemer, the pre-existent being from the heavenly world, whose earthly body is only an outward garb."[54]

However, in contrast to Nietzsche's reading of the New Testament (especially Paul's writings) as the origin of the Hellenization of Jesus' original teaching, as the origin of the infection of Jesus' message with the nihilistic doctrine of a cosmological dualism, Bultmann, who probably more than any other biblical scholar asserts that Gnosticism influenced the New Testament writers, argues that both Paul and John "demythologized" these gnostic concepts. This means, in large part, that both Paul and John emptied this gnostic myth of its cosmic dualism. Although Bultmann argues that both Christianity and Gnosticism teach that there is a great gulf between God and the world, he specifies that in Christianity "this transcendence is not conceived ontologically as in Gnosticism. The gulf between God and man is not metaphysical."[55] Rather, the gulf is the result of human disobedience. "Therefore, transience and death are traced back, not to matter but to sin. It is not, as in Gnosticism, that some tragic destiny has imprisoned the

purely heavenly soul in the body; rather, death is the wages of
sin."[56] While I agree with this distinction between New Testament
and gnostic thought, I believe Bultmann is wrong to argue that both
Paul and John reinterpret Jesus in terms of (a demythologization of)
"the Gnostic redemption myth."[57] Bultmann is correct in identifying John's opposition to Gnostic, or better proto-gnostic, interpretations of Jesus, but he incorrectly uses his program of demythologization to "de-eschatologize" John's gospel.

Nietzsche agrees with the history of religions school of biblical
exegesis when he asserts that the Christian scriptures were influenced by Hellenistic religions. Like Bultmann, he argues that Christianity is based upon a gnostic anthropological and cosmological
dualism.

Christianity has accustomed us to the superstitious concept of the "soul,"
the "immortal soul," soul-monads that really are at home somewhere else
and have only by chance fallen, as it were into this or that condition, into
the "earthly" and become "flesh." (*WP* 765)

Nietzsche, ignoring or ignorant of the New Testament's repeated
attacks on proto-gnostic ideas, blames Christianity for the continued
influence of gnostic concepts in Western thought.

At times, Nietzsche begins to make a distinction between original
Christianity and Hellenized Christian theology, especially in notes
in *The Will to Power*. "Christianity has absorbed diseases of all kinds
from morbid soil: one can only reproach it for its inability to guard
against any infection" (*WP* 174). But after blaming the nihilism of
Christianity on external forces, Nietzsche goes on to explain that this
inability to guard against the influence of nihilistic philosophies and
theologies, its tendency to become ontotheology, "precisely is its
essence: Christianity is a type of decadence" (*WP* 174).

I am arguing that this charge of syncretism is false if we confine
our attention to the New Testament writings. I have been arguing
that the Hebraic anthropology and cosmology presented in the Old
Testament continues to be the basis of New Testament thought,
despite the translation into the Greek language. Gerhard von Rad
argues the same thesis at the conclusion of his seminal work on Old
Testament theology.

Now, it is simple fact that the primitive Christian community was able to
continue to use the language of the Old Testament, to link on to it, and to
avail itself of this linguistic tool. This is a theological phenomenon of great

significance ... It is, of course, extremely important that the language of the New Testament is Greek and not Hebrew. Nevertheless, almost because of this difference, we are soon made aware that in a deeper sense the language of the Old Testament and the New are the same.[58]

The same thesis is at work in the Kittel's monumental *Theological Dictionary of the New Testament* in which each New Testament word is linked to its Old Testament origin and differentiated from its previous uses in Greek thought.

For a moment, Nietzsche appears to realize the importance of the Judaic background of the New Testament when he writes in *The Antichrist* that "the earliest Christianity uses only Jewish-Semitic concepts," but he dehistoricizes the New Testament writings by belittling the importance of this fact, arguing that the use of Jewish-Semitic concepts is the result of "accidents of environment, of language, of background." Therefore, "one should beware of finding more than a sign language in this, a semeiology, an occasion for parables." Nietzsche uses this assertion to read the teachings of Jesus "symbolically," arguing that Jesus was an "anti-realist," and "that not a word is taken literally is precisely the presupposition of being able to speak at all." Jesus is thus the "symbolist par excellence" (*AC* 32).

These assertions allow Nietzsche to read into the gospels, against all historical context, his own view of Jesus' gospel. He robs the gospel's concepts of redemption of all temporal and historical meaning, the very elements which set Christianity apart from Platonic and gnostic philosophies.

The concept of "son of man" is not a concrete person who belongs in history, something individual and unique, but an "eternal" factuality, a psychological symbol redeemed from the concept of time ...

The "kingdom of heaven" is a state of the heart – not something that is to come "above the earth" or "after death" ... The "kingdom of God" is nothing that one expects; it has no yesterday and no day after tomorrow, it will not come in "a thousand years" – it is an experience of the heart; it is everywhere, it is nowhere. (*AC* 34)

Nietzsche thus turns Jesus' teachings about redemption and eschatology into timeless, eternal truths which apply only to the inner, subjective state of the believer. Ironically, Nietzsche, who opposes the nihilistic denial of time and the world, approves of this anti-historical reading of Jesus' teaching over an historical, eschatological reading of the New Testament which does not turn the kingdom of God into a non-temporal, other-worldly hope.

Nietzsche's symbolic reading of Jesus' teachings bears a remarkable resemblance to the existential reinterpretation of the New Testament by Bultmann who considers eschatology part of the mythical husk of the New Testament which must be discarded in order to discover its existential kernel. Just as Nietzsche discards Christian eschatology, "every kind of temporal expectation and promise," as the product of the early Christian's misunderstanding of Christ's message, so does Bultmann see primitive Christianity's Judaic eschatology as an "obstacle" to an understanding of Jesus' true existential message.

> The understanding of Christian existence as a life ... which is always a future possibility is, of course, not always fully explicit in the New Testament in all its ramifications. In fact, there was at the outset a serious obstacle to its full realization. That obstacle was the eschatology which the early Church took over from Judaism, with its expectation of an imminent end of the world, and the ushering in of ultimate salvation by a cosmic catastrophe.[59]

Bultmann's reference to the "understanding of Christian existence ... as a life which is always a future possibility" summarizes his existential interpretation of the New Testament, his interpretation of the *kerygma* of the gospel as centered in the meaning of the *kerygma* for the individual's own existence. "For Bultmann the cosmic eschatology of the world's destruction and the Last Judgment took over the position of the kerygma and its unmediated summons to 'existence.'"[60]

Against this eschatological interpretation, Bultmann interprets the New Testament doctrine of redemption in Heideggerian terms to mean the deliverance from a reliance upon the world, *das Man*, which allows the believer to be "freed from anxiety, from frantically clinging to what is available and disposable [Bultmann's Heideggerian understanding of 'world'] and 'open for others.'"[61] But as Cullman asserts,

> it is simply not true that one can give up this entire redemptive history of the New Testament with a perfectly free conscience and yet hold fast to the Christian faith. This attitude ... proceeds from the false presupposition that the redemptive history is only an external framework which the Christian faith can unhesitatingly discard. In reality that which then remains as alleged "kernel" is not at all a particularly characteristic feature of the Christian revelation.[62]

Ricoeur argues that Bultmann's existential reading distorts the message of the New Testament because by not paying sufficient attention to the specificity of the redemptive either/or in the biblical *kerygma*, "there is a great risk of reducing the rich content of eschatology to a kind of instantaneousness of the present decision at the expense of the temporal, historical, communitarian, and cosmic aspects contained in the hope of the Resurrection."[63] And Nietzsche runs this same risk, for, like Bultmann, he reads all the redemptive–eschatological categories of the New Testament in symbolic-existential terms (*WP* 170).

Such a reading of the New Testament which ignores its historical eschatology, the belief in the resurrection of the dead and the end of world history at the *parousia* of Christ, has been discredited in much of twentieth-century biblical scholarship. Amos Wilder writes as early as 1939 that "There is an increasingly general consent among biblical scholars today that when Jesus announced the coming of the Kingdom of God he envisaged an imminent divine intervention in the world or dramatic judgement and world-renewal similar in nature to the phenomena of the end-time pictured in the Jewish apocalyptic writings."[64]

Both Nietzsche and Bultmann ignore this future aspect of biblical eschatology to focus upon Jesus' statements which refer to "realized eschatology," eschatological statements which refer to the present enjoyment of eternal life by believers. But this realized eschatology is only one aspect of the redemptive eschatology of the Bible. The biblical writers also stress "future eschatology" alongside these pronouncements.

Since the work of Schweitzer, this future eschatology, the belief in the imminent return of Christ and the establishment of the kingdom of God on earth, has been recognized as an essential element of Jesus' teaching and of the New Testament *kerygma*. Schweitzer rejects this belief as an illusion of Jesus, but whether one believes Jesus was right or not, the temporal promise of the return of Christ and the redemption of the world has been recognized as the core of the New Testament message.

Schweitzer in his *konsequent* or consistent eschatology focuses exclusively on the sayings of Jesus which refer to the future, imminent coming of the kingdom of God, explaining the references to a realized eschatology in the biblical writings as later reinterpretations of Jesus' message after his prediction of his imminent return failed to come true.

Bultmann attempts to overcome this problem by demythologizing the eschatological concepts of the New Testament. "Mythical eschatology is finished basically by the simple fact that Christ's parousia did not take place immediately as the New Testament expected it to, but that world history continues and – as every competent judge is convinced – will continue."[65] The future realization of the kingdom of God on the earth is consequently reinterpreted to mean the unlimited future possibilities of the individual believer.

Similarly, C. H. Dodd, in his "realized eschatology," argues that Jesus taught that the kingdom of God was present in his time; therefore, Jesus was not mistaken because he made no predictions about a future breaking in of the kingdom. Dodd, like Nietzsche, attributes any futurist expectations of the kingdom of God to the early Christians. Like Bultmann, Dodd also reinterprets the futurist eschatological language of the Bible. He understands this language as a symbolic expression of ultimate realities belonging to a realm beyond time and space. Thus Dodd ends by interpreting the New Testament with Platonic categories, understanding the kingdom of God as a timeless, eternal realm of truth.

Both Bultmann and Dodd, as well as Nietzsche, were influenced by the liberal theology which reigned in the nineteenth century. "The theological establishment of the day was social liberalism, articulated, for example, by Albert Ritschl (1822–1889), who argued that the kingdom of God was 'this-worldly, monistic and ethical in character.'"[66] Bultmann and Dodd, in agreement with their liberal predecessors, interpreted the eschatological message of the New Testament in the same way as Nietzsche. All these writers distort the meaning of New Testament eschatology with a "radically individualistic and experiential interpretation of the kingdom as the rule of God in one's heart."[67]

These writers misunderstood biblical eschatology because they "saw Hellenism as the primary milieu for Jesus and early Christianity."[68] But "it is not the categories of a second-century Hellenistic Gnosticism (however easily they may be read back), but the categories of first-century rabbinic/apocalyptic Judaism which demand first claim upon the critical historian's mind."[69] In his study of Paul's thought, Beker concludes that

the intrusion of Hellenistic categories in the history of doctrine has pushed aside the apocalyptic coordinates of the resurrection of Christ and the final resurrection of the dead, with the result that the triumph of God through

Christ has become solely the triumph of Christ over our personal death, and the kingdom of Christ as present in the church has displaced the expectation of the coming triumph of God over this creation.[70]

Nietzsche, nineteenth-century liberal theology, and the history of religions theology of the early twentieth century all push aside the eschatological categories of the New Testament in favor of secular ethical and existential categories.

Much of contemporary biblical scholarship and Christian theology has begun to devote itself to a recovery of the original eschatological message of the Bible through an archeology beneath the accretion of Hellenistic thought upon this original biblical *kerygma*. These post World War I scholars have not responded to Schweitzer by focusing upon either realized or futurist eschatology, to the exclusion of the other. Instead they argue that both Jesus and the early Christians taught that the kingdom of God is present in the ministry of Jesus and the life of the believer, but that its consummation, its full realization, is yet to come.

Kümmel in his seminal work, *Promise and Fulfillment*, argues convincingly against the liberal and *religionsgeschichtliche* schools of interpretation of biblical eschatology.

Since the New Testament announces as its central message an act of God at a definite moment in history to be a final redemptive act, the mythological form of the conception cannot simply be detached from this central message: for it would mean that the New Testament message itself is abrogated if a timeless message concerning the present as the time of decision or concerning the spiritual nearness of God replaces the preaching of the eschatological future and the determination of the present by that future ... Therefore it is impossible to eliminate the concept of time and with it the "futurist" eschatology from the eschatological message of Jesus (and from the New Testament altogether).[71]

But Kümmel continues to follow Schweitzer in arguing that Jesus was mistaken in arguing that the kingdom of God would be realized within his own generation.

The American biblical scholar George Eldon Ladd agrees that Jesus taught both "futurist" and "realized" eschatology, but he attempts to harmonize both types of Jesus' eschatological pronouncements. Ladd stresses the Old Testament background to New Testament eschatology to conclude:

The Kingdom of God is the redemptive reign of God dynamically active to establish his rule among men, and this Kingdom, which will appear as an apocalyptic act at the end of the age, has already come into human history in the person and mission of Jesus to overcome evil, to deliver men from its power, and to bring them into the blessings of God's reign. The Kingdom of God involves two great moments; fulfillment within history, and consummation at the end of history.[72]

This interpretation takes into account all of the New Testament sayings about the eschatological kingdom of God, unlike previous interpreters who have had to explain away much of the New Testament material as the result of "primitive" or "mythological" misunderstandings of Jesus or the early Christians. This interpretation maintains the Judaic, biblical view of time and history.

Ladd's exegesis agrees with Niebuhr's presentation of the Christian view of history as a wisdom which resists the Hellenistic dualisms of time and eternity, which Nietzsche attacks, and the naturalistic equation of time and eternity, which Nietzsche uses to counter the nihilistic denigration of the world and time. In Niebuhr's words, Christianity holds that the "eternal is revealed and expressed in the temporal but not exhausted in it."[73] Thus biblical Christianity opposes Nietzsche's object of attack, any cosmological dualism in which time and eternity "are separated so that a false supernaturalism emerges, a dualism between an eternal and spiritual world without content and a temporal world without meaning or significance." Biblical theology also opposes Nietzsche's substitute for Judaeo-Christian eschatology, the eternal return of the same in which "the temporal in its totality is equated with the eternal."[74]

Moltmann has developed this insight into biblical eschatology to show that Christianity should not teach a nihilistic withdrawal from the world, but rather a hope for the redemption of the world. In his seminal work, *The Theology of Hope*, which the *New York Times* announced on its front page as the deathknell to the "God is dead doctrine," Moltmann argues that "Christianity is eschatology, is hope, forward looking and forward moving, and therefore also revolutionizing and transforming."[75] And in his encyclopedia article on the course of theology in the twentieth century, he argues that "Christian theology must be developed in terms of eschatology ... The traditional doctrine of the rescue of the soul into a heaven beyond must become the doctrine of the future of the kingdom of God which renews heaven and earth. The traditional other-worldly hope must be supplemented by hope for the transformation and renewal of the earth."[76]

Moltmann is in part developing the unfinished work of Dietrich Bonhoeffer who rejected the purely other-worldly interpretation of the Christian hope.

Redemption now means redemption from cares, distress, fears, and long-ings, from sin and death, in a better world beyond the grave. But is this really the essential character of the proclamation of Christ in the gospels and by Paul? I should say it is not.[77]

Bonhoeffer, like Ladd and Moltmann, comes to this understanding of New Testament eschatology through reading it in its historical context as writings dependent upon the Old Testament.

Nietzsche's reading of the New Testament gospels is based upon two profound misunderstandings. First of all, Nietzsche falsely asserts that the New Testament teaches a cosmological dualism which condemns the world. According to Nietzsche, the Bible tells Christians to despise the world as a vale of tears and to hope for their removal from this world into a static, divine heaven. Through an analysis of the Bible's redemptive–eschatological separation between this world and the world to come, I have shown Nietzsche's reading to be mistaken.

Nietzsche also sets up an unfounded distinction between the teaching of the biblical writers and the preaching of Jesus. He asserts that Jesus actually taught only an ethic of passivity toward the world out of his inability to tolerate the hatred of men. He sets Jesus against the New Testament writers by absolving him of any *ressen-timent* and of the redemptive-eschatological doctrines which Nietzsche argues originate out of this *ressentiment*. Nietzsche thus uses Jesus to criticize the central doctrines of New Testament theology. However he does not then call for a return to the original teachings of Jesus, but rather calls for an acceptance of his own doctrine of redemption as taught in his replacement for the Bible, *Zarathustra*.

CHAPTER 5

On redemption: the eternal return or biblical eschatology

"Whither is God?" he cried; "I will tell you. *We have killed him –* you and I. All of us are his murderers ... God is dead. God remains dead. And we have killed him ... What was holiest and mightiest of all that the world has yet owned has bled to death under our knives: who will wipe this blood off us? What water is there for us to clean ourselves? What festivals of atonement ... ? Must we ourselves not become gods simply to appear worthy of it?"
Nietzsche, The Gay Science

You disowned the Holy and Righteous One and asked that a murderer be released to you. You killed the author of life, but God raised him from the dead ... Repent, then, and turn to God, so that your sins may be wiped out.
Peter in Acts 3:14–15, 19

Nietzsche presents his own gospel, his counter-gospel, in *Thus Spoke Zarathustra*. Just as readings of Nietzsche's philosophy have emphasized Nietzsche's opposition to metaphysics, so have readings of Nietzsche's narrative focused upon parodies of Socrates/Plato. Kathleen Higgins writes that "neither the parody of the New Testament nor that of the Platonic dialogues ultimately proves to be the more dominant parody."[1] The best recent work on *Zarathustra*, Laurence Lampert's *Nietzsche's Teaching*, while doing a thorough job of mentioning parodies of the Bible and noting allusions, focuses upon Nietzsche's attack on Socratic rationalism. He argues in his conclusion that *Zarathustra* "enacts a battle between philosophers, the protagonists being Plato and Nietzsche."[2] Nietzsche certainly does attack Socratic rationalism and Platonic idealism throughout his works, including *Zarathustra*, but Nietzsche held his principal enemy to be not Greek rationalism, but rather Christian morality. As he reiterates so forcefully in his later works: "Have I been

understood? – Dionysus versus the Crucified. – " (*EH* 335). Not
Nietzsche vs. Plato but Dionysus vs. the Crucified. Parodies of the
New Testament are far more numerous in Nietzsche's *Zarathustra*,
which parodies in its form as well as content not the Platonic
dialogues but the biblical gospels.[3]

In his myth of Zarathustra's progress toward the overman and
his "glad tidings" of the eternal return of the same, Nietzsche
parodies the messianic eschatology of the New Testament. In a
passage which recalls the madman's lament that "I have come too
early ... my time is not yet" (*GS* 125), Zarathustra realizes that
instead of predicting a coming Messiah and preparing his way he
should be preparing the way for himself to become the overman.
"But why do I speak where nobody has *my* ears? It is still an hour
too early for me here. I am my own precursor among this people"
(*Z* 172).

Nevertheless Nietzsche retains the structure and rhetoric of
biblical eschatology in looking forward to Zarathustra's self-
overcoming and enlightenment. Just as Jesus proclaims that the
kingdom of God is near and at hand, so does Zarathustra announce
that " 'Verily, it is at hand, it is near, the great noon!' " (*Z* 191).
Notice Zarathustra's use of Christ's phrase, "Verily," which Jesus
often uses to precede his eschatological pronouncements (for
example, Matthew 16:28 and Luke 21: 31–32). The great noon is the
moment of Zarathustra's acceptance of the doctrine of eternal recurrence without the nihilism of Jesus and the *ressentiment* of Christianity, grouped together now under the concept of the will's desire
for revenge against time and becoming. It is also, as in biblical
eschatology, the time of apocalypse and judgment, a day that
Zarathustra prophesies "is now at hand, the change, the sword of
judgment, *the great noon*: much shall be revealed there" (*Z* 191).
What is revealed there is not the separation of the righteous and the
sinners, as in Jesus' day of judgment, but rather a separation
between those who can accept the teaching of eternal recurrence
with joy and those who are broken by the nihilistic interpretation of
this doctrine. This is why Nietzsche can call the doctrine of eternal
recurrence a "principle of selection" for entrance into his "new
nobility," just as belief in Christ is the basis for inclusion in the
kingdom of God. "In place of 'metaphysics' and religion, the theory
of eternal recurrence (this as a means of breeding and selection)"
(*WP* 462).

And what is the opposite of Nietzsche's new principle of selection? "Christianity is the counterprinciple to the principle of *selection*" (*WP* 246). Whereas Christianity calls for the comfort and redemption of the weak and the suffering, Nietzsche's principle of selection calls for the destruction of the weak and the enhancing of the power of the strong: "A doctrine is needed powerful enough to work as a breeding agent: strengthening the strong, paralyzing and destructive for the world-weary" (*WP* 862).[4]

That Zarathustra's revelation comes at the "great noon" recalls the biblical history of redemption in which Christ's ministry is considered the "midpoint" in the *Heilsgeschichte*, the redemptive history of the Bible.[5] In his narrative of the overman, in which Zarathustra's redemption through his joyful affirmation of eternal recurrence is the "midpoint" of history (*WP* 1057), Nietzsche remains reliant upon the biblical conception of time and history.[6] Nietzsche borrows from biblical eschatology because his "neo-paganism" is "remote from being genuinely pagan," and is rather "essentially Christian, by being anti-Christian."[7] Nietzsche's intense desire to have himself replace Jesus Christ as the center of history and to have his philosophy replace Christian doctrine causes him to secularize biblical eschatology in order to declare that Zarathustra/Nietzsche the overman rather than Jesus the Christ brings redemption to the earth at the midpoint of history. According to Nietzsche the midpoint of time occurs not when Jesus brings redemption to the world, but rather when Nietzsche destroys this Christian doctrine of redemption. Like Jesus before him, Nietzsche/Zarathustra "breaks the history of mankind in two. One lives before him, or one lives after him" (*EH* 333).

Nietzsche claims to have marked the midpoint of history with the announcement of his gospel because he wants to use the doctrine of eternal return as a myth to counter the redemptive history of Christianity and its moral world order. I want to follow Bernd Magnus who at one point interprets the doctrine of eternal recurrence as an "anti-Christian myth,"[8] and Karl Löwith who consistently explains how Nietzsche's doctrine was designed to counter the Christian view of time and history.

The discovery of this *circulus vitiosus deus* is to Nietzsche "the way out of two thousand years of falsehood," liquidating the Christian Era, when man believed in a progressive history determined by an absolute beginning and end, by creation and original sin at one end, by consummation and redemption at the other end.[9]

Magnus, unlike Löwith, argues that Nietzsche's teaching is "utterly indifferent to the truth-value of the doctrine,"[10] but, although Nietzsche sometimes presented eternal recurrence as only an ethical imperative,[11] Heidegger is right to interpret eternal recurrence as the basis of Nietzsche's ontology. In *Zarathustra* the doctrine is presented as true in both an existential and cosmological sense. I do not want to place emphasis on his "proofs" of the doctrine, but rather to recall Nietzsche's criterion of truth announced in *The Antichrist*:

Whatever a theologian feels to be true *must be false*: this is almost a criterion of truth ... Wherever the theologians' instinct extends, *value judgments* have been stood on their heads and the concepts of "true" and "false" are of necessity reversed; whatever is most harmful to life is called "true"; whatever elevates it, enhances, affirms, justifies it, and makes it triumphant, is called "false." (*AC* 576)

In Nietzsche's view, the Christian moral world-order is based upon a denial of reality, upon the nihilistic will, and in direct contrast he wills, in order to overcome it, the eternal return, "the highest formula of affirmation that is at all attainable" (*EH* 295).

Nietzsche sees his doctrine of eternal recurrence as the antidote to the denigration of the natural world and the devaluation of time and becoming in Platonic/metaphysical and Christian/religious worldviews:

the countermyth represents his counterhypothesis to the traditional flight from experience, from becoming; a flight which Nietzsche thought shapes and sustains the dominant tradition. He sought to overcome this traditional retreat from transient experience, represented by metaphysics, Christianity, and nihilism within a single formulation: the doctrine of eternal occurrence.[12]

I argue in the previous chapter that this equation between Platonic metaphysics and Christian theology is based upon a misunderstanding of the biblical view of creation and the world. The biblical writings do not denigrate the earth and becoming, and these writings actually fight against all such dualistic philosophies. But the equation of Platonism and Christianity is crucial to Nietzsche's project. "Nietzsche's substantive assumption is, that there is a sense in which 'philosophy,' 'morality,' 'Christianity' ... can properly be said to have univocal denotation. This is not at all obvious, yet it sustains much of Nietzsche's perspective."[13] This assumption is, I

will argue, shared by Heidegger and Derrida in their attacks on
ontotheology. But, as I have demonstrated in my analysis of the
eschatology of the New Testament, this assumption is unfounded.
There is a profound difference between Platonism and Christianity;
Christianity is not simply Platonism for the people.

But in Nietzsche's view both metaphysics and Christianity are
based upon a devaluation of the world of becoming in favor of an
imaginary other world of being. Through his doctrine of eternal
return, Nietzsche attempts to deconstruct this dualism in which
being represents the realm of the true and the good and becoming
the realm of falsehood and error.

Nietzsche argues that every philosophy that "knows some *finale*,
some final state of some sort, every predominantly aesthetic or
religious craving for some Apart, Beyond, Outside, Above" is based
upon a devaluation of the natural world of time and becoming.
Although the Bible does not view the end as apart or outside of time,
Christian eschatology does look forward to a finale, the *eschaton*.[14]
And "Zarathustra makes clear that the teaching on eternal return
opposes any teaching on the linearity of time that points toward
some future eschatological fulfillment of time."[15] Nietzsche/
Zarathustra's view of time is clearly closer to the Greek view of time
which held that time is cyclical not linear. But Nietzsche does not
merely adopt a Greek or Stoic conception of time, for the Greek view
of history as cyclical led to hope for an escape from the bounded
circle of time to a beyond and the Stoic view of eternal return led to
striving for an apathetic resignation to fate.[16] Nietzsche, on the
contrary, wants the overman to celebrate this world and this life as
the only one, and yet to strive to assert his will to power in the
creation of new values.

But most vigorously Nietzsche wants his doctrine of eternal return
to refute the belief that time has an end and a goal, a goal which can
be used to denigrate this world and this life.[17] Nietzsche sees in the
eschatological view of time the source of the moral world order
which he despised. The teleology of Christian eschatology leads to a
moral condemnation of time and becoming as the cause of sin and
suffering.

This moral condemnation of time and becoming is based upon the
will's resentment towards its inability to change the past. "'It was' –
that is the name of the will's gnashing of teeth and most secret
melancholy. Powerless against what has been done, he is an angry

spectator of all that is past" ($\mathcal{Z}$ 139). Faced with its impotence toward the past, the will seeks revenge against time which limits its scope of creation. Instead of overcoming the past through a will to accept the past as willed and a creative will to power over the future,[18] the will seeks revenge against time and becoming.

> Alas, every prisoner becomes a fool; and the imprisoned will redeems himself foolishly. That time does not run backwards, that is his wrath; "that which was" is the name of the stone which he cannot move ... Thus the will, the liberator, took to hurting; and on all who can suffer he wreaks revenge for his inability to go backwards ...
> *The spirit of revenge*, my friends, has so far been the subject of man's best reflection; and where there was suffering, one always wanted punishment too ...
> Because there is suffering in those who will, inasmuch as they cannot will backwards, willing itself and all life were supposed to be – a punishment ...
> "Things are ordered morally according to justice and punishment. Alas, where is redemption from the flux of things and from the punishment called existence?" Thus preached madness. ($\mathcal{Z}$ 139–140)

The progress of time and this earthly life are understood as a penance for guilt.

Although this "madness" sounds like Schopenhauer's view that our temporal lives are nothing but suffering caused by and penance for our guilt, Nietzsche follows Schopenhauer in asserting that Judaeo-Christian morality taught this denial of life. "What is Jewish, what is Christian morality? Chance done out of its innocence; misfortune besmirched with the concept of 'sin'" (*AC* 25). Higgins explains how Nietzsche understood Judaeo-Christian morality as denigrating our temporal lives:

> Nietzsche argues that the moral perspective of Christianity denigrates the actuality of our lives. It does so in a variety of ways, but one of the most fundamental is evident in the doctrine of sin's implications regarding the proper view of our temporal nature. The doctrine of sin interprets the present, which is relatively unimportant by comparison with the past, the location of sin that establishes our guilt, and the distant future, the location of the reward or punishment.[19]

In philosophy an imaginary realm of being is used to denigrate the world of becoming, and in religion an imaginary realm of truth is used to denigrate our temporal lives as guilty and sinful. These two doctrines are combined in Schopenhauer to condemn both the apparent world and our temporal lives and to look forward to the escape from these through a negation of our will to live which keeps us tied to our temporal life in this world.

Nietzsche saw Zarathustra/Zoroaster as the original author of the moral world order who influenced Judaeo-Christianity through the Hebrew prophets during the Babylonian captivity.[20] He therefore depicts Zarathustra overturning his own teaching and thereby liberating the world from the moral world order.

Nietzsche understood redemption to mean the destruction of this moral world order. The world of becoming and our temporal lives need not be redeemed from any real guilt or sin, but rather only from the false doctrines of the world-weary. "He whom they call Redeemer has put them in fetters: in fetters of false values and delusive words. Would that someone would yet redeem them from their Redeemer" (*Z* 91). Nietzsche believed his doctrine of eternal return freed the world from the ontotheological Lords of Necessity, Purpose and Guilt through the elevation of Lord Chance.

Verily, it is a blessing and not a blasphemy when I teach: "Over all things stand the heaven Accident, the heaven Innocence, the heaven Chance, the heaven Prankishness."

"By Chance" – that is the most ancient nobility of the world, and this I restored to all things: I delivered them from their bondage under Purpose. (*Z* 166)

Zarathustra redeems the world not from bondage to guilt and sin, as Jesus is said to do in the Bible, but rather from the false belief in a moral world order which falsely condemns the world as guilty and sinful.

Zarathustra achieves this redemption at the end of part III in a section entitled "The Convalescent." This scene is intended to replace the myth of Jesus' redemption of the world through his death and resurrection. In an allusion to Jesus' facing of his passion when his "hour" has come, Zarathustra, after bravely facing "his hour" by summoning forth his most abysmal thought, is, like the shepherd in Zarathustra's prophetic vision, choked by the black snake of nausea. He is choked by the negative, nihilistic side of the doctrine of eternal return which laments the return of all that is weak and small and is consequently overcome by the feeling of valuelessness. As a result of this nausea, "he fell down as one dead and long remained as one dead" (*Z* 216). Nietzsche's analysis of nihilism in the notes from *The Will to Power* explain what is happening to Zarathustra in his final transformation into the overman.

Having reached this standpoint, one grants the reality of becoming as the *only* reality, forbids oneself every kind of clandestine access to afterworlds and false divinities – but *cannot endure this world though one does not want to deny it.*

What has happened, at bottom? The feeling of valuelessness was reached with the realization that the overall character of existence may not be interpreted by means of the concept of "aim," the concept of "unity," or the concept of "truth." Existence has no goal or end. (*WP* 12)

Zarathustra is experiencing the "last form of nihilism" which precedes the affirmation of the doctrine of eternal return. But when he revives Zarathustra realizes that "nihilism, as the denial of a truthful world, of being, [is] *a divine way of thinking*" (*WP* 15).

Zarathustra lies as if dead in his cave not for three days, as did Jesus, but rather for seven days, the time it takes for God to create the world in Genesis. And when Zarathustra revives he awakens to a new and innocent creation. He takes an apple and enjoys it innocently, in a parodic reversal of Adam and Eve's fall into sin in the Genesis narrative.[21] Zarathustra reflects upon mankind's ability to name things, Adam's founding act in the garden of Eden, without a lament over any fall, but rather in a celebration of the distance between signifier and the signified: "How lovely it is that there are words and sounds! Are not words and sounds rainbows and illusive bridges between things which are eternally apart?" (*Z* 217). Things are not apart due to a "fall" but are rather separated "eternally." Mankind's ability to bridge things with language is a sign of his creative powers, now unhampered by any external truth. Zarathustra agrees with his animals that "the world lies before me like a garden." The innocence of the garden of Eden has been restored, not through a removal of God's curse on humanity, but rather through a removal of humanity's curse of the earth.

Zarathustra blesses this newly redeemed creation in the final chapter of part III, the original end of his work, "The Seven Seals (Or: The Yes and Amen Song)" which clearly alludes to the final book of the Bible, Revelation.[22] But whereas the final book of the Bible records the events at the end of the world, Nietzsche's final book celebrates the eternal return, the lack of an end of the world.

If history returns eternally, it is not bound by necessity and guilt and is not a place of punishment to be escaped, as in Schopenhauer. Rather, history is free from any external goal or purpose. The overman is therefore free to establish his own values for himself –

"This is *my* way . . . For *the* way – that does not exist" (*Z* 195) – and his own purpose for the earth – "He, however, creates man's goal and gives the earth its meaning and its future. That anything at all is good and evil – that is his creation" (*Z* 196).

This postmodern rejection of any belief in "*the* way," especially Jesus' claim that "I am the way" (John 14:6), does not necessarily lead to a tolerance and celebration of diversity.[23] In Nietzsche, it leads to the imposition of the will of the strong over the weak. " 'Each of us would like to be master over all men, if possible, and best of all God.' This attitude must exist again" (*WP* 958). Nietzsche's doctrine mandates the radical freedom of humanity, but only for the noble overmen like himself.[24]

Nietzsche claims to redeem mankind from guilt, not as Christianity does by showing a way to be freed from the real guilt of sin through forgiveness, but rather by asserting that guilt and sin are illusions invented by priests out of *ressentiment* against the noble, the strong, and the free. Heidegger notes in his analysis of Nietzsche that "Christian dogma knows another way in which the 'It was' may be willed back – repentance. But repentance takes man where it is meant to take him, to the deliverance from the 'It was,' only if it maintains its essential relation to the forgiveness of sin, and thus is generally and from the outset referred to sin" (*WCT* 105). Nietzsche uses his doctrine of eternal return to repudiate the Christian doctrine of sin and to thereby overcome the need for repentance.[25] It is here that we find the motivation for Nietzsche's murder of God.

If there is one sentence in Nietzsche which best sums up his philosophy, I think it would be the following one from *Zarathustra*: "But let me reveal my heart to you entirely, my friends: *if* there were gods, how could I endure not to be a god! *Hence* there are no gods" (*Z* 86). I believe that Nietzsche has truly revealed his "heart" here, the heart of his philosophy, and his "heart" in the biblical sense, his heart towards God. "Away from God and gods this will has lured me; what could one create if gods existed?" (*Z* 87). Here is Nietzsche's real objection to God and a divinely ordered world. If God existed, the overman would not be his own master and would not be free to follow his own will to power.

Nietzsche argues that the problem with Christianity is that it devalues the natural world of time and becoming, that it labels this life as a punishment, the body as sinful, and this world as evil. But the Bible does not assert that the earth, the body or time is evil in itself; rather, it claims that it is humanity's rebellion against God which has made this "world" sinful. Nietzsche's philosophy glorifies this rebellion against God.

Jesus tells a parable in Luke which I believe explains Nietzsche's parable of the death of God. Jesus tells of a man who planted a vineyard and who sent servants to collect a share of the produce of the vineyard. But each time the owner sent servants, the servants were beaten and sent away.

Then the owner of the vineyard said, "What shall I do? I will send my son, whom I love; perhaps they will respect him."
But when the tenants saw him, they talked the matter over. "This is the heir," they said. "Let's kill him, and the inheritance will be ours." So they threw him out of the vineyard and killed him. (Luke 20: 14–15)

Nietzsche believed that once the overman "killed the author of life" (Acts 3:15), that he would then become lord of his own life; after he murdered the creator of the earth, he could create his own world. The beginning and end of Nietzsche's philosophy is the death of God, and this desire for the death of God originates out of the desire for freedom and autonomy.

PART TWO

Heidegger's forgetting: the secularization of biblical anthropology

It would undoubtedly be the greatest error, if one were to explain the existent essence of man, as though it were the secularized translation of a thought about man by Christian theology via God.   Heidegger, "Letter on Humanism"

CHAPTER 6

From the death of God to
the forgetting of Being

Being able to estimate, to esteem, that is, to act in accordance with the standard of Being, is itself creation of the highest order. For it is preparation of readiness for the gods; it is the Yes to Being. "Overman" is the man who grounds Being anew.

Heidegger, *Nietzsche*, volume I

Nietzsche, the thinker of the thought of will to power, is the *last metaphysician* of the West. The age whose consummation unfolds in his thought, the modern age, is a final age. This means an age in which at some point and in some way the historical decision arises as to whether this final age is the conclusion of Western history or the counterpart to another beginning.

Heidegger, *Nietzsche*, volume III

Heidegger follows Nietzsche in attempting to uncover the essence of metaphysics, to encapsulate the history of Western philosophy from Plato to the present within this essence, and to inaugurate a new way of thinking. "Heidegger agrees with Nietzsche on the basic matter: all previous philosophy is governed by Platonism and what is needed is the overcoming of Platonism."[1] But Heidegger places Nietzsche within, even though at the end of, the metaphysics Nietzsche claimed to have overcome. Whereas Nietzsche wants to deconstruct the metaphysical distinction between two worlds, between the true world of being and the apparent world of becoming, Heidegger wants to reinstate a distinction, the difference between Being and beings, without falling back into a metaphysical distinction between a noumenal and physical world or a theological distinction between the earthly and the heavenly. According to Heidegger, metaphysics originates not in the distinction between the true and apparent worlds, but rather in the more originary "differentiation of Being and beings." If metaphysics arises from the ontological difference, "then by referring back to the differentiation we have reached the origin of metaphysics and at the same time attained a more original concept of metaphysics" (*N* IV 184).

According to Heidegger, Nietzsche's reversal of the Platonic, metaphysical distinction between the true and apparent worlds does not mean the overcoming of metaphysics, but rather the "entrenchment" in metaphysics. Whereas Nietzsche wants to free the higher men from the shadow of God by abolishing the "true" world of Being, Heidegger wants to free Being from the shadow of beings. But Heidegger believes we can descry "this shadow *as* a shadow" only by thinking Nietzsche's thought. "Then we will experience first and foremost how decisively Being is already overshadowed by beings" (*N* III 157).

But prior to this critical reading of Nietzsche as the last metaphysician, Heidegger in his early works seems to take Nietzsche's metaphysics as a starting-point. This includes Nietzsche's atheism. I disagree with Gadamer's assertion that "it was only after *Being and Time* that Nietzsche fully entered into Heidegger's horizon, and ... an understanding of Heidegger as an atheistic thinker can be based upon only a superficial appropriation of his philosophy."[2] Heidegger, in his 1925 lecture course "Prolegomena to the History of the Concept of Time," which was the first development of the themes of *Being and Time*, quotes Nietzsche to assert that:

Philosophical research is and remains atheism, which is why philosophy can allow itself the "arrogance of thinking." Not only will it allow itself as much; this arrogance is the inner necessity of philosophy and its true strength. Precisely in this atheism philosophy becomes what a great man called the "joyful science."[3]

In *Being and Time* Heidegger will more cautiously bracket out any consideration of the other-world and after-death in a phenomenological approach,[4] rather than rejecting transcendence in an atheistic approach, in an effort to avoid being "a mere countermovement" which "necessarily remains, as does everything 'anti,' held fast in the essence of that over against which it moves" (*QT* 61). Nevertheless, Heidegger's practice in *Being and Time* of considering the "this-worldly interpretation" of *Dasein* as more fundamental than "other-worldly speculation" (*BT* 292) is in part due to the influence of Nietzsche's atheism.

More than one commentator has noted that Heidegger's early work, prior to his prolonged "confrontation" (*Auseinandersetzung*) with Nietzsche in his lectures and writings in the decade between 1936 and 1946, appropriates Nietzsche's thought without criticism, and that, even though his early works, such as *Being and Time*, do not refer to Nietzsche extensively,[5] Nietzsche's thought has a great influence on Heidegger's *Dasein* analysis.

However rarely cited in *Being and Time*, Nietzsche may well be the regnant genius of that work – Nietzsche, who exposes the anthropomorphic base of metaphysical projections and the evanescence of Being understood as permanence of presence; supplies genealogical accounts of time and eternity in such a way that the latter appears as vengeance wreaked on the former; confronts without subterfuge human existence as irredeemably mortal, bursting with possibility yet bound to fatality.[6]

Heidegger is indebted to Nietzsche's concept of "the herd" in his analysis of "*das Man.*" Heidegger's concept of "authentic" *Dasein* parallels in some respects Nietzsche's teaching that the overman must not be a disciple, but must follow his "own" way. And Heidegger interprets Zarathustra's experience of the "Moment" when he overcomes nihilism by affirming the eternal return as representing the achievement of an authentic understanding of *Dasein*'s temporality, "the temporality in which humanity stands; preeminently humanity and, so far as we know, humanity alone" (*N* II 99).

The strongest evidence for the influence of Nietzsche's teaching on humanity (the overman) and time (eternal recurrence) is found in Heidegger's early lectures on Nietzsche, collected in volume I of the German edition, in which Heidegger "often makes sympathetic use of the vocabulary of the fundamental ontology of *Being and Time*, of a '*Daseinanalytik*', to interpret Nietzsche."[7] I will explore these parallels between Nietzsche and Heidegger's thinking in more detail when I turn to an analysis of *Being and Time*, but I want to begin by looking briefly at Heidegger's confrontation with Nietzsche in the thirties and forties.

Heidegger's later lectures on Nietzsche turn about to consider Nietzsche not as an ally in the new thinking of fundamental ontology, but rather as the "last metaphysician" who brings metaphysics to its end. Many have argued, following Hannah Arendt,[8] that this change resulted from Heidegger's experience with National Socialism, but whether or not the change in Heidegger's valuation of Nietzsche can be specifically dated and his motives made transparent, it does seem clear that the change resulted from a "turn" in

Heidegger's own thinking, a turn away from the focus on the analysis of *Dasein*'s experience of Being toward an investigation of Being itself, as traced in the history of metaphysics.

This is seen most clearly in Heidegger's treatise "Nihilism As Determined by the History of Being," composed during the years 1944–46 but not published until 1961. Here Heidegger argues that the essence of metaphysics, from Plato to Nietzsche, is nihilism, and that Nietzsche does not overcome nihilism as he claims. Rather, Nietzsche's metaphysics is "utterly completed, perfect nihilism ... the fulfillment of nihilism proper" (*N* IV 203). Heidegger's judgment is based upon his definition of the essence of metaphysics.

According to Heidegger, the essence of metaphysics is nihilism because it fails to think Being itself as Being.

> Nietzsche acknowledges the being as such. Yet, in such acknowledgement, does he also recognize the Being of beings, and indeed It itself, *Being*, specifically *as Being*? He does not. (*N* IV 201)

Nietzsche's omission of the thought of Being itself is common to metaphysics as a whole. Being is always thought of as the Being of beings. This is the essence of metaphysics according to Heidegger. "The Being of beings is examined *in terms of* beings as what is thought *toward* beings" (*N* IV 206). Being is not thought as Being itself, but rather as the "answer" to the question of the meaning of the Being of beings.

> Accordingly, how does metaphysics comport itself to Being itself? Does metaphysics think Being itself? No, it never does. It thinks *the being* with a view to Being. Being is first and last what answers the question in which being is always what is interrogated. What is interrogated is not Being as such. Hence, Being itself remains unthought in metaphysics. (*N* IV 207)

Because metaphysics thinks of Being only in terms of beings, as the answer to the question of the meaning of the Being of beings, metaphysics is ontotheological. Metaphysics, since "the beginning of metaphysics in Plato and Aristotle," considers Being as "the first cause and the highest existent ground of being." According to Heidegger this means that "Metaphysics is inherently theology" (*N* IV 209).

Recall that Nietzsche made the same claim about metaphysics, that he castigated "our whole philosophy" for having "theologians' blood in its veins" (*AC* 8). Although defining the theological character of metaphysics in distinctive ways, both Nietzsche and

Heidegger seek to free philosophy from theology, to overcome and destroy the theological character of metaphysics. Nietzsche and Heidegger's critiques of the theological character of metaphysics are not unrelated. Heidegger asserts that the "*coherence* of ontology and theology in the *essence* of metaphysics is enunciated with particular clarity where metaphysics, following the thrust of its own name, identifies the fundamental trait by which it knows the being as such. That is *transcendence*" (*N* IV 210). And Nietzsche's abolition of the transcendental world of philosophy and the transcendent world of theology is at the heart of his thinking.

Nevertheless, Heidegger accuses Nietzsche's thought of being theological. "As an *ontology*, even Nietzsche's metaphysics is *at the same time* theology." Because Nietzsche, according to Heidegger's *eisegesis*, divides the Being of beings into the *essentia* of beings, as will to power, and the *existentia* of beings, as eternal recurrence of the same, Nietzsche's thought "is an expression not of atheism but of ontotheology" (*N* IV 210). Heidegger qualifies this startling assertion by noting that his "metaphysical theology is of course a negative theology of a peculiar kind" (*N* IV 210). I think what Heidegger means here is that by trying to overcome ontotheology by inverting its metaphysical distinction between being and becoming, Nietzsche's thought remains held fast in metaphysics as anti-metaphysics, as a mere counter-movement to metaphysics rather than as a more originary thinking of the question of Being.

Heidegger argues that Nietzsche accepts the traditional meta-physical understanding of Being as permanentizing presence. "Often he calls that which is steadily constant – again remaining true to the manner of speaking of metaphysical thinking – 'Being'" (*QT* 84). Nietzsche does speak of Being in this manner, but he rejects this idea of "Being" as a vacuous concept, a fictional projection of the weak. In *Ecce Homo*, Nietzsche, when referring to the affinity between his affirmation of eternal return and Heraclitus' "Yes" to becoming, acknowledges that his philosophy involves "the radical rejection of even the concept '*Being*'" (*EH* 273). For Heidegger, this means to succumb to nihilism, for the essence of nihilism means "There 'is' nothing to Being as such: Being – a *nihil*" (*N* IV 201). Nihilism for Heidegger means not only the falsification of beings, the actual world, through the ontotheological concept of Being (as in Nietzsche's definition of nihilism), but also the falsification of Being through an occupation "solely with 'reality'" (*N* II 208).

According to Heidegger, Nietzsche continues to think Being, for all metaphysics thinks the Being of beings, but in Nietzsche's thought "Being has been transformed into a value" (*QT* 102). "Being is determined as value and is consequently explained in terms of beings as a condition posited by the will to power, by the 'being' as such" (*N* IV 201). In attempting to overcome nihilism through value thinking, through the devaluation of the highest values, including Being, and the revaluation of all values on the basis of will to power, Nietzsche remains trapped in the forgetting of Being itself.

For it is precisely in the positing of new values from the will to power, by which and through which Nietzsche believes he will overcome nihilism, that nihilism proper first proclaims that there is nothing to Being itself, which has now become a value ... Consequently, Nietzsche's metaphysics is not an overcoming of nihilism. It is the ultimate entanglement in nihilism. (*N* IV 203)[9]

Nietzsche attempts to overcome nihilism, the meaninglessness which results from the devaluation of the highest values hitherto, through a "mere assigning of sense and meaning" (*QT* 54). This causes Nietzsche to be trapped within the modern metaphysics of sub-jectivity.

Heidegger places Nietzsche at the end of Western metaphysics as a whole which began with Plato, but he more specifically places Nietzsche's thinking at the end of the modern metaphysics of sub-jectivity which began with Descartes. It is here that I think Heidegger's analysis is most perceptive. Heidegger has been criti-cized for conflating Descartes and Nietzsche, especially for not acknowledging Nietzsche's attack on the unified subject and its will. "Heidegger simply ignores the innumerable passages in which Nietzsche caustically attacks the modern notion of a self-grounding, or even a stable, enduring, causally efficacious 'subject'."[10] But Heidegger does take into account the differences between Descartes and Nietzsche. He notes that for Descartes the will is "merely self-legislation for representational reason, which is active only as representing," while for Nietzsche the "will is now pure self-legislation of itself" (*N* III 224). He also acknowledges "Nietzsche's exceedingly sharp rejection of the Cartesian *cogito*" (*N* IV 123), Nietzsche's critique of the Cartesian subject "in the sense of the I-ness of conscious thought" (*N* III 132ff.).

But according to Heidegger, Nietzsche inverts Descartes' anthropological dualism to assert that "what underlies is not the 'I' but the 'body'" (*N* IV 133); therefore, Nietzsche's conception of man is still metaphysical. Just as he merely inverts the metaphysical dualism of being and becoming, so does he merely invert the metaphysical dualism of mind and body. He still conceives of man as *animal rationale* even though he gives priority not to the soul and consciousness but rather to the body and its drives (will to power). But that "Nietzsche posits the body in place of the soul and consciousness alters nothing in the fundamental metaphysical position which is determined by Descartes" (*N* IV 133).

Descartes grounds truth in the self-certainty of human consciousness, and Nietzsche grounds truth in the will to power of the overman. Nietzsche's thought is a radicalization of Descartes' preliminary attempt to transpose "all of mankind and its history from the realm of the speculative truth of faith for Christian man into the representedness of beings grounded in the subject" (*N* IV 134). Descartes gives man the power to represent the true, apart from Christian revelation ("I have always thought that two questions – that of God and that of the soul – are chief among those that ought to be demonstrated by the aid of philosophy rather than theology"[11]). Nietzsche gives the overman the "absolute power to enjoin what is true and what is false" (*N* IV 145).

It is in the doctrine of the overman that Heidegger locates, correctly I think, the completion of the modern metaphysics of subjectivity. But is Heidegger's thinking free from the same modern metaphysics of subjectivity in his conception of authenticity as the autonomy of individual *Dasein*? Heidegger begins to admit it is not in his lecture "European Nihilism" when he says that "the attempt and the path it [*Being and Time*] chose confront the danger of unwillingly becoming merely another entrenchment of subjectivity." But Heidegger blames the problem on the "noncomprehension" caused by the modern reader's "habituation, entrenched and ineradicable, to the modern mode of thought: man is thought as subject, and all reflections on him are understood to be anthropology." Heidegger gives yet another reason, which again implies that the subjectivist reading is mistaken. "On the other hand, however, the reason for such noncomprehension lies in the attempt itself, which ... evolves from what has been heretofore; in struggling loose from it, it necessarily and continually refers back to the course of the past and even calls on it for assistance, in the effort to say something entirely different" (*N* IV 141). In my analysis of *Being and Time* which follows I will demonstrate the extent to which Heidegger relies upon Christian anthropology in his attempt to "struggle loose" from it, but I will argue that what Heidegger says as a result is not "something entirely different" from the modern metaphysics of subjectivity.

In his analysis of modern philosophy, Heidegger asserts that:

What is new about the modern period as opposed to the Christian medieval age consists in the fact that man, *independently and by his own effort*, contrives to become certain and sure of his human being in the midst of beings as a whole. The essential Christian thought of the certitude of salvation is adopted, but *such "salvation" is not eternal, other-worldly bliss, and the way to it is not selflessness*. The hale and the wholesome are sought exclusively in the free self-development of all the creative powers of man ... In the context of man's liberation from the bonds of revelation and church doctrine, the question of first philosophy is "In what way does man, *on his own terms and for himself*, first arrive at a primary, unshakable truth, and what is that primary truth?" (My emphases, *N* IV 89)

But while Heidegger considers Descartes' philosophy "in the context of man's liberation from the bonds of revelation and church doctrine," he refuses to consider Nietzsche's philosophy in this context, despite the fact that Nietzsche insisted upon this aspect of his project. In failing to consider Nietzsche's anti-Christianity, Heidegger runs the risk of repeating it. Like Descartes and Nietzsche, Heidegger wants to determine how man can exist "independently and by his own effort ... on his own terms and for himself." In fact we will see that this latter phrase becomes the very definition of authenticity in Heidegger's *Being and Time*. And although neither Nietzsche nor Heidegger is interested in securing the "certitude" of our salvation, Nietzsche does insist that "redemption," and Heidegger after him insists that "authenticity," is not "other-worldly bliss, and the way to it is not selflessness." Both define this freedom and autonomy in opposition to Christianity; both continue to see Christianity as "that *against which* the new freedom – whether expressly or not – must be distinguished" (*N* IV 99).

Heidegger fails to appreciate the extent to which Nietzsche's proclamation of the death of God refers to the God of Christianity. In fact in the close of his essay, "Nietzsche's Word: God is Dead,"

Heidegger equates the death and murder of God with the killing of Being.

Then, thinking in terms of values is radical killing. It not only strikes down that which is as such, in its being-in-itself, but it does away utterly with Being ... The value-thinking of the metaphysics of the will to power is murderous in a most extreme sense, because it absolutely does not let Being itself take its rise, i.e., come into the vitality of its essence. (*QT* 108)

Heidegger wants to displace Nietzsche's emphasis upon the death of God with his own concern with the forgetting of Being.[12] This is appropriate, according to Heidegger, because "the destiny of Being" is "more essential and older ... than the lack of God" (*N* IV 248).

Just as Heidegger's criticism of Nietzsche is limited by his unwillingness to consider Nietzsche's opposition to Christianity, so is his critique of the history of Western thought limited by his unwillingness to discuss the role of biblical thought in this history. Is Heidegger unwilling to do so – as he states, directly after asserting that "Metaphysics is ontotheology" – because someone who "has experienced theology in his own roots – both the theology of the Christian faith and that of philosophy – today prefers, in the realm of thinking to be silent about God" (*ID* 54–55)? If so, then Heidegger's own theological origins would account for his unwillingness to consider the role of biblical theology in his own thinking. Like Nietzsche, Heidegger grew up in a religious home and inherited a philosophical tradition permeated with Christian doctrine. But, whereas Nietzsche set out to attack Christianity head on, Heidegger seeks to avoid his Christian origins, to separate his thought from Christian theology. As Heidegger admits toward the end of his life: "Without this theological background [origin] I should never have come upon the path of thinking. But origin always comes to meet us from the future" (*OWL* 9–10). It is to this origin we now turn.

CHAPTER 7

Heidegger's theological origins: from biblical theology to fundamental ontology

I am a Christian theo-logian.
Heidegger, letter to Karl Löwith (1921)[1]

Without this theological background [origin] I should never have come upon the path of thinking. But origin always comes to meet us from the future.
Heidegger, "A Dialogue on Language" (1959)

I will be focusing in the following chapters on a comparison and contrast between Heidegger's analysis of *Dasein* and Paul's Christian anthropology. I am less interested in proving that Christian anthropology was a "source" for Heidegger's hermeneutic of *Dasein* than I am in analyzing the ways in which Pauline concepts undergo a modification when they resurface in *Being and Time*. Ultimately I will contrast Heidegger's "godless" (*gott-lose*) analysis of *Dasein* (*ID* 72), which insists that we must first develop an adequate understanding of human existence before considering the question of God, with the biblical understanding of humanity, which insists that we must begin with the divine/human relationship in order to understand human existence.

There has recently been a renewed interest in the "young Heidegger" as a result of the publication of Heidegger's early Freiburg lectures in the *Gesamtausgabe*.[2] There have also been new biographical studies of the young Heidegger resulting from the renewal of the controversy over Heidegger's involvement in National Socialism.[3] I will be drawing upon this new research on the early Heidegger in order to reopen the debate concerning the relationship between Heidegger's fundamental ontology, especially his *Dasein*-analysis, and Christian theology, especially biblical anthropology.

It is my contention that the use of Heidegger in Christian theology was a grave mistake that must be corrected. And it is my hope that the recent criticism of Heidegger's involvement in Nazi politics might be a catalyst for a reconsideration of Heidegger's relationship to Christian theology. This is certainly true of Derrida's recent works on Heidegger, both *Aporias* and *Of Spirit*, which although they are motivated by a discussion of the Nazi question, end by focusing upon Heidegger's relationship to Christian theology. Hugo Ott makes an interesting connection between Heidegger's politics and theology when he uses the following passage from a 1935 letter from Heidegger to Jaspers to guide his biography of Heidegger: "I am finding the two great thorns in my flesh – the struggle with the faith of my birth, and the failure of the rectorship – quite enough to have to contend with."[4] I will be investigating the first of these struggles, Heidegger's struggle with Christianity.[5]

I will begin this investigation with an examination of Heidegger's theological background, thus taking up Macquarrie's suggestion that one could, and I will argue *should*, "reverse" the method of his own study (i.e. using Heidegger's philosophy to re-articulate Christian theology) in order to "investigate the influence of Christian theology – and ultimately biblical thought – upon the philosophy of existentialism."[6]

Heidegger's theological background has been outlined in great detail in the recent work of Sheehan, Kisiel, van Buren, and Ott,[7] but it is important that I summarize this research as background for my analysis of Heidegger's use, and more importantly his modification, of Christian theological concepts in his *Dasein*-analysis.

Heidegger was raised in a devout Catholic family. He began to study for the Jesuit priesthood as a young man, but decided to study philosophy instead.[8] Heidegger began his academic career as a Catholic theologian, then came under the influence of Protestant thought through the works of Schleiermacher, Luther, Pascal, and Kierkegaard, and eventually abandoned all faith in Christianity under the influence of Husserl's phenomenology, Franz Overbeck's Christian skepticism, and Nietzsche's anti-Christian atheism.

Ott accounts for these changes through a study of Heidegger's biography, especially in reference to Heidegger's disappointments in pursuing academic appointments as a Catholic philosopher. Husserl's letters demonstrate that suspicion of Heidegger's "religious [*konfessioneller*] narrowness" were a hindrance in the advancement of his academic career and that had he not abandoned his "confessional ties" he would have been disqualified for the posts he was seeking.[9]

Rather than emphasizing these practical motivations, Sheehan accounts for Heidegger's loss of faith in terms of his philosophical development, arguing that "a new phase is inaugurated when the more formal pathos of *radical questioning* ('skepsis') as such wins out over any specific content or 'worldview,' especially the Christian, and that passion is itself called the 'fundamental atheism indigenous to philosophy.'"[10]

Ott and Kisiel's accounts are linked by Heidegger's rejection of the Vatican's demand that Catholic scholars swear an oath against modernism, for those Catholics who swore this oath were discriminated against in seeking academic posts since they had given up their ability to "question radically."

Heidegger announces his abandonment of his Catholic faith in a now famous letter to the Catholic priest Engelbert Krebs: "Epistemological insights encroaching upon the theory of historical knowledge have made the system of Catholicism problematic and unacceptable to me – but not Christianity and metaphysics (these, of course in a new sense)."[11] Kisiel begins his monumental study of the genesis of *Being and Time* with a discussion of this letter, concluding that "by 1919, the young Heidegger had had a radical change of heart and mind in both [Christianity and metaphysics], which in a deep sense are linked, perhaps even one."[12] Here, in 1919, Heidegger has only abandoned his allegiance to the "system" of Catholicism, but in the 1920s, both Christianity and metaphysics will also become "problematic and unacceptable" to Heidegger.

Before adopting Husserl's methodological and Nietzsche's ideological atheism, Heidegger became for a brief period of time a Protestant, a member of the "Free Christianity" movement with which Husserl also identified himself. Husserl writes that being a "free Christian" means being an "'undogmatic Protestant' ... by which I mean that someone has set an ideal goal of religious longing for himself and understands it as an infinite task."[13] I want to stress that this vaguely defined, liberal theology was adopted by Heidegger *before* his concentrated attention upon Paul's epistles in his courses on the phenomenology of religion at Freiburg in the early 1920s and his seminars on Paul's writings with Bultmann at Marburg in the mid 1920s. This liberal Christianity will determine to a large extent Heidegger's reading of Paul's epistles.[14]

In his seminal study on Heidegger's lecture course on "The Introduction to the Phenomenology of Religion" (1920–21), Thomas Sheehan points out that while knowledge of the influence of Aristotle and Kierkegaard on Heidegger's *Dasein*-analysis have been investigated: "another major influence on the uniqueness of *Being and Time* lay concealed in the background: Heidegger's reading of St. Paul and early Christianity ... we are only beginning to gather the evidence which will allow us to document, rather than just to surmise, the strong influence which early Christianity exerted on *Being and Time*."[15] Most of this evidence has now been documented, and in the remainder of my Heidegger analysis I will investigate in detail this relationship between Heidegger's *Being and Time* and St. Paul's epistles to the early Christian church.

Heidegger's lecture course on the phenomenology of religion provides an invaluable starting-point for my investigation. Since Heidegger's own notes on this course are too sketchy to be published, Sheehan's analysis of the *Nachschriften* written by Heidegger's students during the lecture course has become a kind of primary text for scholars discussing Heidegger's theological origins. Sheehan's work can now be supplemented by Kisiel's thorough paraphrase of the students' notes in his recently published work on the genesis of *Being and Time*.

The lectures were divided into two parts, "Introduction to the Phenomenon of Factical Life-Experience" and "A Phenomenological Interpretation of Original Christianity in St. Paul's Epistles to the Galatians and Thessalonians." The first part of the course dealt with a phenomenon forgotten by the entire Western tradition but understood, though not explicitly, by the early Christians: "life in its here-and-now facticity, factical life-experience ... This is the technical term and an awkward one, which *Being and Time* will replace with the more manageable term *Dasein*, 'existence.'"[16] According to Sheehan, Heidegger develops his concept of human existence, of *Dasein*, in part from his reading of the epistles of St. Paul. Pöggeler agrees that it was by "reflecting upon primordial Christian religiosity as the model of factical life-experience [that] Heidegger obtains the guiding concepts which present the structure of factical life or, as Heidegger says later, of 'factical existence.'"[17]

Kisiel has shown how indebted Heidegger is, in his analysis of "factic life experience," to Dilthey's analysis in *Introduction to the Human Sciences* of Christian lived experience.[18] In glossing Dilthey in his course on the phenomenology of religion, Heidegger asserts that it is from Christianity, especially Paul's writings (as interpreted by Augustine, Luther and Kierkegaard) that he learned that: "Philosophy [as] universal phenomenological ontology ... takes its departure from the hermeneutic of Dasein, which, as an analytic of *existence*, has made fast the guiding-line for all philosophical inquiry at the point where it *arises* and to which it *returns*" (*BT* 62). Heidegger's "universal phenomenological ontology," the project of *Being and Time*, flows out of "the hermeneutic of Dasein," and both his conception of hermeneutics and of *Dasein* originate in his studies of Christian theology.

According to Sheehan, not only was Heidegger's concept of human existence influenced by Paul, but also his conception of temporality was in part developed through his reading of the epistles of St. Paul. In the second part of the lecture series, Heidegger gives a reading of St. Paul's epistles to the Galatians and the Thessalonians in terms of their representation of factical life-experience and the temporality of this experience. Here Heidegger develops his "second thesis, namely, that original Christian experience generates primordial temporality and lives out of it."[19]

Heidegger applies his conception of primordial temporality to his reading of the eschatology of St. Paul. Paul writes in 1 Thessalonians 5: "Now as to the times [*chronoi*] and epochs [*kairoi*], brethren, you have no need of anything to be written to you. For you yourselves know full well that the day of the Lord will come just like a thief in the night." (Heidegger translates the terms *chronoi* and *kairoi* by the German *Zeit* and *Augenblick*, respectively.) He gives a reading of the *parousia* in Paul's distinctive use of the term, tracing it back to its roots in the Old Testament "Day of the Lord" and distinguishing it from the Greek concept. Heidegger correctly defines *parousia*, as used by Paul, not as presence, but as the second coming of Jesus Christ.

According to Heidegger, the question as to the "when" of Christ's second coming is answered not,

by any reference to objective time, not even to the time of everydayness. Rather the question, as it were, is bent back and referred to factical life-experience. "You yourselves well know" (*oidate*) – and this *oidate* refers to that knowledge which the Thessalonians have insofar as they have already become what they are. This is the knowledge inherent in *Gewesensein*, the already-dimension of their existence. The question of temporality in Christian religious experience becomes a matter of how one lives one's facticity.[20]

Therefore Sheehan can claim that Heidegger's concept of temporality was derived not from his reading of the Greeks, but from his interpretation of early Christianity: "From out of the context of the enactment of factical life-experience before the unseen God (i.e., 'being awake') there is generated primordial temporality ... we can see that already in 1920–21 the basic lines of Heidegger's doctrine of temporality were set and that they issued not from his reading of the Greeks but from his interpretation of early Christianity."[21]

Kierkegaard argues in *The Concept of Anxiety*, the work of Kierkegaard which most strongly influenced Heidegger, that history is a Judeao-Christian discovery and that this Judeao-Christian conception of temporality is incompatible with the Greek dualism of the temporal and eternal.[22] Zimmerman argues that Heidegger opposes to the Greek conception of temporality "the conception of time from an equally respected, but different, tradition: the one represented by the New Testament."[23] But I want to argue that Heidegger developed his conception of authentic temporality not from the New Testament conception of time, but rather from the misinterpretation of New Testament eschatology as presented in the liberal theology of the late nineteenth and early twentieth century. "As part of the generation following Dilthey and Nietzsche, and as a theology student exposed to the views of the liberal theologians of the era, Heidegger was influenced by the attitude that belief in a literal life after death and in the Second Coming (*paraousia*) [sic] as an actual historical event were remnants of an other-worldliness whose time had passed."[24]

Not only must we point out the origin of Heidegger's insights into authentic temporality in his readings of the New Testament, but we should also note the way in which Pauline concepts undergo a modification in Heidegger's formal indication of the biblical texts.

The Christian – or Pauline – meaning of eschatology has shifted from the expectation of a future event to a presence before God, what Heidegger calls a *Vollzugszusammenhang mit Gott*, a context of enacting one's life in uncertainty before the unseen God. The weight has shifted to the "how" of existence. Yes, the Parousia seems to St. Paul to be imminent, but for Heidegger that imminence serves only to characterize the "how" of factical life: its essential uncertainty.[25]

Like Nietzsche and Bultmann in their reading of Christian eschatology, Heidegger interprets Pauline eschatology existentially as referring only to a here and now attitude divorced from any realistic, historical expectation of Christ's *parousia*.

Although Heidegger makes a distinction between the Greek meaning of *parousia* (presence) and the biblical meaning of *parousia* (second coming of Christ), he nevertheless de-historicizes Paul's writings by focusing solely on the realized eschatology in Paul's conception of the *parousia*. "Heidegger was not interested in the theology of the second coming ... but in the ontology of the *kairos*, i.e., in the ontological structure of kairological time."[26] By interpreting *parousia* in Paul's letters as referring not to a future event but to the time of an existential decision, Heidegger has turned the historical, temporal term of Paul's Judaeo-Christian thought into an a-historical, a-temporal Greek term. This existential interpretation of the Bible, adopted by Bultmann, marks, according to Ricoeur, an "emptying of the eschatological dimension and a return to the philosophy of the eternal present."[27] Heidegger turns the Hebraic eschatology of the Bible into a modern, secularized version of the Greek philosophy of presence.

Whereas Paul writes that the Thessalonians have "turned to God and away from idols in order to serve a living and true God and to wait for His Son from Heaven" (1 Thessalonians 1:10), Heidegger, in his *eisegesis*, insists that the "authentic Christian relation to the Parousia is fundamentally not the awaiting of a future event."[28] Although there is an "already" dimension to the eschatology of the New Testament, the Christian has already been saved and been transferred to the kingdom of the Son, there is also a "not yet" dimension to this eschatology, for the Christian awaits the return of Jesus to the earth. The prophetic dimension of New Testament eschatology is ignored by Heidegger.

Thus the process by which Heidegger turns the structures of biblical thought into the formality of an ontology, his "formal indication" (*BT* 361) of biblical theology, dislodges the biblical texts from their specifically Judaeo-Christian context. Bruce Ballard is correct when he argues that "it is important to distinguish between Heidegger's derivation of the concept of understanding in *BT* and its theological origin ... For Heidegger's phenomenology of the Being of human beings, there can be no appeal to a transcendent God ... But the factical life experience out of which the Thessalonians' special knowledge arises, *is* in relation to God and would be senseless without such relation."[29] Although Heidegger proclaims this process to be a neutral one which merely brackets the question of God, this process is the same as secularization, the retaining of a religious conception stripped of its religious import. Theology, talk about God, becomes anthropology, talk about humanity. In this specific example, the uncertainty of life lived in faith before God (creaturehood) becomes the uncertainty of life lived authentically in the face of death (finitude).

In addition to Heidegger's use of the New Testament understanding of temporality, Sheehan also observes Heidegger's early development of the concepts of authenticity and inauthenticity in his reading of St. Paul. Paul writes in 1 Thessalonians 5:

While they are saying "Peace and safety!" then destruction will come upon them suddenly like birth pangs upon a woman with child; and they shall not escape. But you, brethren, are not in darkness, that the day should overtake you like a thief . . . so then let us not sleep as others do, but let us be alert and sober.

The first group in this description, "they," are those who live inauthentically. "They are, says Heidegger, absorbed in and totally dependent on the world in which they live. Their 'waiting' is all for this world. They cannot be saved because *they do not possess themselves*, they have forgotten the authentic self."[30] Here we see Heidegger not only developing his concept of inauthenticity out of his interpretation of Paul, but also the beginning of the change which Heidegger will introduce into the biblical concept. Just as in Paul the human experience of time, *chronos*, is determined by a moment of decision, so in Heidegger must *Dasein* face such a moment of decision in order to achieve authenticity.

But according to Heidegger authenticity is based not on one's relationship to God, as in Paul, but rather on one's relationship to his or her own self: "they do not possess themselves." Heidegger reverses Paul's biblical doctrine, that to live by the Spirit one must die to self and follow Christ, to assert that authenticity means self-possession, following the dictates of one's own Self. "'They' have *forgotten themselves* in favor of the world, they cannot *save themselves* because they do not *have themselves*, they do not *seek themselves* in the clarity of their *own* knowledge and so live 'in the dark'" (my emphases).[31] Heidegger secularizes Paul's analysis of the life of sin to make it refer to forgetting one's own Self rather than the forgetting of God.

In contrast to those who are asleep, those who live in the light –

not only the light of God, but also, more fundamentally according to Heidegger, the light of self-comprehension and self-possession – relate authentically to the *parousia*. For these, "the question of the 'when' of the Parousia reduces back to the question of the 'how' of life – and that is '*wachsam sein*,' to be awake. And further, by way of contrast with the first group who cry out 'Peace! Security!' the Christian's state of wakefulness in factical experience means a *constant, essential and necessary uncertainty.*"[32] In Sheehan's analysis, *Entschlossenheit* (resolve) has its roots in this Christian conception of "being awake" or watchful, and the concept of the anticipation of death takes shape out of the tension in Christian existence of living between the already of the resurrection and the not yet of the *parousia*.

Pöggeler, Gadamer, and Sheehan have correctly stressed the importance of Heidegger's early lectures in religion and theology in the development of concepts which came to maturity in the writing of *Being and Time*, but what van Buren and Kisiel have stressed is that it is Heidegger's fundamental ontology, his phenomenological method, which directed his interpretation of Paul. The young Heidegger gave a formal indication of not only Paul's biblical anthropology, but also of Aristotle's philosophical anthropology in his interpretation of the *Nicomachean Ethics*. Kisiel emphasizes how the introduction Heidegger wrote for a proposed book on Aristotle, which came out of his Aristotle courses of 1921–22, "incorporates Heidegger's declaration of independence of philosophy from theological questions, thereby announcing for the very first time a change in direction from the immediately preceding years of his academic development."[33] Heidegger lectured even more often on the works of Aristotle during this same period, and the influence of early Greek philosophy is at least as strong as the influence of primitive Christianity on the development of Heidegger's thought.

So Kisiel is right to argue, regarding Heidegger's early lecture courses, that their interest "is more methodological than theological and religious."[34] He correctly emphasizes Heidegger's formal indication of Christian theology and Greek philosophy in his interpretation of Paul and Aristotle. Kisiel further asserts that "formal indication is perhaps the very heart and soul of the early Heidegger,"[35] including *Being and Time*. I fully agree, but I want to criticize the supposed "neutrality" of Heidegger's formal indication, arguing first of all that there is not a universal or fundamental ontology underlying Greek and Judaeo-Christian anthropology. "Heidegger thought the hermeneutic unfolding of either the Aristotelian world or the world of the New Testament ... would lead to the same result and uncover the same, universal factical structures."[36] To attempt to formulate such a synthesis involves combining elements from Greek philosophy and biblical theology; thus Heidegger, who defines ontotheology as the synthesis of Greek and Christian thought, rather than destroying actually creates his own ontotheology in *Being and Time*.

And, as in all ontotheologies, the biblical paradigm is subordinated to the Greek. In Heidegger's analysis of Dasein, the biblical paradigm is distorted by "the less God-centered and more self-centered ontological framework of human action that Heidegger finds in Aristotle."[37] And Heidegger no doubt knew that Luther had condemned Aristotle's *Ethics* as "the worst enemy of grace."

Zimmerman and Kovacs use Bultmann's terminology to describe Heidegger's formalization of Paul's theological anthropology as a "de-mythologizing" of biblical thought.[38] This term does not seem appropriate to me, for Heidegger is not objecting to the mythological dimension of the biblical worldview, but is, rather, following Nietzsche, objecting to the theological dimension of the New Testament worldview. Heidegger insists that he is objecting to the *ontology* of Christianity, not its theology, but, since the Bible grounds its concepts theologically rather than ontologically, Heidegger's critique of biblical ontology still involves a rejection of the theological character of Christian thought. Like Nietzsche, Heidegger wants to develop a "this-worldly" understanding of human being. Considering Heidegger's appropriation of biblical thought as a de-mythologizing fails to take into account the significant changes which Heidegger introduces in his so-called neutral formalization of Christian anthropology.

Thus Zimmerman's equation of Bultmann's description of the faithfulness/sinfulness distinction and Heidegger's description of the authenticity/inauthenticity distinction fails to take into account how the exclusion of God from Heidegger's analysis leads to an overturning of the basic principles of Paul's anthropology. Zimmerman writes that Heidegger's "distinction between authenticity and inauthenticity stems from his "de-mythologizing" analysis of the Christian distinction between faithfulness and sinfulness ... Inauthenticity is an intensification of everyday egoism; authenticity is a diminution of it."[39] But I will show in my following chapters that inauthenticity does not refer to someone controlled by "egoism." On the contrary, inauthenticity in *Being and Time* refers to someone who is controlled by others rather than one's own self. And inauthenticity does not refer to someone who has "died to self," as in Paul's concept of faithfulness, but rather to someone who has resolutely heeded the call of one's own Self.

While Zimmerman's work, *The Eclipse of the Self*, has given the most complete interpretation of the relation between Heidegger's concept of authenticity and Christian theology, he does not present a detailed analysis of the modifications which the biblical concepts of sinfulness and faithfulness undergo in Heidegger's description of inauthenticity and authenticity. Zimmerman does emphasize that the role of the will, the "voluntaristic or willful strain in resoluteness," as the way to "conversion" from inauthenticity to authenticity is different from Paul's description of the role of grace in the Christian understanding of conversion. Zimmerman quotes Barth to assert that "If Karl Barth is correct in his estimation that 'There is one thing, and only one thing which [Bultmann] does not get from Heidegger, and that is his description of the transition [to redemption] as an act of God,' then a consideration of Bultmann's interpretation of the New Testament would provide considerable insight into Heidegger's thinking."[40]

But, by using Bultmann to represent Christian theology, Zimmerman fails to explain adequately the differences between the role of the self in Heidegger's *Dasein*-analysis and the role of the self in biblical theology. Zimmerman quotes Bultmann's antithetical descriptions (in "Romans 7 and the Anthropology of Paul") of the man of sin and the man of faith: " 'the man who wants to be himself loses himself; instead of the 'I,' 'sin' becomes the subject . . . his self is not realized when he himself tries to lay hold of it by disposing of his existence, but only when he surrenders himself to the claim of God and exists from him.' "[41] Although Bultmann uses Heidegger's term "authenticity" to name Paul's analysis of the life of faith, Bultmann is describing well the Pauline, biblical conception of faithful existence. But what neither Bultmann nor Zimmerman realize is that this Pauline concept is *opposed* to Heidegger's description of authentic existence. For laying hold of one's own existence, willing to be one's own self, is *the* mark of authentic existence according to Heidegger. But according to Paul, this is *the* mark of the life of sin. Zimmerman consistently misses this crucial distinction.[42]

The best works in English on the relation between Heidegger's *Dasein*-analysis and Christian anthropology (Macquarrie, Zimmerman, and Kovacs) all focus upon a comparison of Heidegger and Bultmann. These critics, as well as the theologians who appropriate Heidegger's thought, all tend to accept without question Heidegger's claim that he is performing a neutral formalization of biblical theology. According to Kovacs, Heidegger "clearly describes the place of man in his philosophy, and he can develop his thought without a theistic or an atheistic orientation ... The 'neutrality' of SZ [regarding theology and atheism] does not preclude an openness toward other dimensions of There-being that are not considered in the existential analysis."[43] This approach, which I will certainly agree is in line with Heidegger's own interpretation of his philosophy, forces Kovacs to explain away the "seemingly 'atheistic'" statements in *Being and Time*.[44]

But such a neutral, ontological formalization is impossible. I want to focus on Heidegger's formal indication of Pauline anthropology to criticize Heidegger's claims that (1) it is not a secularization of Christian anthropology; (2) it is neutral in regard to the theological claims of Christian faith; and (3) Christian theology must use his fundamental ontology in order to make itself understood conceptually.

Kovacs admits that the "word *demythologization* is not found in *SZ*," but he argues that it is the best term to "emphasize the questioning (rethinking and 'criticizing') attitude of SZ toward the traditional approach to the philosophical problem of God."[45] I want to argue that the term Heidegger uses to describe the modern transformation of the Christian definition of man also describes Heidegger's own transformation of Christian anthropology in his *Dasein*-analysis. Like modern philosophy, Heidegger has not demythologized, but rather "detheologized" (*enttheologisiert*) the Christian conception of humanity (*BT* 74). We can make this even more specific, designating which God is excluded, by using Derrida's term, "de-Christianize,"[46] to describe Heidegger's formal ontology of Pauline anthropology.

The early twenties were crucial in Heidegger's development. Around this time he abandoned his Christian faith and began to work on what would become his major work, *Being and Time*. I am not the first to see a connection between these two events, despite Heidegger's attempts to avoid characterizations of his work as theological or anti-theological. Karl Löwith, a student of

Heidegger's during this period, argues that "it was no mere misunderstanding when so many hearers of Heidegger's lectures and readers of *Being and Time* understood the author at that time other than he understands himself today [1953], namely as the composer – attuned to Kierkegaard, Pascal, Luther, and Augustine – of an irreligious [*unglaubigen*] 'analytic of Dasein'."[47]

Most works on Heidegger and theology to date take him at his word when he disavows any irreligious motivations for his thought, although Gadamer has forcefully asserted that Heidegger's philosophical project does belie theological motivations,[48] and Derrida has questioned "whether, in order to sustain this existential analysis, the so-called ontological content does not surreptitiously reintroduce, in the mode of ontological repetition, theorems and theologemes pertaining to disciplines that are said to be founded and dependent – among others, Judeo-Christian theology, but also all the anthropologies that are rooted there" (*A* 54–55). While the language of *Being and Time* does reflect the influence of Judeao-Christian theology in Heidegger's *Dasein*-analysis, the distortions of Christian theology belie not a theological, but rather an anti-theological motivation.

Heidegger's formal indication of Pauline anthropology looks forward to his later violent anti-Christian polemics and actions during his membership in the National Socialist movement[49] more than it looks back to his early identification of himself as a "Christian theo-logian." Kisiel argues correctly that in 1922, "when Heidegger first proclaims the fundamental 'atheism' of philosophy, we can add another famous German – alongside Eckhart and Luther – to whom Heidegger is heir: namely, Friedrich Nietzsche."[50] Rather than accusing Heidegger of being an "underhanded Christian" (as Nietzsche accuses Kant), I want to demonstrate that Heidegger in *Being and Time* is an underhanded atheist.

CHAPTER 8

The redemptive–eschatological separation of flesh and Spirit in the epistles of the Apostle Paul

> For the mind set on the flesh is death, but the mind set on the Spirit is life and peace, because the mind set on the flesh is hostile toward God; for it does not subject itself to the law of God, for it is not even able to do so; and those who are in the flesh cannot please God. However, you are not in the flesh but in the Spirit, if indeed the Spirit of God dwells in you ... And if Christ is in you, though the body is dead because of sin, yet the spirit is alive because of righteousness. But if the Spirit of Him who raised Jesus from the dead dwells in you, He who raised Christ Jesus from the dead will also give life to your mortal bodies through His Spirit who indwells you.   Romans 8:6–11

Nietzsche criticizes Christianity for denigrating the body and defining the essence of man through the fictitious concepts of the soul and spirit. Heidegger criticizes Nietzsche for remaining entrenched in the metaphysical conception of man as *animal rationale*, for merely reversing Platonism and Christianity to define the essence of man in terms of the body.[1]

> The overman is the expressly willed negation of the previous essence of man. Within metaphysics man is experienced as the rational animal (*animal rationale*). The "metaphysical" origin of this essential definition of man, a definition that sustains all Western history, has to this hour not been understood, has not been made a matter of decision for thinking. This means that our thought has not yet emerged from the division between the metaphysical question of Being, which asks about the Being of beings, and the question that inquires more primordially; that is, inquires into the truth of Being and thus into the relationship of the essence of Being with the essence of man. (*N* III 217)

Heidegger accuses the thought of "all Western history" of relying upon this metaphysical dualism of the mind and body, and we can see that he is pointing here to his own *Dasein*-analysis in *Being and*

123

Time as the only way beyond this metaphysical conception of human being.

But biblical thought, because it is based on the Hebraic not the Greek conception of humanity, does not understand human beings as a dualism of body and spirit, as Platonism does, nor as a dualism of mind and body, as Descartes does. Paul's division between the flesh and the Spirit is not a metaphysical–ontotheological dualism, but rather a redemptive–eschatological separation between those alienated from God and those reconciled to God.

Both Paul and Heidegger draw upon a traditional vocabulary in developing their anthropological concepts, and yet both thinkers give new meaning to this used linguistic currency. Paul uses the everyday vocabulary of the Greco-Roman world of his time and the language of the Torah (especially from the Septuagint translation), while Heidegger uses the language of modern metaphysics and also borrows terminology from the New Testament and Christian theology (especially Augustine, Luther and Kierkegaard). Both writers reshape the language of Greek metaphysics and contemporary, everyday uses of their language in an attempt to express a vision of humanity that is radically different from the metaphysical anthropologies of ontotheology.

In comparing Heidegger's analysis of *Dasein*[2] with Paul's description of *anthropos*,[3] we must first consider Heidegger's claim that his analysis of Dasein in *Being and Time* is not anthropology. The purpose guiding Heidegger's *magnum opus* is not to construct a philosophical anthropology, but rather "to raise anew *the question of the meaning of Being*" (*BT* 19). Nevertheless, the analysis of Dasein, "*man*'s Being" (my emphasis, *BT* 47), assumes a privileged position for Heidegger in working out the question of Being: "the first way which leads away from metaphysics to the ecstatic existential nature of man must lead through the metaphysical conception of human selfhood."[4]

In Heidegger's hermeneutics, the formal structure of the question of Being is divided into three parts: "that which is asked about," which is Being (*Sein*); "that which is interrogated," which are entities (*Seiendes*) as they are in themselves; and "that which is to be found out by the asking," which is the meaning of Being (*BT* 24). Among those entities which are to be interrogated, "Dasein" is given priority in asking the meaning of Being: "If to Interpret the meaning of Being becomes our task, Dasein is not only the primary entity to be interrogated; it is also that entity which already comports itself, in its Being, towards what we are asking about when we ask this question" (*BT* 35). Therefore, Dasein is not to be analyzed as an end in itself. Dasein, the Being of man, is to be analyzed only because of its distinctive relationship to Being itself. Consequently, Heidegger denies that his work is a "philosophical anthropology"; rather, he calls his analysis of Dasein "fundamental ontology," for it provides the basis for the "universal phenomenological ontology." None the less, "*fundamental ontology*, from which alone all other ontologies can take their rise, must be sought in the *existential analytic of Dasein*" (Heidegger's emphasis, *BT* 34).

But a similar qualification must be made about the so-called "theological anthropology" of the Apostle Paul. Paul is in no way interested in developing an independent definition of the essence or constitution of man. He is not interested in humanity as an end in itself, but in humanity as created and redeemed by God. Here we can make a preliminary connection between Paul and Heidegger. Just as Heidegger is interested in Dasein only in its relation to Being (including Being-in-the-world and Being-with-others), so is Paul interested in anthropos only in its relationship to God (and how this relationship should determine the way one conducts him or herself in the world, especially towards others). This is not to equate Heidegger's "Being" with Paul's "God." I do not want to make this equation which Heidegger explicitly denies and which leads away from the God revealed in the Bible towards another god of ontotheology. But the structural parallels between Paul's biblical theology and Heidegger's fundamental ontology should not be overlooked.

Paul begins his epistle to the Romans with a description of anthropos in terms of our relationship to God. He states that even though we were given an understanding of God – "that which is known about God is evident within them; for God made it evident to them" (Romans 1:19) – we have chosen to forget God – "since they did not think it worthwhile to retain the knowledge of God" (Romans 1:28).

They exchanged the truth of God for a lie, and worshiped and served created things rather than the Creator. (Romans 1:25)

Just as Paul begins his most complete theological treatise with the claim that we were given an understanding of God, so does Heidegger begin his *magnum opus*, *Being and Time*, by stating that "we

already live in an understanding of Being."[5] Heidegger calls this
Dasein's "pre-ontological understanding of Being," and the later
Heidegger will claim that it is Being which "gives" Dasein this
understanding, just as God has given anthropos a basic understanding of Himself according to Paul. And just as in Paul anthropos has
forgotten to acknowledge God, worshipping creatures instead of the
Creator, so in Heidegger has Dasein forgotten the question of Being,
investigating beings instead of Being ("the meaning of Being is still
veiled in darkness"). In his early lecture courses on Paul's epistles,
Heidegger equates the Pauline term, "darkness" (which means in
Paul a forgetting of God), with his own concept of inauthenticity,
which means in Heidegger's later thought the forgetting of Being.

Heidegger analyzes the Being of Dasein in order to understand
the revelation of Being: Paul lays bare the nature of anthropos in
order to understand the revelation of God. Therefore, the term
"anthropology" must be written with scare quotes in our description
of the writings of both Paul and Heidegger. Both Paul and Heidegger
attempt to present an "anthropology" which opposes a philosophy
based upon the independent, subjective ego, a philosophy like
Nietzsche's in which "the world [is] thought according to the
paradigm of man" (*N* III 154).

In some ways then Heidegger shares with Christianity the opposition to modern philosophy's exaltation of man which began with
Descartes. As I have noted, he identifies Descartes' metaphysics as
the beginning of "that emancipation of man in which he frees
himself from obligation to Christian revelational truth and church
doctrine to a legislating from himself that takes its stand upon itself"
(*QT* 148). Of course Heidegger would not have us return to an
obligation to Christian revelational truth, but he concurs with
Christianity in his opposition to defining man as an isolated ego and
therefore making him the ground of all knowledge and truth.
Heidegger objects to defining Dasein apart from its Being-in-the-
world, while Paul objects to defining anthropos apart from our
relationship to God.

But Heidegger is as suspicious of the view of humanity presented
by Christian theology as he is of philosophical anthropology: "what
stands in the way of the basic question of Dasein's Being (or leads it
off the track) is an orientation thoroughly coloured by the anthropology of Christianity and the ancient world" (*BT* 74). In Christian
theology, according to Heidegger in *Being and Time*, the nature of

man's Being is defined as "in the image of God" (*imago dei*), taken from Genesis 1:26: "Let Us make man in Our image, according to Our likeness." Despite Heidegger's characterization of Christian theology, according to the Bible humanity lost this image when we fell away from God, for Paul speaks of the "restoration" of the *imago dei* through humanity's relationship with Jesus Christ. Thus even the most basic concept from biblical anthropology is misrepresented and unexplored by Heidegger. Rather, Heidegger turns immediately to the "Helleno-Christian" description of mankind in early Christian theology in order to justify his rejection of Christian anthropology.

Heidegger goes on to point out that Christian theology did not develop its definition of humanity solely from the standpoint of faith, but rather looked to philosophy, to the ancient Greeks, in constructing a conceptual understanding of man. "But just as the Being of God gets Interpreted ontologically by means of ancient ontology, so does the Being of the *ens finitum*, and to an even greater extent" (*BT* 74). Descartes marks the culmination of theology's appropriation of ancient ontology, for in Descartes, " 'God' is a purely ontological term" (*BT* 125). In Descartes, theological speculation abandons its biblical foundation and becomes onto-theology. (This "relation between the Word of Holy Scriptures and theological-speculative thinking," split asunder after Descartes, is the subject of Heidegger's studies in biblical hermeneutics which he claims led him upon the path of thinking the relation between language and Being (*OWL* 9–10).)

Heidegger, following Luther,[6] criticizes Christian theology for adopting its ontology from the ancient Greeks. At one point in *Being and Time*, Heidegger even looks forward to a return to a primordial Christian faith, called for by Luther, which no longer relies upon metaphysics for its foundation:

Theology is seeking a more primordial interpretation of man's Being towards God, prescribed by the meaning of faith itself and remaining within it. It is slowly beginning to understand once more Luther's insight that the "foundation" on which its system of dogma rests has not arisen from an inquiry in which faith is primary, and that conceptually this "foundation" not only is inadequate for the problematic of theology, but conceals and distorts it. (*BT* 30)

I am certainly in sympathy with this call by Heidegger for Christian theology to cease to try to use modern metaphysics to articulate its teachings and beliefs. At the time Heidegger wrote this passage,

Barth had already begun to articulate the recovery of a Christian theology "in which faith is primary," but Heidegger himself, after dividing theology and philosophy, chose the path of philosophy.

I could simply agree with Heidegger's analysis of the division between philosophical and theological inquiry had he not asserted, on the very same page of *Being and Time* that calls for theology to cease building upon modern philosophy's foundation, that his ontological inquiry "is indeed more primordial" than the "ontical inquiry of the positive sciences." For we know from his lecture, "Phenomenology and Theology," that he considered theology a positive science, and in this lecture he asserts that his "genuine ontology" should "function as a guide for ... theological explication" (PT 19). Ironically, Heidegger claims that theology must use his phenomenological analysis of Dasein in order to make its claims about the nature of man conceptually understood. Thus Heidegger calls upon theology to repeat the mistake he has just charged it with, i.e. turning to philosophy to gain conceptual understanding of faith, turning biblical theology into ontotheology. Using Heidegger's fundamental ontology as the foundation for Christian theology "conceals and distorts" biblical faith as much as Greek metaphysics.

Despite the fact that Heidegger calls for the "residues of Christian theology within philosophical problematics" to be "radically extruded" (*BT* 272), this theology still provides Heidegger with a "clue" in defining the essence of man as Dasein. "But the idea of 'transcendence' – that man is something that reaches beyond himself – is rooted in Christian dogmatics" (*BT* 74). This definition of transcendence as belonging to man, as defining his essence, is central to Heidegger's description of Dasein. And it is my contention that Heidegger in fact takes much more from Christian theology than this one clue. But like all the "clues" Heidegger takes from Christianity, Heidegger excludes God and therefore secularizes the borrowed concept. In this case, "transcendence," which in *Being and Time* Heidegger equates with the "spiritual" (*BT* 419), is explained as a "basic constitutive feature of Dasein" rather than as a gift from God.[7]

Heidegger draws most heavily upon the language of biblical theology in his Dasein-analysis. He insists that he is not secularizing Christian theological anthropology, but is rather merely formalizing Pauline (and Aristotelian) structures in terms of their fundamental, ontological implications. He acknowledges that his analysis of Dasein comes out of his interpretation of "the Augustinian (i.e., Helleno-Christian) anthropology with regard to the foundational principles reached in the ontology of Aristotle" (*BT* 243, note vii). Yet at the same time Heidegger insists that "what stands in the way of the basic question of Dasein's Being (or leads it off the track) is an orientation thoroughly coloured by the anthropology of Christianity and the ancient world, whose inadequate ontological foundations have been overlooked" (*BT* 74). Heidegger claims to overcome this problem by providing an ontological foundation, a fundamental ontology, for the ontic structures of Christian (especially Pauline) and Greek (especially Aristotelian) anthropology, which "have become intertwined in the anthropology of modern times" (*BT* 75). But these strands of Western thought are radically different, and one cannot provide a single, ontological foundation for these two ways of thinking without misinterpreting one or both.

In what follows I will attempt to tease apart the intertwining of biblical theology and Greek philosophy in modern anthropology through an exegesis of the description of anthropos in Paul's epistles. I will distinguish the biblical redemptive-eschatological interpretation of humanity from the dualistic description of man as *animal rationale* in ontotheology, building upon and extending my analysis of the related redemptive-eschatological division between this *aion* and the *aion* to come in the first part of my study.

Six key terms are used to describe anthropos in the New Testament: *kardia*, *nous*, *pneuma*, *psyche*, *sarx*, and *soma*.[8] By far the most important of these terms is kardia ("heart"), which Paul borrows from the Old Testament. The use of this term throughout the Old Testament (the Hebrew "*leb*" and "*lebab*"), in all the gospels, and in the rest of the New Testament is one of many indications of a consistent image of humanity which is presented throughout the Bible. But the Pauline epistles are the most important texts in determining the biblical image of humanity, as Werner Kümmel explains: "Paul is, indeed, particularly important, for he is the only New Testament writer who to any great extent offers us direct statements about man's nature, and uses extensively the anthropological terminology of his time."[9]

In Hellenistic thought, kardia means the seat of both emotion and thought. At times kardia has this meaning for Paul, but it also takes on the more inclusive meaning of "the inner life of man and the source or seat of all the forces and functions of soul and spirit."[10] Thus kardia signifies the whole of the inner being of anthropos, the ego, the person.

But Paul uses kardia in a more specific sense as well which differs both from its use in ancient Greek thought and from the popular use of this term in the Greco-Roman world of Paul's time. This distinctive use of the term kardia, even though it is expressed in Greek, derives from the Hebrew Bible. In this sense, kardia refers to the part of anthropos to which God's revelation is addressed and the part of us which in turn responds either positively or negatively to this revelation. Therefore, kardia refers to anthropos' standing before God. As Paul writes in Romans 10:10, "with the heart man believes, resulting in righteousness." And because anthropos believes or rejects God with his or her heart, it is the heart which God judges, "for God sees not as man sees, for man looks at the outward appearance, but the Lord looks at the heart" (1 Samuel 16:7).

Paul does not draw only from the Old Testament in his description of the inner person (*esothen anthropos*). As the apostle sent to proclaim the gospel to the Gentiles, Paul also uses the Greek term *nous* to speak of the inner person, especially in his or her relation to God. The term sometimes has the connotation of "mind" and "understanding," and is therefore somewhat distinguished from kardia. But nous is often used interchangeably with kardia to designate anthropos in his or her response to God.

Although psyche ("soul") and pneuma ("spirit") have another more specific connotation in Paul, the two terms are also used interchangeably to designate the inner person. When using these terms in their general sense, "Paul speaks of *pneuma* in much the same sense of a *psyche*, at least so long as he intends the human spirit and not the Spirit of God given to believers (as is usually the case when he speaks of *pneuma*). Just as *psyche*, *pneuma* denotes man in his natural existence, approached from within."[11] This use of pneuma as an anthropological concept, a general term, like psyche, for the inner person, is borrowed from popular anthropological ideas[12] and must be distinguished from Paul's distinctive use of pneuma to mean the Spirit of God. Before explaining the more specific, and more important, meaning of these terms in Paul, let us first add to our discussion Paul's vocabulary for talking about the "outer person" (*exo anthropos*).

As Paul uses psyche and pneuma in a general sense to refer to the inner person or as a metonymic designation of the whole person, so too does he use sarx ("flesh") and soma ("body") to refer to the outer person or as a metonymic designation of the whole person:

One can take his point of departure here in the general popular usage by which "body" denotes the tangible and visible organism in which various "members" are to be distinguished ... In this sense "body" is frequently synonymous with "flesh," insofar as flesh sometimes also denotes only the material corporeality of man.[13]

Thus kardia, nous, psyche, and pneuma are all used interchangeably to designate the inner person, and sarx and soma are used interchangeably to designate the outer person. This is so only when Paul uses these terms in the general sense, borrowed from popular anthropological ideas. But although Paul "uses a series of anthropological terms in his description of human existence which are not clearly defined one from the other" in this general, popular sense, this does not mean that "he uses these terms in a quite careless way."[14] The context makes it clear when Paul is using these anthropological terms in a popular sense and when he is using them in their more specifically biblical denotations.

When Paul uses the above anthropological terms from the specific perspective of the Christian revelation concerning anthropos, important distinctions are made between the various terms for the inner and outer person. These distinctions differentiate Paul's separation of sarx and pneuma from anthropological dualisms. In Paul, "the distinction itself is of a very general and formal significance, describing the outward, visible, physical, and the inward, invisible, spiritual side of human existence. No general anthropological conclusions are to be drawn from this, however, e.g., of a dualistic man consisting of two 'parts,' or of a more or less 'real' or 'essential' part of man."[15] The division which permeates Paul's epistles is not the anthropological dualism of Platonic or Cartesian metaphysics, but the redemptive division of biblical theology.

This redemptive division is most often designated as the antithesis of flesh and Spirit.

Flesh (body) and Spirit do not stand over against one another here as two "parts" in the human existence or in the existence of Christ. There is no question here ... of a dichotomistic distinction in an anthropological sense.

Nor is the contrast ethical as is indeed the case in other contexts … Rather, "flesh" and "Spirit" represent two modes of existence, on the one hand that of the old aeon which is characterized and determined by the flesh, on the other that of the new creation which is of the Spirit of God.[16]

Used in this sense, in distinguishing the new nature given to the Christian who has been redeemed by Christ (the redemptive division), and in distinguishing the new aeon from the old, inaugurated by Christ's death and resurrection (the eschatological division), flesh and Spirit take on new meaning. Paul's division between flesh and Spirit is not the basis of an ontotheological–anthropological dualism between the material body and the immaterial soul. Rather, it is a redemptive–eschatological division which describes two possible responses to the revelation of Jesus Christ and to the subsequent existence in either the new aeon of the Spirit or the old aeon of the world.

When used in the antithesis of flesh and Spirit, flesh no longer means the outward person, but rather the whole person in his or her limited and mortal nature, in his or her dependence upon God's Spirit. "But '*sarx*' is more frequently used to indicate the opposite of God or '*pneuma*', and it then denotes the *whole* man, who faces the Creator as a sinner."[17] Spirit is now a theological term for the Spirit of God, not an anthropological term for the inner person. Therefore, the division that Paul teaches is the antithesis of the human apart from God and the human in relation to God, of human weakness and dependency on the one hand, and human pride and self-proclaimed autonomy on the other.

In this distinctive sense, flesh means the human as a sinful (sarxic) mode of existence. Although Paul's division, in opposing "flesh" and "Spirit," often sounds like a Platonic or even Gnostic dualism in which the body is evil and the soul or spirit is good, Paul means to express a very different division. In his letter to the church at Rome, Paul is supplanting the popular anthropological conceptions of the Gentile Christians. The sinfulness of sarx is not inherent in the physical or material, for the "*sarx* has thoughts (*phronema*, Romans 8:6–7), desires (*epithumia*, Galatians 5:16), [and] mind (*nous*, Colossians 2:18)."[18] Even sarx as the whole person does not necessarily indicate a sinful mode of existence:

Just as in the Old Testament concept "flesh" (e.g., Isa. 31:3; Jer. 32:27; Job 10:4), or "flesh and blood," it denotes in Paul especially the human as such and taken by itself, as distinguished from and in contrast to the divine.

There is not yet here *per se* an indication of human sinfulness, but only of human limitation and weakness ... Regarding this meaning of "flesh" one is thus able to conclude with Gutbrod: "As the whole man, man is therefore *sarx*, absolutely distinct from God, i.e., he has nothing divine in him, which is not yet to say that he is evil, but simply that he is man, who is created, and not God, who created him."[19]

Barth begins to recover this biblical understanding of humanity when he draws upon Kierkegaard in his commentary on Romans to argue forcefully that the basic biblical division is not a dualism between body and spirit but rather "the qualitative distinction between man and God."[20]

Although sarx is not necessarily evil, the only example the Bible gives of a sinless flesh is Jesus Christ. Our flesh only becomes sinful when we turn away from God to assert our independence. And according to Paul, even though flesh is not necessarily sinful, in fact all humanity since Adam has rebelled against God. As Paul writes in Romans: "through one man sin entered into the world, and death through sin, and so death spread to all men, because all sinned" (Romans 5:12).

But, with the advent of Christ, humanity was offered the opportunity to be set free from its sinful mode of existence. Thus Paul writes of the opposition of natural, fleshly anthropos and the new spiritual anthropos, both as an antithesis of the Christian and non-Christian (1 Corinthians 2:14) and in the antithesis between the pre-Christian (the old self) and the Christian (the new self). Paul exhorts his readers that,

in reference to your former manner of life, you lay aside the old self [*palaios anthropos*], which is being corrupted in accordance with the lusts of deceit, and that you be renewed in the spirit of your mind, and put on the new self [*kainos anthropos*], which in the likeness of God has been created in righteousness and holiness and truth. (Ephesians 4:22–24)

This change from the old man to the new man (King James translation), or better, from the old self to the new self (New American Standard and New International translations), is more than an ethical dualism. The new self "does not join on to and restore what is already in existence; it revolutionizes the world and the hearts of men through a new birth."[21] In order to emphasize the radicalness of this division between the old and the new self, a division which no Hegelian *Aufhebung* can synthesize, one could translate this division as a separation between the old life and the new life.

This second birth involves "the putting on" of both a new body and a new spirit. Whereas the old self is characterized by a fleshly mind (*nous tes sarkos*, Colossians 2:18), the new self is given a new mind, the mind of Christ (*nous Christou*, 1 Corinthians 2:16). This change from the fleshly mind to the mind of Christ is called "*metanoia*." Again the term is borrowed from everyday Greek but is given a profound new significance. Psychologically, *metanoia* refers to a change within one's own mind, but in Paul's theology *metanoia* comes to mean conversion, the impartation of the new creation or new life to the one who is given the mind of Christ.

A similar distinction applies to the outer person of the old and the new self. In this context, soma can be distinguished from sarx. Although the sarx can be put in the service of the new life, it is not renewed, but sacrificed. Paul uses the word soma or body to refer to the new outer life. Just as Paul does not use the term *kosmos* to refer to the new *aion*, so does he refrain from using the term sarx to refer to the new soma. In order to distinguish his new distinctive use of the term soma from the popular anthropological use, Paul speaks of the spiritual body as opposed to the natural body. "If there is a natural body, there is also a spiritual body," and it is in the resurrection of the dead that the natural body "is raised a spiritual body" (1 Corinthians 15:44).

Paul goes on in this crucial passage to explain the source of this new spiritual body:

So also it is written, "The first man, Adam, became a living soul." The last Adam became a life-giving spirit. However, the spiritual is not first, but the natural; then the spiritual. The first man is from the earth, earthy; the second man is the Lord out of heaven. As is the earthy, so also are those who are earthy; and as is the heavenly, so also are those who are heavenly. And just as we have borne the image of the earthy, we shall also bear the image of the heavenly. Now I say this, brethren, that flesh and blood cannot inherit the kingdom of God. (1 Corinthians 15: 45–50)

After distinguishing between the natural body and the spiritual body (and asserting that the soul and the body will be resurrected, in opposition to the gnostic tendencies of the Corinthian church),[22] Paul then aligns the flesh with the perishable natural body when he writes "that flesh and blood cannot inherit the kingdom of God." Thus in his division of the old life and the new, Paul distinguishes between sarx and soma. "Involved here ... is the characteristic distinction between 'flesh' and 'body' in the Pauline usage ... 'Flesh,' even when it does not have the pregnant significance of human sinfulness, always has man in his weakness, transitoriness, especially in view; 'body,' on the contrary, represents the image of man as he was created by God, was intended for God, and will therefore be saved from death by God."[23] So although flesh (sarx) and blood will not inherit the kingdom of God (1 Corinthians 15:50), yet God has promised to give life through his Holy Spirit to the Christian's mortal body (soma) (Romans 8:11).

Paul's redemptive division also allows him to make a distinction between soul and spirit, though not as two parts of the inner person. Rather, Paul uses psyche to denote the inner being, the ego, of the natural self while he uses pneuma to refer to the new "self" of the Christian. The old "I" is characterized by the term psyche, just as the natural body is called the "psychical body" ("*soma psychikon*," 1 Corinthians 15:44). Thus psychic is used in a manner parallel to sarxic and in opposition to the pneumatic. Again in 1 Corinthians, Paul distinguishes between the natural person ("*psychikoi*") and the spiritual person ("*pneumatikoi*"):

Now we have received, not the spirit of the world, but the Spirit who is from God, that we might know the things freely given to us by God, which things we also speak, not in words taught by human wisdom, but in those taught by the Spirit, combining spiritual thoughts with spiritual words. But a natural man [*psychikoi*] does not accept the things of the Spirit of God; for they are foolishness to him, and he cannot understand them, because they are spiritually appraised. (1 Corinthians 2:14)

Thus, the Spirit also refers to a hermeneutical gift. All claims to human autonomy are humbled, for we need the Spirit both to understand and to live out the new life.

Paul's model for the new anthropos is Jesus Christ who sacrificed his sarx and psyche, though sinless, in order to redeem humanity's sinful psyche and sarx, in order to make available the Spirit and the spiritual body. The Christian is baptized into Christ's death whose flesh was crucified for us:

don't you know that all of us who were baptized into Christ Jesus were baptized into his death? We were therefore buried with him through baptism into death in order that, just as Christ was raised from the dead through the glory of the Father, we too may live a new life. (Romans 6:3–4)

So just as God sent "His own Son in the *likeness of sinful flesh* ... as an offering for sin," so will God, through Christ who "condemned sin in the flesh" (Romans 8:3), "transform the body of our humble state into *conformity with the body of His glory*" (Philippians 3:21). Christ took on the likeness of sinful flesh that we might put on the likeness of his glorified, spiritual body. And just as Jesus came "to give His life [*psyche*] for many" (Mark 10:45), so those who do not "love their life [*psyche*] even to death" (Revelations 12:11) will be given a new life through the pneuma of God.

So neither the body (soma) nor the soul (psyche) nor the mind (nous) is immortal: All is flesh and will fade like grass. But the new spiritual body and the new self, the pneuma, the *nous Christou*, will abide forever. Herein lies the Pauline division:

[Paul] sets this individual pneuma, which is transcendent to man and proper to God, in antithesis to both soul and body. This may be seen positively in the strict differentiation of the human nous (1 C. 14:14) but also negatively in the fact that he avoids pneuma when he wants to describe the innermost I of the pre-Christian man ... For this reason the pneuma, though always God's Spirit and never evaporating into the pneuma given individually to man, is also the innermost ego of the one who no longer lives by his own being but by God's being for him.[24]

Paul separates not the soul and the body, not the inner and outer man, but rather those who live by their own being and those who live for God. It is this separation which must be compared to Heidegger's distinction between authentic and inauthentic existence.

In direct contrast to philosophical anthropology, Paul sees anthropos as a being "who cannot be determined in the light of his own self. His existence stems from outside himself."[25] Käsemann goes on to explain how the category of the individual is not applied to those who live their own free and independent lives but to those who live according to God's Spirit.

Paul only applies the category of the individual to the believer ... For him man under the rule of sin could never be an "individual" but was, as representative of his world, a victim of its powers. For him, the "individual" is not the premise of an anthropological theory but the result of the grace which takes people into its service ... According to the apostle, individuation does not follow from already existing individualities; it is a crystallization of our calling, in which the point at issue is the universal lordship of Christ.[26]

This separation between the self as a victim of the powers of the world and the self that has been called to become free to be an individual is very similar to Heidegger's distinction between *das Man* and the authentic self.

But, unlike Paul, Heidegger believes that the authentic self is one's own (this is the root meaning of authenticity), and results from a call from one's own self. This concept of the authentic self directly contradicts Paul's concept of the redeemed self: "The fully interior or self-conscious ego is the ego of sin ... Within this [Pauline] tradition or mode of consciousness there can be no spiritual 'I,' or no spiritual 'I' which is my own, for it is the ownness or self-conscious ego which is the antithesis of Spirit."[27]

This is seen most clearly in Paul's definition of the Christian "I" in Galatians 2:20:

I have been crucified with Christ; and it is no longer I who live, but Christ who lives in me; and the life which I now live in the flesh I live by faith in the Son of God, who loved me and delivered himself up for me.

The ego of the old life has been crucified with Christ, and the "I" of the new self is not a mystical depersonalization of the self, but the surrender of the self to the lordship of the crucified and resurrected Jesus Christ. "Thus, Paul's view of man distinguishes itself completely from every purely humanistic or descriptive view of man, as much as from every idealistic or dualistic conception."[28] And also from Heidegger's conception of Dasein in his fundamental ontology.

CHAPTER 9

Inauthenticity and the flesh

As it is, it is no longer I myself who do it, but it is sin living in
me.   Paul, Romans 7:17

Proximally, it is not "I," in the sense of my own Self, that "am,"
but rather the Others, whose way is that of the "they."
                                     Heidegger, *Being and Time*

Theologians such as Bultmann, Tillich, and Macquarrie have been
the quickest to recognize the affinities between the Heideggerian
analysis of Dasein and the Pauline description of anthropos, but
· instead of demonstrating how Heidegger borrowed extensively from
the New Testament, they have used Heidegger's analysis of Dasein
to formulate a new existentialist Christian theology.

Bultmann, in defense of his use of Heidegger's existential analysis
in his New Testament theology, seems to understand that Heidegger
is borrowing directly from the New Testament: "Above all,
Heidegger's existentialist analysis of the ontological structure of
being [Dasein] would seem to be no more than a secularized,
philosophical version of the New Testament."[1] More often,
however, Bultmann fully accepts Heidegger's claim that his ontological description of Dasein must *precede* any "ontic" claims made by
theology about the nature of man in order for these claims to be
conceptually understood.[2]

But surely this is a reversal of the proper way to assess the
relationship. Heidegger read and studied the Bible and Christian
theology before he wrote *Being and Time*. Hans Jonas formulates the
relationship correctly in his essay "Heidegger and Theology":

But does the consonance on the philosopher's part arise from independent
philosophical reflection, or was the Biblical model itself a factor in the
reflection? I think, there can be no doubt that the latter is the case. We are

simply in the presence of that well-known and always known fact that there is much secularized Christianity in Heidegger's thought.[3]

This "fact" may have been well known in German theological circles, but it was long unknown or ignored in the appropriation of Heidegger by Anglo-American theologians and literary critics. And a criticism of this secularization, of Heidegger's "neutral" formal indication, is long overdue.

Heidegger himself specifically denies the claim that he is merely secularizing the description of man presented by Christian theology:

> It would undoubtedly be the greatest error, if one were to explain the existent essence of man, as though it were the secularized translation of a thought about man by Christian theology via God (*Deus est suum esse*); for ex-sistence is neither the actualization of an essence, nor does ex-sistence itself realize and constitute the essential. (*LH* 279)

This is a difficult statement to assess, because the reason Heidegger gives for denying that his phenomenological description of Dasein is a secularization of Christian theology's image of man is based not upon a statement concerning the New Testament description of human existence but upon subsequent reinterpretations of the New Testament by theologians who drew upon Greek ontology in their interpretation of man. That Heidegger is referring to ontotheology in which Greek conceptuality is primary and not to biblical theology in which Hebraic thought is fundamental is made clear by the definition of God as *suum esse*. Biblical theology makes no use of the metaphysical distinction between existence and essence, and although God is called "the most high" in the Bible, He is nowhere called the "highest being."

Heidegger destroys the essence/existence dichotomy by beginning his preparatory analysis of Dasein with the claim that "*The 'essence' of Dasein lies in its existence*. Accordingly those characteristics which can be exhibited in this entity are not 'properties' present-at-hand; they are in each case possible ways for it to be, and no more than that" (*BT* 67). According to Heidegger then, Dasein is not a "what" or a substance; consequently, Dasein should not be described in terms of categories, but in terms of "existentials." Categories describe attributes of things that are present-to-hand while existentials describe ways in which Dasein can be.

We have seen that in Paul's division between the flesh and the Spirit there is a similar distinction. "Flesh" does not refer to the body as a physical substance, and "Spirit" does not refer to a soul substance; rather, these terms refer to possible ways in which humans can be (in relationship to God). As with Heidegger, these are not two different substances which are somehow mingled together in human beings: they are not the basis for a metaphysical dualism. Rather they are ways in which humans can be, ways which correspond, with a difference, to Heidegger's distinction between authenticity and inauthenticity. And Heidegger was aware of the specifically biblical connotations of Paul's use of the terms sarx and pneuma as evidenced in his course on Paul's letters to the Thessalonians.[4] So while Heidegger's analysis of Dasein may not be a secularized translation of Christian theology's thought about man when this theology appropriates Greek metaphysics, Heidegger's Dasein-analysis may still well be a secularized translation of biblical, especially Pauline, thought about anthropos.

Heidegger attempted to distance himself from both a Christian and an anti-Christian stance during the late 1920s when he was writing and publishing *Being and Time*. He makes a distinction between "Christianness," i.e., the life of faith testified to in the New Testament and still lived today, and "Christianity," the subsequent historical movement which, although based upon the original faith of Christianness, did not always remain faithful to the original conception. At times, Heidegger appears to claim that, while his thinking is critical of Christian theology, he has nothing to say about Christian faith.

Therefore, a confrontation with Christendom is absolutely not in any way an attack against what is Christian, any more than a critique of theology is necessarily a critique of faith, whose interpretation theology is said to be. (*QT* 64)[5]

Although it may appear that Heidegger is making a Kierkegaardian distinction here, the basis of his division, which is made clear in his 1928 lecture, "Phenomenology and Theology," is the thought of Franz Overbeck, who in *Concerning the Christianness of Our Contemporary Theology* (1873) separates "Christianness," the essence of Christianity, from its actual historical manifestations in the church and in theology.[6] Overbeck's distinction is based upon a skeptical stance toward the possibility of Christianness, not a critical stance toward Christendom from the standpoint of faith (as in Kierkegaard). Therefore Heidegger's distinction between Christianness and Christianity should not be read as an affirmation of Christianness, just as his distinction between metaphysical theiology and Christian theology[7] does not mean that he is supporting the latter. Rather, he is excluding Christian theology from the realm of thinking, for Heidegger also followed Overbeck in "bracketing revelation in the pursuit of the exigencies of philosophical thinking" (PT 114).

Heidegger denies that his analysis of Dasein either affirms or rejects any theological claims about the nature of human beings:

Through the ontological interpretation of *Dasein* as Being-in-the World, there is neither a positive nor a negative resolution of a possible Being-towards-God. However, through the elucidation of the transcendency there is first obtained *an adequate concept of Dasein*, in consideration of which one may now ask what exactly is, ontologically, the relationship between God and *Dasein*. (Heidegger's emphasis; LH 294)

Heidegger claims that, while his thinking does not decide for or against faith, faith must appropriate his analysis of Dasein *before* attempting to understand humanity's relationship to God. These two claims will be tested here. Does Heidegger's analysis of Dasein make no claims about the possibility of man's "Being-towards-God" in terms of the biblical conception of anthropos' relationship to God? And does Heidegger's analysis provide the first adequate description of Dasein which enables us to begin to understand the relationship between God and man? Continental, British and American theologians have often accepted these claims in their appropriation of Heidegger's thinking for theological purposes,[8] but these claims should not be accepted without a more careful investigation of the relationship between the analysis of Dasein in *Being and Time* and the New Testament description of anthropos.[9]

Heidegger, in the first sentence of his preparatory analysis of Dasein, writes that "We are ourselves the entities to be analysed. The Being of any such entity is *in each case mine*." In a note to this passage, Heidegger refers to Augustine's *Confessions* where Augustine writes "But what is closer to me than myself? Assuredly I labour here and I labour within myself; I have become to myself a land of trouble and inordinate sweat" (*BT* 67, note i). This is one of many examples of Heidegger's use of the Christian conception of humanity's fall to guide his interpretation of the self of Dasein. The description of Dasein's alienation from its self in inauthenticity is guided in part by Christianity's theological description of humanity's fall away from the *imago dei*. Throughout his analysis of Dasein,

Heidegger uses biblical idioms to describe how "Dasein has in every case already gone astray and failed to recognize itself" (*BT* 184).

Heidegger draws upon Christian theology to describe not only the fact of Dasein's fallenness, but also the cause of Dasein's fall. He begins his analysis of inauthenticity by investigating the "who" of Dasein in its everydayness. "Proximally and for the most part Dasein is fascinated with its world. Dasein is thus absorbed in the world" (*BT* 149). According to Heidegger, Dasein loses its authentic self, its own (*eigentlich*) self, in the world. Heidegger's description of Dasein's possibilities as either being absorbed in the world or being authentically one's Self repeats, at least structurally, Christ's rhetorical question: "For what will a man be profited, if he gains the whole world [*kosmos*], and forfeits his soul" (Matthew 16:26). This theme in Heidegger of the world as "tempting" (*BT* 221) to Dasein parallels closely the same long-standing theme in Christianity. According to Dreyfus and Rubin, "That Heidegger is secularizing original sin is clear when he treats lostness in the one not as a structural *tendency* but as a psychological *temptation*."[10]

"World" is for Heidegger an "ontologico-existential concept," often referred to in this sense as "worldhood" in *Being and Time*. "Worldhood" refers not to the totality of beings in the world, but rather "to a kind of Being which belongs to Dasein." "World" is then an existential of Dasein, a description of a way Dasein can be. In this sense Dasein can be called "worldly" (*BT* 93). Paul also uses "world" in this sense to refer to the way of being of those who live according to the present age, who live according to the flesh. Thus "worldhood" or "Being-in-the-world" is used by Heidegger in the same way that "world" is used in Paul, not as the totality of things present-to-hand, but in reference to a mode of being for Dasein.

Hans-Georg Gadamer claims that Heidegger took his concept of "world" from the New Testament. "Heidegger had himself sketched the history of this concept of the world [in *Vom Essen des Grundes*], and in particular, had called attention to and historically legitimated the difference between the anthropological meaning of this concept in the New Testament (which was the meaning he used himself), and the concept of the totality present-at-hand."[11] In this historical sketch of the term "world," Heidegger himself admits that the New Testament significantly advanced the understanding of the concept "world":

It is no accident that in connection with the new ontical understanding of existence that appeared in Christianity the relationship of *kosmos* to human Dasein, and so even the concept of the world, was focused and clarified . . . In Paul (cf. I Corinthians and Galatians), *kosmos houtos* means not merely, or even primarily, the condition of the "cosmic," but the condition and the situation of man, the character of his stance *with regard to* the cosmos and of his evaluations of what is good. *Kosmos* is the Being of man in the How of a way of thinking that is estranged from God (*he sophia tou kosmou*: wisdom of the world). (*ER* 51)

Note that Heidegger, while admitting that "world" was first used to describe a way of being in Paul, still separates his use of the term "world" from its use in the New Testament by calling the Christian analysis "ontic." This same rhetoric will be used by Heidegger throughout *Being and Time* when he refers to the influence of Christian theology on his own thought.[12]

In his "Letter on Humanism," Heidegger works to separate his use of the term "world" from its New Testament precedent, now defining world as "the clearing of Being."

To refer to "Being-in-the-world" as the basic trait of the *humanitas* of the *homo humanus* is not to claim that man is simply a secular being, in the Christian sense, and so turned away from God and devoid of "transcendency" . . . "World" . . . does not in any way signify, in the term "Being-in-the-world," the earthly being in contrast to the heavenly . . . "World" is the clearing of Being, wherein man stands out from his thrown essence . . . Thought of from the point of view of ex-sistence, "world" is in a way transcendence within and for existence. (LH 293)

Heidegger is of course correct in pointing out that the Pauline redemptive division (earthly/heavenly), as well as the medieval distinction between secular and sacred, has been eliminated in his use of the concept. Nevertheless, in both Paul and Heidegger, "world" is used to describe a way humanity can be, but in Paul the term has the negative connotation of a way of being apart from God, while in Heidegger the term has the positive connotation of Dasein's ex-sistence, its "transcendence within and for existence."

Nevertheless the existential meaning of "world" as used in the New Testament is retained by Heidegger: "Throughout the foregoing, 'world' serves as the name of the essence of human Dasein. This concept of world corresponds perfectly to Augustine's existentiell concept" (*ER* 79). But Heidegger follows the Enlightenment tradition in that "the uniquely Christian evaluation of 'worldly'

Dasein, of the *amatores mundi*, has dropped away" (*ER* 79). He has merely excluded the possibility of a spiritual transcendence and thereby stripped this existential of its negative connotation.[13] Heidegger's "world" refers to Dasein's relatedness to Being, while Paul's "world" refers to anthropos' alienation from God.

However, the structure of Paul's distinction between "worldly" and "spiritual" anthropos, between living according to the flesh and living according to the Spirit, returns in Heidegger's distinction between authentic and inauthentic existence. Heidegger secularizes Paul's exhortation: "Do not conform any longer to the pattern of this world [*aion*], but be transformed by the renewing of your mind" (Romans 12:2).

Heidegger vigorously denies that his concept of the inauthentic self has any negative moral or religious implications: "our own Interpretation is purely ontological in its aims, and is far removed from any moralizing critique of everyday Dasein" (*BT* 211). He writes that "even in its fullest concretion Dasein can be characterized by inauthenticity – when busy, when excited, when interested, when ready for enjoyment" (*BT* 68). The inauthentic Self, then, is not a sinful self which must be redeemed. It rather means, as the German word "*uneigentlich*" indicates more clearly, that the inauthentic self is not one's own. This is the defining characteristic of the inauthentic self: it is the "They-self" (*das Man*). Dasein's self, proximally and for the most part, is not one's own:

Dasein, as everyday Being-with-one-another, stands in *subjection* to Others. It itself *is* not; its Being has been taken away by the Others. (*BT* 164)

As Heidegger questions in Pauline terms, "It could be that the 'who' of everyday Dasein just is *not* the 'I myself'" (*BT* 150).

Despite the significant changes made by Heidegger, his model for the inauthentic self is still taken from Christian theology. We can see the parallel most clearly in the epistle to the Romans in which Paul describes the condition of his self before his conversion: "I am of flesh [*sarkikos*], sold into bondage to sin [*hamartia*]" (Romans 7:14). This "bondage" of the self to sin, which is not simply an ethical condition, is the structural paradigm for Heidegger's presentation of the inauthentic self's "subjection" to the Others. Heidegger also learned from Paul that it is due to this subjugation that the "'who' of everyday Dasein . . . is *not* the 'I myself.'" As Paul asserts: "But if I am doing the very thing I do not wish, I myself am no longer the one doing it, but sin which dwells in me" (Romans 7:20). Paul is explaining that if he cannot do the good which he, his "authentic" self ("I myself"), desires to do, then the "I myself" is no longer the acting self. The fleshly self has come under the power of sin, just as in Heidegger the inauthentic self has come under the sway of the Others.

In neither Paul nor Heidegger is this intended to be an excuse for our actions, but rather a description of a possible way to be. Neither "sin" in Paul nor the "They" in Heidegger are "substances" which are present-to-hand. But whereas the "They" represents alienation from Dasein's authentic Self, "sin" designates anthropos' alienation from God.

Paul uses the term "flesh" to describe anthropos as a creature, as created by God and therefore finite, mortal. Heidegger, while avoiding the question of whether Dasein was created or not,[14] describes the finitude of Dasein by the term "thrownness." Because Dasein finds itself already in the world, Heidegger says that Dasein is "thrown." And just as this initial use of the term "flesh" by Paul makes no conclusions about whether anthropos is dominated by sin but merely designates humanity's finitude, so too does Heidegger's term "thrownness" apply to both the authentic and inauthentic self. In both cases, it is humanity's refusal to accept its finitude which causes it to fall under subjection, the power of *hamartia* in Paul and the power of *das Man* in Heidegger.

It is Dasein in its "fallenness" which designates its absorption by the world and its subjugation to the they-self, just as it is the fall of humanity in Paul which determines that all flesh has become alienated from God. Steiner points out the theological overtones of Heidegger's analysis: "Again, and pre-eminently, the tonality is theological. It was as if Heidegger's whole diagnosis of inauthenticity amounted to a quasi-secular version of the doctrine of fallen man."[15]

Heidegger protests in advance against theological interpretations of his concept of fallenness.[16] But why does he use terminology with such deep theological overtones if he wants to avoid misunderstanding? I believe there are two reasons for this. The first is that Heidegger drew upon Christian theology as a primary paradigm of human existence in formulating his description of Dasein's inauthentic existence. The second is that Heidegger wanted his analysis of Dasein to replace the Christian interpretation of humanity as the "primordial" description of human being.

Ontically, we have not decided whether man is "drunk with sin" and in the
status corruptionis, whether he walks in the *status integritatis*, or whether he
finds himself in an intermediate stage, the *status gratiae*. But in so far as any
faith or "world view", makes any such assertions, and if it asserts anything
about Dasein as Being-in-the-world, it must come back to the existential
structures we have set forth, provided that its assertions are to make a claim
to *conceptual* understanding. (*BT* 224)

Heidegger, after basing his description of Dasein on Christian
anthropology, now tells Christian theology that it must use his
existential structures if it is to have any hope of being understood!

Heidegger, in his hermeneutic of Dasein, borrows the structure of
Paul's description of anthropos, but secularizes it by taking God out
of the biblical paradigm. Humans have not fallen from God; rather,
Dasein has fallen away from its authentic self. "Dasein has, in the
first instance, fallen away from itself as an authentic potentiality for
Being its Self, and has fallen into the 'world'. 'Fallenness' into the
'world' means an absorption in Being-with-one-another, in so far as
the latter is guided by idle talk, curiosity, and ambiguity" (*BT* 220).
But, according to the Bible, we are alienated from ourselves because
we are alienated from God. Our alienation from God is more
"primordial." We are fallen and guilty because of a defiant rebellion
against God.

In Heidegger, "fallenness" and "thrownness" describe our ontological condition in the "world," a condition which we did not
cause, a condition without origin. In defining guilt as an ontological
condition rather than as the result of an act of the will, Heidegger
has introduced a gnostic element into Paul's doctrine. Therefore,
Heidegger's fundamental ontology cannot provide the ontological
foundation for Christian theology.

Christian theology would be foolish to rely upon Heidegger's
"god-less" thinking (as Heidegger later terms his thought) in conceptually formulating its faith. Karl Barth gives a clear affirmation
of the position of biblical theology regarding analyses which "seek to
understand man primarily without God ... as though he were in a
position to understand himself":

We cannot try to understand man even hypothetically without God in
order to find out whether the last in the matter is an open question, or a
statement borrowed from theology, or perhaps atheistic dogma. On the
contrary, we must advance from the starting-point that man is not to be
understood without God.[17]

According to Barth there can be no "neutral" description of human being which brackets the relationship between human beings and God. To bracket this relationship is to begin in opposition to Christian theology.

In order to demonstrate the dangers of beginning with Heidegger's existential analytic in conceptualizing Christian theology (as Heidegger claims we must), I will consider an example which Heidegger gives us in his lecture, "Phenomenology and Theology." In discussing the relationship between his fundamental ontology and Christian theology, Heidegger asserts:

All theological concepts necessarily contain that understanding of Being which is constitutive of human Dasein, insofar as it exists at all. Thus, for example, sin is manifest through faith, and only the believer can factually exist as a sinner. But if sin, which is a phenomenon of existence, is to be interpreted in theological concepts, then the *content itself* of the concept ... calls for a return to the concept of guilt. And guilt is an original ontological determination of Dasein. The more radically and appropriately the basic constitution of human existence is brought to light in terms of genuine ontology [i.e. Heidegger's ontology], e.g., the more the concept of guilt is grasped in its origin, the more clearly can it function as a guide for the theological explication of sin. (PT 18–19)

Heidegger is here speaking specifically of Christian theology, and he directs the Christian theologian to his existential analysis of guilt in section 58 of *Being and Time*. Let us begin with Heidegger's existential concept of guilt and see if it can work as a "guide" and "corrective" to the Christian theological conception of sin, as Heidegger claims it should.[18]

In his analysis of guilt, Heidegger follows his method of looking first at the "everyday" meanings of the term. He rejects all these meanings, whose common root is a principle of lack. In this common conception of guilt, Dasein is lacking something in regards to an external standard. Heidegger thereby separates guilt from any relation to an ethical law: "it must also be detached from relationship to any law or 'ought' such that by failing to comply with it one loads himself with guilt" (*BT* 328).

According to Heidegger, guilt must be understood not as man's awareness of his spiritual condition, but as an existential of Dasein's kind of Being. Guilt in this sense refers to Dasein's condition of being thrown: "As being, Dasein is something that has been thrown; it has been brought into its 'there', but *not* of its own accord" (*BT* 329).

Therefore: "Not only can entities whose Being is care load them-selves with factical guilt, but they *are* guilty in the very basis of their Being" (*BT* 332). According to Heidegger, this condition of being guilty, of being thrown, is the basis of Dasein being "morally" good or evil (*BT* 332). Dasein is finite and therefore has a "nullity" in its existence. This opens the possibility of Dasein choosing an inauthen-tic existence. But it also opens up Dasein's Being-free for all its existentiell possibilities, including the possibility of accepting its guilt authentically, of realizing that it is thrown and still able to project its future. In both Heidegger's analysis and in biblical revelation, human beings are finite and yet free to choose their own possibilities, authenticity or inauthenticity in Heidegger and obedi-ence or autonomy in the Bible.

Heidegger's assertion that Dasein is "guilty in the very basis of its being" is clearly reminiscent of Paul's teaching on anthropos' fall into sin through Adam (Romans 5:12), and yet Heidegger's concept of guilt relates not to the Christian doctrine of sin, but rather to the Christian doctrine of humanity's finitude as created. Heidegger's analysis of Dasein as thrown, as existing "but *not* of its own accord" (*BT* 329), agrees with Christian theology in acknowledging that humanity did not create itself, but Heidegger's philosophy has no place for God as Dasein's Creator, as the Judge before whom Dasein is guilty.

In biblical revelation, guilt is the awareness of sin. Sin is not a subsequent existentiell possibility based upon the existential cate-gory of guilt. Rather, sin is the basis of guilt, and guilt is a sub-sequent subjective realization of one's sin before God. It is not Heidegger's category of guilt which determines the meaning of sin, but rather the category of "before God." In Ricoeur's terms, "guilt designates the *subjective* moment in fault as sin is its *ontological* moment. Sin designates the real situation before God."[19] Although he claims that his fundamental ontology should become the basis of Christian theology, Heidegger has reversed the biblical understand-ing of the relationship between sin and guilt. In Paul, guilt is a possible realization of anthropos' actual spiritual sinfulness; in Heidegger, sin is one possible existentiell understanding of Dasein's more primordial ontological guilt. According to the New Testa-ment, it is not "only the believer [who] can factually exist as a sinner" (*PT* 18); rather, all are sinners, "for all have sinned and fall short of the glory of God" (Romans 3:23).

Heidegger essentially replaces the Judaeo-Christian doctrine of guilt with a Greek conception. The description of the understanding of guilt in sixth-century Greece in Kittel's *Theological Dictionary* closely parallels Heidegger's definition: "Guilt is associated with human limitation ... and is thus posited by life itself. It has to be accepted and confessed."[20] So too in Heidegger is guilt an expression of Dasein's finitude, of its being thrown, and Heidegger calls for Dasein not to free itself from guilt, but rather to accept it authentically.

Whereas in Heidegger Dasein becomes aware of its guilt, i.e. its finitude, through the internal call of its own conscience, in Paul anthropos becomes aware of his or her sin, and therefore becomes guilty, through the law revealed in God's Word. Heidegger's existential category of guilt serves not to "correct" the biblical conception of sin, but rather to distort it through reducing the terms to human experience alone. Our rebellion against the God who created us is reduced to a philosophical finitude, a finitude based not upon Dasein's Being, as Heidegger claims, but upon our subjective consciousness, our realization that we have not decided to come into the world and that we will not decide when we will leave it through death. This leads to a conception of the "I" as guilty in its own being, in relation to its own Self, and not in its relation to God. The category of the individual being guilty before God, i.e. sinful, is "corrected" out of the picture. As Ricoeur continues in his phenomenological interpretation of sin and guilt:

Let the "I" be emphasized more than the "before thee," let the "before thee" be even *forgotten*, and the consciousness of fault becomes guilt and no longer sin at all; it is "conscience" that now becomes the *measure*.[21]

This is very similar to what happens in Heidegger: in excluding humanity's position before God, the measure of Dasein's guilt becomes its own conscience in Heidegger's subsequent analysis of Dasein's authentic acceptance of its Being-guilty.

If we use Heidegger's existential conception of guilt to "guide" and "correct" our conception of sin, we will not elucidate the biblical revelation concerning sin, but rather replace this revelation with a philosophical conception of finitude which excludes the biblical understanding of anthropos as created and in sinful rebellion against its Creator. This will lead us yet further astray from biblical revelation when we come to understand what it means to authentically accept our guilt. In Heidegger this will mean to accept our ownmost possibilities in resolve, made known to us by the internal voice of our conscience, while in Paul this will mean to admit our sin, made known to us through the law of Scripture and the conviction of the Holy Spirit (for we can't even understand the law of Scripture on our own), and to surrender our own lives to God.

CHAPTER 10

The eigentlich Selbst *or the* pneumatikos anthropos

Anticipatory resoluteness is not a way of escape, fabricated for the "overcoming" of death; it is rather that understanding which follows the call of conscience and which frees for death the possibility of acquiring *power* over Dasein's *existence*.
Heidegger, *Being and Time*

Since the children have flesh and blood, he too shared in their humanity so that by his death he might destroy him who holds the power of death – that is, the devil – and free those who all their lives were held in slavery by their fear of death.
Hebrews 2:14–15

In Heidegger, it is the state-of-mind or mood of anxiety which "brings Dasein back from its falling, and makes manifest to it that authenticity and inauthenticity are possibilities of its Being" (*BT* 235). In a footnote to this passage, Heidegger admits that his analysis of the phenomenon of anxiety is based upon his theological studies:

It is no accident that the phenomena of anxiety and fear ... have come within the purview of Christian theology ontically and even (though within very narrow limits) ontologically. This has happened whenever the anthropological problem of man's Being towards God has won priority and when questions have been formulated under the guidance of phenomena like faith, sin, love, and repentance.

Heidegger goes on to refer to Augustine, Luther,[1] and Kierkegaard,[2] but in borrowing from Christian theology, Heidegger has made some significant changes. Again, all the changes result from a "detheologizing," from the exclusion of God. Instead of God calling humanity to repentance through his word, Heidegger believes that "Dasein itself must, in its Being, present us with the possibility and the manner of authentic existence" (*BT* 277). In biblical theology, anthropos is unable to apprehend or to live "authentically" (i.e. faithfully) without the revelation of God through Jesus Christ. The life of Jesus presents us with "the possibility and the manner of authentic existence." Kierkegaard makes this same point in *Training in Christianity*: "Christ's life here upon the earth is the paradigm: it is in likeness to it that I along with every Christian must strive to construct my life."[3]

Whereas in Paul and the whole of the New Testament, anthropos must die to his or her self in order to truly live, in Heidegger Dasein must accept its death, not as a future, indefinite possibility, but as a present possibility, in order to regain its authentic Self.[4] At first glance, Heidegger's doctrine seems to be merely a secularized version of Christian baptism, in which the old self dies so that the new self might be born again of God.[5] In both cases one encounters death before the end of his or her existence. Heidegger notes that, "In its Interpretation of 'life,' the anthropology worked out in Christian theology – from Paul right up to Calvin's *meditatio futurae vitae* – has always kept death in view" (*BT* 293, note vi). But, despite Heidegger's extensive use of the language and concepts of Pauline .anthropology, his analysis of the way to authenticity has elements which serve to work directly against the Christian doctrine of the way to salvation. And it is Heidegger's desire to distance himself from his Christian origins which causes him to invert the Christian paradigm.

Although Heidegger insists that theology should adopt his existential analysis, his doctrine leaves no place for the belief in Christ's victory over the power of death. Zimmerman writes that, "Evidently, there is not much room within this existential concept of authentic Being-towards-death for an existentiell concept permitting an individual to de-fuse *Angst* by believing he will not really die after all but will be saved from death by divine intervention."[6] In his discussion of death, Heidegger writes:

No one can take the Other's dying away from him. Of course someone can "go to his death for another." But that always means to sacrifice oneself for the Other "in some definite affair." Such "dying for" can never signify that the Other has thus had his death taken away even in the slightest degree. (Heidegger's emphasis; *BT* 284)

This is a direct denial of the New Testament teaching on the meaning of the death and resurrection of Jesus Christ. Jesus said that "I am the resurrection and the life; he who believes in Me shall live even if he dies, and everyone who lives and believes in Me shall never die" (John 11:25–26). The New Testament teaches that Christ defeated sin and death by "dying for" humanity: He has taken away the power of death over those who believe. This is the gospel announced by Paul to the Gentiles: "'Death has been swallowed up in victory'" (1 Corinthians 15:54). Heidegger explicitly denies this possibility. He reverses Paul by calling upon Dasein to accept the power of death over its existence. Even Kovacs, who repeatedly follows Heidegger's self-interpretations in which he insists that he is performing a theologically neutral description of Dasein, admits that "the great distance between Heidegger's phenomenology and Christian thought remains. In the final analysis, this is the primal distance and the basic difference between the certainty of death and the hope of resurrection, the distance between the inescapable finitude of human existence and the expectation of salvation that 'breaks into' the human condition."[7]

For both Heidegger and Nietzsche, freedom from death promised by Christianity is a nihilistic denial of Dasein's mortality and finitude. Even though the New Testament insists upon the mortality and finitude of human beings, the fact that it offers a way of attaining eternal life makes Christianity a lie and a danger for both Nietzsche's overman and Heidegger's authentic Dasein.

Taminiaux has "explored the context in which the first reference to Nietzsche is made [in *Being and Time*]. It punctuates the analysis of Being-authentic precisely with the possibility *not-to-be-outstripped* of death."[8] When discussing how authentically anticipating one's death delivers Dasein from the illusions of the they into the freedom of authentic existence, Heidegger quotes from the section of *Thus Spoke Zarathustra* entitled "On Free Death" (*Z* 71–74). Taminiaux summarizes the convergence between Zarathustra's teaching "on free death" [*vom freien Tod*] and Heidegger's analysis of "freedom for death" [*Freiheit zum Tode*]:

Free anticipation of death, subscription to one's own demise is at the very core of the *Selbstsucht* [quest for the self] inherent in the Nietzschean notion of the will-to-power. The free acceptance of finite existence is therefore the first point of convergence between the Heideggerian analysis and the teaching of Zarathustra.[9]

Both Zarathustra/Nietzsche and Heidegger's teachings about the free acceptance of one's own death oppose the Christian belief in the resurrection of the dead made possible through the sacrifice of Jesus.

In "On Free Death," Zarathustra castigates those who die too late and those who die too soon. Jesus is the prime example of the latter. "Verily, that Hebrew died too early ... Believe me my brothers! He died too early; he himself would have recanted his teaching, had he reached my age" (*Z* 73). Jesus died a decadent, too immature to have accepted Nietzsche's gay science. Furthermore, his death filled his disciples with *ressentiment*, and their thirst for revenge caused them to invent the fictions of the other world and life after death. Heidegger also opposes the belief in freedom *from* death taught by Christianity, and he opposes to this inauthentic view of death the anticipation of one's own death as not to be outstripped, "freedom *for* one's own death" (*BT* 308). "Anticipation, however, unlike inauthentic Being-towards-death, does not evade the fact that death is not to be outstripped; instead, anticipation frees itself *for* accepting this" (*BT* 308).[10]

Thus it is simply not true when Heidegger says that "in the ontological analysis of Being-towards-the-end there is no anticipation of our taking any existentiell stand toward death. If 'death' is defined as the 'end' of Dasein – that is to say, of Being-in-the-world – this does not imply any ontical decision whether 'after death' still another Being is possible" (*BT* 292). If we accept Heidegger's analysis of the "mine ownness" of death, there can be no belief in the Pauline doctrine of Christ's "dying for" our salvation from sin and death and therefore no belief in a life after death in the sense revealed in the Bible. Other "ontical" decisions about life after death may remain, but the Christian, biblical conception is denied and excluded.

Nevertheless, Heidegger claims that any questioning of the possibility of life after death must be made on the basis of his analysis of the meaning of death for Dasein:

Only when death is conceived in its full ontological essence can we have any methodological assurance in even *asking* what *may be after death*; only then can we do so with meaning and justification ... The this-worldly ontological Interpretation of death takes precedence over any ontical other-worldly speculation.[11] (*BT* 292)

In Derrida's analysis of this aspect of Heidegger's argument, he correctly asserts that "It is impossible to overemphasize the importance of what is *being decided*, so authoritatively and so decisively, at the very moment when what is in question is to decide on what *must remain undecided"* (*A* 54). Derrida stresses the "contamination" of Heidegger's supposedly "neutral" formal indication with Judaeo-Christian anthropology (*A* 79), but, by resolving to leave the question of life after death undecided, Heidegger has decided to exclude the Christian view of death. In the end, Heidegger's anti-Christianity contaminates his analysis of Dasein's death more than his theological origins do.

Therefore, if Christian theology accepts Heidegger's claim that it must begin with his analysis of the meaning of death, as it unfortunately has done in many cases, it would have to reject the central doctrine of the New Testament: that faith in the cross (Paul's metonymic designation for the death and resurrection of Jesus Christ) redeems humanity from the power of sin and death. Bultmann, who more than any other theologian has relied on Heidegger's existential analysis of Dasein in his own theological writings, has done just this: he has denied that Jesus rose from the dead. But as Paul states emphatically, "if Christ has not been raised, your faith is worthless" (1 Corinthians 15:17).

Heidegger's interpretation of death as uniquely one's own also leads to a conclusion opposed to the Bible regarding the nature of the "authentic" Self. "But if 'ending,' as dying, is constitutive for Dasein's totality, then the Being of this wholeness itself must be conceived as an existential phenomenon of a Dasein which is in each case one's own" (*BT* 284). If Dasein's dying is fully accepted as its own possibility in anticipatory resoluteness, as always a part of Dasein's being as a whole which is "not to be outstripped," then one's life is also one's own or "authentic." Seneca, another influence on Heidegger's conception of care, argues, according to Derrida's paraphrase, that "there is a right of property to one's own life" and therefore also to one's own death (*A* 3). Heidegger's supposedly neutral analysis privileges this Greco-Roman conception of death over the Judaeo-Christian.

In Heidegger, because man must die for himself, then he must also live for himself. The opposite conclusion is drawn by Paul:

not one of us lives for himself, and not one dies for himself; for if we live, we live for the Lord, or if we die, we die for the Lord; therefore whether we live or die, we are the Lord's. (Romans 14:7–8)

For Paul neither one's life nor one's death should be one's own, for Christ is "Lord both of the dead and the living" (Romans 14:9).

In the Heidegger of *Being and Time*, it is not Being or Nothing which takes the place of God, but the authentic Self. Kovacs writes that "it may seem that man (There-being) replaces God [in *Being and Time*] ... However, neither the notion of There-being nor the concept of Being in Heidegger's thinking takes the 'place' of God of classical (Western) metaphysics."[12] Dasein may not replace the God of "classical (Western) metaphysics," but it does take the place of the biblical God in calling Dasein out of its absorption in the world. Instead of God calling anthropos into relationship with him, into faithful existence, through the person of Jesus Christ (Romans 1:6), Dasein is called by its own (authentic) Self out of absorption in the world, out of the they-self, back to its own Self. This call in Heidegger is the call of conscience, which calls Dasein to authentically accept its Being-guilty.

Just as in his analysis of guilt, Heidegger's analysis of conscience is in some ways similar to the use of the same term in the Bible. (Both "guilt" and "conscience" are used rarely in the Bible, originating in Hellenic not Hebraic thought.) Heidegger is consistent with the Christian conception of the conscience in saying that it originates with the self. The conscience is never equated with the voice of God in the Bible (even though it has been in later ontotheologies). Although it is a gift from God, this gift has been corrupted along with humanity's understanding as a result of our alienation from God (1 Corinthians 8:7).

But, again as in his analysis of guilt, Heidegger's "conscience" replaces a different biblical term. Just as his analysis of guilt formally indicates not the biblical conception of guilt, but rather the biblical conception of creatureliness, so does his analysis of conscience formalize not the use of conscience in the New Testament, but rather the biblical description of God's call to redemption.

The function of the conscience in Heidegger is radically different from its limited function in the Bible. The Old Testament has no word for "conscience," for as W. D. Davies explains: "Hebrew thinking is theocentric, not introspective ... The obedience demanded by God has been revealed to man from a source outside him in the Law and the prophets. Not knowledge of the self (including conscience) but the fear of the Lord was the beginning of wisdom (Proverbs 1:7; 9:10)."[13] Paul uses the term conscience only to refute its use by those under the influence of Greek thought in the church at Corinth, as Davies points out:

In 1 Corinthians, following his policy of being all things to all men, he had used his opponents' term. But that he did not give to "conscience" the overriding significance in ethics that they did appears in 1 Cor. 4:4. There . . . he makes it clear that conscience is not his ultimate court of appeal. This is Christ himself. Open to corrupting influences, as it is, conscience is to be quickened by the Spirit and enlightened by Christ.[14]

According to Heidegger, the call of the conscience is not open to corrupting influences because it comes from the authentic Self, and only the they-self is open to external influence. The call of conscience only appears as an alien, external call because Dasein, in its subjugation to the they-self, is alienated from its authentic Self from whence the call of the conscience arises.

The caller is unfamiliar to the everyday they-self; it is something like an *alien* voice. What could be more alien to the "they," lost in the manifold "world" of its concern, than the Self which has been individualized down to itself in uncanniness and been thrown into the "nothing"? (*BT* 321–322)

The conscience is the call from the Self (the authentic Self) to the self (the they-self), beckoning Dasein to return to its authentic Self. "*In conscience Dasein calls itself*" (320). "And to what is one called when one is thus appealed to? To one's *own Self*" (*BT* 317).

At the beginning of the third part of *Thus Spoke Zarathustra*, in which Zarathustra accepts his call to be the teacher of the eternal recurrence, Nietzsche writes that for Zarathustra, "what finally comes home to me, is my own self and what of myself has long been in strange lands and scattered among all things and accidents" (*Z* 152). Zarathustra is liberated from the herd into the freedom of his own self just as Dasein is delivered from its lostness in the they into the freedom of its own, authentic self. Just as Zarathustra bids his disciples to "lose me and find yourselves" (*Z* 78), so does Heidegger tell us that "because Dasein is *lost* in the 'they', it must first *find* itself" (*BT* 313). Jesus' teaching of the selflessness of his disciples thus stands opposed to both Nietzsche's parody and Heidegger's secularization: "He who has found his life shall lose it, and he who has lost his life for My sake shall find it" (Mathew 10:39).

Despite the Nietzschean distortions of the biblical paradigm, the Christian overtones of Heidegger's description of the call of the conscience are unmistakable: "The call of conscience passes over in its appeal all Dasein's 'worldly' prestige and potentialities. Relentlessly it individualizes Dasein down to its potentiality-for-Being-guilty, and exacts of it that it should be this potentiality authentically" (*BT* 354). In calling Dasein to authentic existence "without regard to persons" (*BT* 319), this call of the conscience replaces not the biblical conception of conscience, but rather the biblical teachings about the call to faithful existence by God, who in his call is "no respecter of persons" (Acts 10:34) and who calls us to acknowledge our sin and guilt.

The structural pattern of a call to come out of one's absorption in the world and into authenticity is drawn from the Bible (and it must be remembered that Nietzsche in *Zarathustra* is drawing upon the Bible extensively), but again God is excluded in Heidegger's version. It is from Nietzsche that Heidegger learns to turn the "other-worldly" doctrines of Christianity into a "this-worldly" existential teaching (*BT* 292, *Z* 13). In the transformation, the conversion, from inauthenticity to authenticity, all originates from the Self and returns to the Self:

> If Dasein is to be able to get brought back from this lostness of failing to hear itself, *and if this is to be done through itself*, then it must first be able to find itself – to find itself as something which has failed to hear itself, and which fails to hear in that it *listens away* to the "they." (First emphasis mine; *BT* 315)

Zarathustra says that in those who "have long belonged to the herd," the "voice of the herd will still be audible" within them (*Z* 62). Like Zarathustra, Heidegger exhorts his readers to cease listening to the voice of the herd or the they in order to find themselves, to find themselves as something which heretofore has failed to heed the voice of their own conscience. Just as Zarathustra comes to accept and affirm eternal recurrence only after he leaves the marketplace and his disciples, isolating himself from "the herd," so must Dasein accept its own death through ceasing to follow the dictates of *das Man* in order to heed the call of its own, authentic self. Heidegger follows Nietzsche in looking forward to a time when "he who had been lost to the world now conquers his own world" (*Z* 27). And in opposition to Christian redemption, both Nietzsche and Heidegger want their readers to achieve their own salvation, for "if this is to be done through itself" (*BT* 315), Dasein must become its "own redeemer and joy-bringer" (*Z* 141).

Heidegger sets his conception of conscience against those who regard the call to authentic existence as coming from an external source:

If the interpretation continues in this direction, one supplies a possessor for the power thus posited, or one takes the power itself as a person who makes himself known – namely God ... Why should we look to alien powers for information before we have made sure that in starting our analysis we have not given *too low* an assessment of Dasein's Being, regarding it as an innocuous subject endowed with personal consciousness ...? (*BT* 320, 323)

Heidegger's statement here represents the process of secularization in modernism, *par excellence*: A biblical revelation is perceived as the reification of a human desire or power; therefore, the structure of the biblical revelation is preserved but all is explained in natural, human terms.

Although Heidegger writes that because he is only indicating the formal aspects of the idea of existence, "the call ... may undergo a different interpretation in the individual Dasein in accordance with its own possibilities of understanding" (*BT* 318), the Christian interpretation of the call is again specifically excluded. "The fact that the call is not something which is explicitly performed *by me*, but that rather 'it' does the calling, does not justify seeking the caller in some entity with a character other than that of Dasein" (*BT* 321).[15]

Dasein's conscience calls Dasein to accept its own mortality which individualizes Dasein by confronting it with anxiety.

Death does not just "belong" to one's own Dasein in an undifferentiated way; death *lays claim* to it as an *individual* Dasein. The non-relational character of death, as understood in anticipation, individualizes Dasein down to itself ... *the state-of-mind which can hold open the utter and constant threat to itself arising from Dasein's ownmost individualized Being, is anxiety.* (*BT* 308, 310)

And in Heidegger's interpretation of Nietzsche's doctrine of the eternal return of the same, the demon's announcement of the doctrine of eternal recurrence confronts the hearer with this anxiety (*N* II 24).

According to Heidegger, the thought of eternal return does not "come *from* any arbitrary human being, nor does it come *to* any arbitrary human being in his or her most arbitrary everydayness, that is to say, in the midst of all the hubbub that enables us to forget ourselves" (*N* II 24). The same point is made regarding the call of the conscience in *Being and Time*: "If in this lost hearing, one has been fascinated with the 'hubbub' of the manifold ambiguity which idle talk possesses in its everyday 'newness', then the call must do its calling without any hubbub and unambiguously, leaving no foot-hold for curiosity. *That which, by calling in this manner, gives us to understand, is the conscience"* (*BT* 316). The thought of eternal return cannot be heard by the they-self that is lost in the world. The call comes rather from the authentic self to the inauthentic self that has been individualized through the anxiety caused by the confron-tation with the possibility that one's death is one's own and not to be escaped. And just as the call of conscience in Heidegger comes from and leads Dasein to "the Self which has been individualized down to itself in uncanniness" (*BT* 322), so does the thought of eternal return cause, in Heidegger's interpretation, "that kind of individ-uation which we must grasp as *authentic appropriation*, in which the human self comes into its own" (*N* II 24). The acceptance of the eternal return by Zarathustra, of the chaos and finitude of the world, leads to an acceptance of authentic temporality in the same way that Dasein's resolute acceptance of its own death does.

In Nietzsche's description of Zarathustra's confrontation with the thought of eternal return, the thought seems to come from an external source, just as in Heidegger's analysis of the call of con-science:

"It" calls, against our expectations and even against our will ... The call comes *from* me and yet *from beyond me and over me.* (*BT* 320)

Similarly, in *Thus Spoke Zarathustra*, the thought of the eternal return comes from Zarathustra, yet it first comes as the silent voice of an other against Zarathustra's will:

Then it spoke to me again without voice: "You know it, Zarathustra, but you do not say it!" And at last I answered defiantly: "Yes, I know it, but I do not want to say it!"

Then it spoke to me again without voice: "You do not *want* to, Zarathustra?" (*Z* 145)

This call which speaks without voice is similar to the call of the conscience in Heidegger, for "*Conscience discourses solely and constantly in the mode of keeping silent"* (*BT* 318).

According to Heidegger, this call to authenticity must be accepted as one's own in the *Augenblick*,[16] a term used by Paul (in Luther's translation),[17] Kierkegaard,[18] and Nietzsche. In his use of the term we can see Heidegger choosing Nietzsche's existential interpretation of time over Paul's eschatological conception. In

Paul, the *Augenblick* refers to the moment of the *parousia* of Christ when those Christians who have not yet died will "be changed, in a moment, in the twinkling of an eye, at the last trumpet; for the trumpet will sound, and the dead will be raised imperishable, and we shall be changed" (1 Corinthians 15:52).[19] We saw how, in his early Freiburg lectures, Heidegger interprets Paul's eschatological pronouncements existentially as referring to the "here and now" acceptance of the uncertainty and groundlessness of one's own existence. Heidegger considered eschatological interpretations of Paul's pronouncements as referring to an "awaiting" of the *parousia* to be based upon an inauthentic view of time. And in *Being and Time*, Heidegger writes that the "inauthentic future has the character of *awaiting*" (*BT* 386). Heidegger opposes authentic resolve to this inauthentic stance toward the future.

Heidegger finds this authentic resolve in Zarathustra's understanding of the gateway of the "Moment" as the juncture of one's own past and future. In his existential acceptance of eternal recurrence in the moment, the *Augenblick*, Zarathustra comes to understand and live in authentic temporality.

The temporality of the time of *that* eternity which Nietzsche requires us to think in the eternal return of the same is the temporality in which humanity stands; preeminently humanity and, so far as we know, humanity alone. Human beings, resolutely open to what is to come and preserving what has been, sustain and give shape to what is present. (*N* II 98–99)[20]

Heidegger discovers in Nietzsche an anticipation of his analysis of authentic temporality, the ecstatic unity of temporality: "With one's factical Being-there, a potentiality-for-Being is in each case projected in the horizon of the future, one's 'Being-already' is disclosed in the horizon of having been, and that with which one concerns oneself is discovered in the horizon of the Present" (*BT* 416). Thus Taminiaux can write that Heidegger's "ecstatico-horizonal temporality includes an existential reappropriation of the eternal return."[21]

According to Heidegger, it is in anticipatory resoluteness,[22] revealed to Dasein through the state-of-mind of anxiety and the call of the conscience, that Dasein gains its authentic Self. Heidegger does not want to confront and attack Christianity directly as Nietzsche did. Rather, he attempts to differentiate his work from the Christian-moral interpretation of humanity by denying that authenticity is a privileged term that has any moral consequences.

But Heidegger's language belies the connection between his analysis of authenticity and the Christian description of the life of faith and its moral consequences. Heidegger's analysis of a conscience summoning Dasein out of its falling into the "they" (*BT* 322) is his substitution for Christ's call to be the in world but not of it (John 17:15–16). Heidegger continues by expounding the moral consequences of authentic existence:

> Dasein's resoluteness towards itself is what first makes it possible to let the Others who are with it "be" in their ownmost potentiality-for-Being ... Only by authentically Being-their-Selves in resoluteness can people authentically be with one another – not by ambiguous and jealous stipulations and talkative fraternizing in the "they" and in what "they" want to undertake. (*BT* 344)

This description of "authentically being with one another" is merely a god-less version of Christian love, and the avoidance of the ambiguous talk of the "they" is merely a philosophical version of Paul's practical exhortation to "avoid worldly and empty chatter" (2 Timothy 2:16). In spite of Heidegger's denials, it is clear that authentic existence is the ideal of Heidegger's existential analysis.

Although he bases much of his analysis on insights gathered from the New Testament, Heidegger's hermeneutic of Dasein's authentic self must be rejected by Christian theology because his ontological structures, having been influenced by the atheistic reversal of the Christian understanding of the source and meaning of redemption by Nietzsche, are incompatible with the biblical conception of faithful existence. I must concur with Hans Jonas when he writes: "That theology should admit this foe – no mean foe, and one from whom it could learn so much about the gulf that separates secular thinking and faith – into its inner sanctum, amazes me."[23]

In secularizing the New Testament representation of anthropos, Heidegger ends with a reverse image of Paul's description of the *pneumatikos anthropos*. In claiming to be able to present man phenomenologically, as he is in himself, without the aid of revelation, Heidegger repeats the offense of the *sarkikos anthropos*, of proclaiming his independence from God. In so doing, Heidegger defines authentic existence as living according to the commands of the Self which is one's own. Heidegger can thus agree with Nietzsche in describing authentic existence as autonomous existence, "the submission of ourselves to our own command, and the resoluteness of such self-command" (*N* I 50), for "whoever heeds commands does not heed *himself''* (*Z*200). Dasein has two alternative ways to be in Heidegger: we can live according to the dictates of the they in inauthenticity, or we can live according to the demands of our own Self in authenticity.

Paul also presents two alternatives for the human self. We can try to live as if our life and death were completely our own. This is the *eigentlich Selbst* for Heidegger, but this is the *sarkikos anthropos* in Paul. If we try to act on our own, in our own flesh, we become a subject of sin. We are held in subjection by sin, and therefore our subjectivity, our "I," is defined by sin:

it is no longer I myself who do it, but it is sin living in me. (Romans 7:17)

Or, we can lay down our "own" life and crucify our "own" self with Christ. Then we live not according to the flesh, but according to the Spirit. We no longer live for ourselves, but for Christ. Paul makes this clear in his description of the "I" of faith which harks back to his description of the sinful self in Romans:

I have been crucified with Christ; and it is no longer I who live, but Christ lives in me. (Galatians 2:20)

Heidegger avoids a purely subjectivist definition of the self by defining it not as substance, but as a way to be, by describing the self as a way of existing in the world, as the conjunction of self, world, and Being.

Self and world belong together in the single entity, the Dasein. Self and world are not two beings, as subject and object, or like I and thou, but self and world are the basic determination of the Dasein itself in the unity of the structure of being-in-the-world.[24]

This description of being-in-the-world follows directly after a passage in which Heidegger refers to the conception of cosmos in Paul. But, despite this use of the biblical conception of *kosmos* to move beyond the modern metaphysics of subjectivity, Heidegger's description of human being remains, like Nietzsche's, antithetical to the Christian description in that it describes Dasein as independent of God. In so doing, Heidegger describes the natural self, the sinful self. Heidegger admits that there is a "factual *existentiell opposition* between faithfulness and a human's free appropriation of his whole existence ... *faith,* as a specific possibility of existence, is in its innermost core the mortal enemy of the *form of existence* which is an essential part of *philosophy* ... Faith is so absolutely the mortal enemy

that philosophy does not even begin to want to do battle with it"
(PT 20).

But Heidegger's analysis of Dasein, despite his denials, does do
battle with Christianity, for Heidegger, in the end, sets the
Enlightenment ideal of autonomy against the biblical call to death
to the self through Christ.[25] Although Nietzsche and Heidegger's
call for humanity to enter the freedom of autonomy is not based
upon the "courage to use your own reason!," as in Kant, their calls
are still based upon the Enlightenment call to obtain the "resolution
and courage" to base one's existence upon one's own self (autonomy), and not upon God (heteronomy).[26] Habermas may object to
Heidegger's undermining of the rationality of the Enlightenment,
but seen in the larger historical perspective of the modern reaction
against Christianity, Heidegger remains "entrenched" (to use the
term he used against Nietzsche) within the Enlightenment tradition.
What else could be expected from a philosopher who defines his
thinking as "the free questioning of purely self-reliant Dasein?"
(PT 20).

Derrida concludes his deconstruction of Heidegger's analysis of
death by writing:

What is [Heidegger's existential] analysis witness to? Well, precisely to that
from which it demarcates itself, here mainly from the culture characterized
by the so-called religions of the book. Despite all the distance taken from
anthropo-theology, indeed, from Christian onto-theology, the analysis of
death in *Being and Time* nonetheless repeats all the essential motifs of such
ontotheology. (*A* 79–80)

Thus Heidegger's charge against Nietzsche returns upon his own
thought: "Nevertheless, as a mere countermovement it necessarily
remains, as does everything 'anti,' held fast in the essence of that
over against which it moves" (*QT* 61).

PART THREE

Derrida's denials: the deconstruction of ontotheology

What is the function of this Christian model? In what sense is it exemplary for speculative onto-theology?　　Derrida, *Glas*

CHAPTER II

From the ends of man
to the beginnings of writing

In order to make this attempt of thinking recognizable and understandable within philosophy, it was possible at first to speak only within the horizon of the existing philosophy and within the usage of the terms familiar to it.

Heidegger, "Letter on Humanism"

To attempt an exit and a deconstruction without changing terrain, by repeating what is implicit in the founding concepts and the original problematic, by using against the edifice the instruments or stones available in the house, that is, equally, in language. Here, one risks ceaselessly confirming, consolidating, *relifting* (*relever*), at an always more certain depth, that which one allegedly deconstructs.

Derrida, "The Ends of Man"

In reading Derrida's "The Ends of Man," we enter the problem of reading itself. In this essay Derrida gives a reading of Heidegger's existential analytic in *Being and Time,* and he also reads Heidegger's own reading of his existential analytic in his "Letter on Humanism." Both Heidegger and Derrida defend the existential analytic against Sartre's misreading, against his anthropologistic reduction of Heidegger's *Being and Time.*[1] Derrida recalls, as Heidegger had recalled in his "Letter," that according to the opening sections of *Being and Time,* "anthropology and humanism were not the milieu of his thought and the horizon of his questions. The 'destruction' of metaphysics or classical ontology was even directed against humanism" (*M* 118).

Yet after defending Heidegger against this "misreading," a fact that in itself should prevent us from seeing Derrida's deconstructive readings as an opening up of texts to arbitrary interpretations,[2] Derrida goes on to uncover a *relève* of humanism in Heidegger's work. Derrida raises this question before proceeding with his own reading of Hegel, Husserl, and Heidegger:

What must hold our interest ... is the kind of profound justification, whose necessity is subterranean, which makes the Hegelian, Husserlian, and Heideggerian critiques or *de-limitations* of metaphysical humanism appear to belong to the very sphere of that which they criticize or de-limit ... what authorizes us today to consider as essentially *anthropic* or anthropocentric everything in metaphysics, or at the limits of metaphysics, that believed itself to be a critique or delimitation of anthropologism? What is the *relève* of man in the thought of Hegel, Husserl, and Heidegger? (*M* 119)

Derrida raises the question of the *relève* of man in Heidegger's discourse not as an end in itself, for Derrida wants to deconstruct in this essay, "The Ends of Man," not only the metaphysical concept of "man," but, more importantly, the ontotheological ("eschatoteleological") conception of the "end."

Returning his language upon him, we can say that the goal or end of Derrida's essay is a *relève* as well, not a *relève* of man, but a *relève* of Heidegger's concept of the end of metaphysics as the closure of metaphysics, a *relève* of Heidegger's destruction of ontotheology as the deconstruction of logocentric metaphysics, and the *relève* of the ontico-ontological difference as *différance*.

Derrida would probably reject the application of the term *relève/Aufhebung* to his project due to its complicity with the Hegelian concepts of truth and negativity. But the term seems to fit given Derrida's relationship to Heidegger's thought and given Derrida's definition of *relever*: "*Aufheben* is *relever* in the sense in which *relever* can combine to relieve, to displace, to elevate, to replace and to promote, in one and the same movement" (*M* 121). All these pairs, especially "replace and promote," describe Derrida's use and yet rewriting of Heidegger's destruction of ontotheology. Derrida repeatedly admits that his thought is dependent on Heidegger's, but at the same time he insists that his style prevents his thought from belonging to the metaphysics of presence in the way that Heidegger's does. "I sometimes have the feeling that the Heideggerian problematic is the most 'profound' and 'powerful' defense of what I attempt to put into question under the rubric of the *thought of presence*" (*Pos* 54). This relationship is perhaps presented most clearly in *Positions*, but Derrida gives an economical statement of this relation in the section within *Of Grammatology* entitled "The Written Being/The Being Written" (the title is itself a re-*writing* of the question of Being):

The ontico-ontological difference and its ground (*Grund*) in the "transcendence of Dasein" ... are not absolutely originary. Différance by itself would be more "originary," but one would no longer be able to call it "origin" or "ground," those notions belonging essentially to the history of onto-theology, to the system functioning as the effacing of difference. It can, however, be thought of in the closest proximity to itself only on one condition: that one begins by determining it as the ontico-ontological difference before erasing that determination. (*OG* 23–24)

Thus it is only by going through Heidegger's concept of the ontological difference, by preserving it as he replaces it, that Derrida uncovers the play of *différance* and the repression of this play by ontotheology. And Heidegger uncovers the ontico-ontological difference, and the forgetting of this difference by metaphysics, only by way of his hermeneutic of Dasein.

It is in Heidegger's hermeneutic of Dasein that Derrida locates a "hold which the 'humanity' of man and the thinking of Being, a certain humanism and the truth of Being, maintain on one another" (*M* 123–124). It must be stressed that Heidegger's thought of Being is in complicity with a *certain* humanism; therefore, Derrida is not attempting to "emprison all of Heidegger's text in a closure that this text has delimited better than any other" (*M* 123). Derrida follows Heidegger in distinguishing Heidegger's work from philosophical anthropology, and therefore he agrees that Heidegger's hermeneutic of Dasein is not held within metaphysics (according to Heidegger's demonstration that all humanisms are based upon metaphysics in that they determine the essence of man without asking the question of the truth of Being).

But, despite Heidegger's insight into the link between humanism and metaphysics, an insight that Derrida has put to work in the beginning of his essay, Derrida uncovers a less obvious return to metaphysics in Heidegger's analysis of the "proper" of man, "proper" in the sense of man's authenticity, his "ownness," and "proper" in the sense of proximity, the nearness of man and Being. Thus Heidegger both transgresses and is contained within the ontotheological determinations of man:

For, on the one hand, the existential analytic had already overflowed the horizon of a philosophical anthropology: *Dasein* is not simply the man of metaphysics. On the other hand, conversely, in the *Letter on Humanism* and beyond, the attraction of the "proper of man" will not cease to direct all the itineraries of thought ... It is in the play of a certain proximity,

proximity to oneself and proximity to Being, that we will see constituted, against metaphysical humanism and anthropologism, another insistence of man, one which relays, relieves, supplements that which it destroys. (*M* 124)

In keeping with my previous emphasis upon Heidegger's thought before the *Kehre*, I will be concentrating on Derrida's deconstruction of Heidegger's conception of the "proper of man," of his authenticity, his ownness, not in terms of Dasein's proximity to Being but of Dasein's proximity to itself.

Derrida begins with the opening of *Being and Time* in which Heidegger justifies his use of Dasein, of man's Being, as a privileged example in asking the question of Being. He outlines Heidegger's arguments for giving Dasein priority. In both arguments, ontic and ontological, Derrida locates a way in which Heidegger's questioning of the meaning of Being becomes inscribed within the horizon of metaphysics.

In the determination of the ontic priority of Dasein, Heidegger refers to "our" everyday preunderstanding of Being.

[*W*]*e always already* conduct our activities in an understanding of Being. Out of this understanding arise both the explicit question of the meaning of Being and the tendency that leads us toward its conception. We do not *know* what "Being" means. But even if we ask "What is 'Being'?," we keep within an understanding of the "is," though *we* are unable to fix conceptually what that "is" signifies. (*M* 124)

Derrida underscores the "we" in Heidegger's text, for it is in philosophy's use of the "we" that Derrida finds a link between the critique of humanism and its *relève* within this critique. Whether the problem of man be displaced into the question of "rational being" (Kant), "consciousness" (Hegel), "transcendental subjectivity" (Husserl), or "Dasein" (Heidegger), "anthropology regains all its contested authority" by way of the "we," for man operates as the only example of the concept which has replaced him in the philosopher's discourse. For instance in Heidegger: "This way of Being is proper (*eignet*) only to man." Philosophy leaves (empirical) man only to return to him after defining this "essence" or the truth of man.

Heidegger analyzes not man but Dasein in *Being and Time*, but all that is thought about Dasein is applied to man and to man only, for Dasein is nothing other than *man*'s Being. "We can see then that Dasein, though *not* man, is nevertheless *nothing other* than man"

(*M* 127). Derrida locates here the first index of the *relève* of man in Heidegger's thought:

Man and the name of man are not displaced in the question of Being such as it is put to metaphysics. Even less do they disappear. On the contrary, at issue is a kind of reevaluation or revalorization of the essence and dignity of man. (*M* 128)

This new valorization of man is made through the determination of man's essence as existence. Thus in the very same move whereby Heidegger begins to destroy the essence/existence opposition of metaphysics, a certain anthropologism is reinscribed within his text because Heidegger's conception of ex-sistence can be applied only to man. "Ek-sistence can be said only of the essence of man, that is, only of the human 'to be.' For as far as our experience shows, only man is admitted to the destiny of eksistence" (LH 204). We can now see the full irony of Derrida's locating another "insistence" of man in Heidegger's thought, for insistence is the opposite of exsistence for Heidegger, and therefore denotes man's inauthentic resistance to accepting his own dignity as exsistent.

Derrida locates another sign of the *relève* of man in Heidegger's justification for choosing Dasein as the entity which will have priority in asking the question of the meaning of Being. According to Derrida,

It is governed by phenomenology's principle of principles, the principle of presence and of presence in self-presence, such as it is manifested to the being and in the being that *we* are. It is this self-presence, this absolute proximity of the (questioning) being to itself, this familiarity with itself of the being ready to understand Being, that intervenes in the determination of the *factum*, and which motivates the choice of the exemplary being, of the text, the good text for the hermeneutic of the meaning of Being. (*M* 125)

This proximity to itself, its self-understanding in its self-identity, is in fact the defining characteristic of Dasein, the entity which will guide from the beginning Heidegger's questioning of the meaning of Being: "Thus to work out the question of Being adequately, we must make an entity – the inquirer – transparent in *his own* Being ... *This entity which each of us is himself* and which includes inquiring as one of the possibilities of its Being, we shall denote by the term '*Dasein*'" (my emphases; *BT* 27). In his analysis, Derrida asserts that "the name of man remains the link or the paleonymic guiding thread which ties the analytic of Dasein to the totality of metaphysics' traditional discourse" (*M* 127).

Gadamer questions this reading of Heidegger by Derrida, objecting to the way Derrida "reads Heidegger through Husserl."[3] Gadamer admits that Heidegger borrows Husserlian concepts in the transcendental description of Dasein in *Being and Time*, but he asserts that "neither Heidegger nor the hermeneutical turn in phenomenology can be accused of logocentrism, in the sense found in Derrida's critique of Husserl."[4] Gadamer believes that Heidegger's conception of self-understanding, like his own, has more in common with modern Protestant theology than with Husserl's phenomenological idealism. He argues that the concept of self-understanding (*Selbstverstandnis*) "has a pietistic undertone suggesting precisely that one cannot succeed in understanding oneself and that this foundering of one's self-understanding and self-certainty should lead one to the path of faith. *Mutatis mutandis* this applies to the hermeneutical usage of this same term."[5] But I have argued that more changes occur between Heidegger's theological origins and his fundamental ontology than Gadamer here admits, and that Heidegger's conception of the self has more in common with modern metaphysics than it does with Christian theology. Therefore I agree with Derrida that there is a *relève* of (modern, metaphysical) man in Heidegger's Dasein-analysis.

In order to further outline this *relève* not only of man, but also, through man, the *relève* of the metaphysics of presence, Derrida now turns to Heidegger's "Letter on Humanism." Derrida does not have to deconstruct Heidegger's text, but rather simply to provide commentary upon it in order to discover Heidegger's return to the essence and truth of man by way of his Dasein-analysis: "The proper of man, his *Eigenheit*, his 'authenticity,' is to be related to the meaning of Being" (*M* 133). The dignity of man which Heidegger wishes to restore is based upon the valorization of the "*propre*" of man. Derrida, following Heidegger beyond the *Kehre*, emphasizes the continuation of the metaphorics of the proper in Heidegger's analysis of Being, but it must be remembered that this valorization comes out of Heidegger's hermeneutic of Dasein. The proper of man, as determined in *Being and Time*, is his acceptance of his being as "his own."[6] As I have shown, this is revealed to Dasein through the voice of conscience, through the voice of his "authentic" self.

This valorization of self-presence in Heidegger's concepts of authenticity and conscience are the presuppositions that I criticized when comparing Heidegger's analysis of Dasein to Paul's description of anthropos. Derrida will pursue in detail the question of "what unites the values of self-presence [for example, authenticity] and spoken language [for example, the voice of conscience]" in *Of Grammatology* and *Speech and Phenomenon* (and we will turn to these texts in a moment). Derrida is more interested in the phonocentrism behind the voice of Being, but he also notes that the "insistence of the voice also dominates the analysis of *Gewissen* [conscience in *Sein und Zeit*]" (*OG* 324). I want to suggest that the conjunction of Derrida's deconstruction and a Pauline critique of Heidegger's Dasein-analysis points not to an affinity between Derridean and biblical discourse, but rather to an alternative tradition in the West which resists the metaphysics of presence or ontotheology and therefore also resists Derrida's deconstruction.

In the beginning of his essay, Derrida criticizes those who ignore "the history of concepts. For example, the history of the concept of man is never examined. Everything occurs as if the sign 'man' had no origin, no historical, cultural, or linguistic limit" (*M* 116). Heidegger eludes this criticism, and therefore Derrida claims that any "metahumanist" position which "does not make use of the information he provides concerning the genesis of the concept and the value of man ... remains historically regional, periodic, and peripheral" (*M* 128). But, in both Heidegger's analysis of the genesis of the concept of man and in Derrida's brief summary of this information, one of the two major forces determining the West's conception of man is avoided. Two major forces have shaped the West's understanding of humanity: the Greco-Roman and the Judaeo-Christian.[7] But in claiming to work within an historical perspective, both Heidegger and Derrida mention the influence of Christianity only after it has been appropriated by Greek thought. The same avoidance is noticed in a conversation about Heidegger between Paul Ricoeur and Gabriel Marcel. Ricoeur says that "I am always somewhat disturbed by what I might call the prudence with which Heidegger circumvents this [Judaeo-Christian] tradition," and Marcel exclaims in response: "Heidegger is Greek!"[8]

Regarding the Judaeo-Christian understanding of man, Derrida mentions only "the Christianizing of the Latin *humanitas*" (*M* 128), and Heidegger mentions only a Neoplatonic interpretation of the biblical presentation of man:

The Christian sees the humanity of man, the *humanitas* of the *homo*, as the delimitation of *deitas*. He is, in the history of Grace, man as the "child of

God," who hears in Christ the claim of the Father and accepts it. Man is not of this world, in so far as the "world," theoretically and *Platonically understood*, is nothing but a transitory passage into the other world. (My emphasis; LH 275)

Two misreadings of the biblical conception of anthropos are presented here. "The Christian" understands humanity (as *anthropos* not as *humanitas*) not solely within the history of grace as a child of God. The Bible also claims to reveal the nature of humanity apart from God, as a stranger and alien to God.

As I have argued above, Heidegger uses this biblical understanding of the pre-Christian and non-Christian in formulating his hermeneutic of Dasein, but then claims that Christian theology must use his analysis of Dasein in order to conceptually understand both pre-Christian and Christian existence. Heidegger claims that his hermeneutic of Dasein applies to Christian existence because he sees Christian rebirth as an *Aufhebung* of the pre-Christian life:

the sense of the Christian occurrence of rebirth is that one's pre-faith-full, i.e., unbelieving, human existence is sublated (*aufgehoben*) therein. Sublated does not mean done away with, but raised up, kept, and preserved in the new creation ... Hence we can say that precisely because all basic theological concepts, considered in their full regional context, include meanings which are existentielly (factually) powerless, i.e., *ontically* sublated (*aufgehoben*), they have as their *ontological* determinants meanings which are pre-Christian and which can thus be grasped purely rationally. (PT 18)

But this philosophical model of rebirth as *relève* distorts the biblical text. Paul speaks not of a raising up of the old self, but rather of the need to *put to death* this old self. The old self, the flesh, may continue after the rebirth, hence the need for a continual putting off of the flesh until the physical death, but there is no *relève* of the flesh. The new self (pneuma) is entirely new, completely other than the old self (sarx), and is never reconciled to or synthesized with the old.

Heidegger's second misreading involves his description of the Christian understanding of the world. This description is based wholly upon a Neoplatonic conception, a conceptuality specifically judged as false within the text of the New Testament. Judging the Judaeo-Christian understanding of anthropos by this Hellenized amalgam is like judging the Marxist position by a corrupt Marxist government, or judging a Freudian position by an incompetent psychiatrist. Heidegger passes over, in this case by describing a distorted version of, the biblical conception of "world" in order to disguise his reliance upon this New Testament model, in order to claim originality and "primordiality" for his analysis. This also explains the intensity of Heidegger's denials ("It would undoubtedly be the greatest error") that his concept of the existent essence of man as Being-in-the-world is a secularization of the Christian conception of man.

Derrida, in adopting Heidegger's historical analysis, also inherits an historical blindness towards an understanding of the historical force of the non-metaphysical biblical revelation of anthropos. Thus there is an historical alternative other than that with which Derrida closes his essay, the Nietzschean distinction between the superior man and the overman.

Heidegger, in his essays on Nietzsche, had turned this distinction against Nietzsche, calling him the superior man, the last great metaphysician of the West. Derrida returns this judgment upon Heidegger: "Or, on the contrary, are we to take the question of the truth of Being as the last sleeping shudder of the superior man?" (*M* 136). Heidegger falls short of the superman in that his style of *Destruktion* repeats the original problematic of metaphysics and uses the language of metaphysics in attempting to overcome it. The overman announced by Nietzsche uses a different "style" of deconstruction:

The latter – who is not the last man – awakens and leaves, without turning back to what he leaves behind. He burns his text and erases the traces of his steps. His laughter then will burst out, directed toward a return which no longer will have the form of the metaphysical repetition of humanism, nor doubtless, "beyond" metaphysics, the form of a memorial or a guarding of the meaning of Being, the form of the house and of the truth of Being. (*M* 136)

This is often taken to be Derrida's "style" of deconstruction, but he makes it clear here that it is not simply a matter of choosing "between [these] two *relèves* of man" (*M* 135): "It also goes without saying that the choice between these two forms of deconstruction [Nietzsche's and Heidegger's] cannot be simple and unique. A new writing must weave and interlace these two motifs of deconstruction" (*M* 135).

Nevertheless, Derrida's discourse does seem to have more affinity with Nietzsche's in that Nietzsche also sees the need for a plural style. This is verified by Derrida in his conclusion to "Différance" where he champions Nietzschean affirmation of play against

Heideggerian nostalgia and hope: "There will be no unique name, even if it were the name of Being. And we must think this without *nostalgia* ... On the contrary, we must *affirm* this, in the sense in which Nietzsche puts affirmation into play, in a certain laughter and certain step of the dance. From the vantage point of this laughter and this dance ... the other side of nostalgia, what I will call Heideggerian *hope*, comes into question" (*M* 27). Derrida vehemently rejects readings of his philosophy as nihilistic,[9] but, while it may be true that he rejects "incomplete nihilism," the lament over the loss of meaning, he does seem to embrace Nietzsche's "complete nihilism," the affirmation of the play of meaning, beyond nostalgia and hope for a transcendental signified.

From the viewpoint of an Arnoldian humanism, this is to reject our last remaining source of meaning.[10] Murray Krieger articulates this humanistic rejection of deconstruction:

> If we share Arnold's loss of faith, we can go either one of two ways: we can view poetry as human triumph made out of our darkness, as the creation of verbal meaning in a blank universe to serve as a visionary substitute for a defunct religion; or we can – in our negation – extend our faithlessness, the blankness of our universe, to poetry ... Stubbornly humanistic as I am, I must choose the first alternative.[11]

But both humanism and postmodernism are based upon the negation of another choice, that of religious faith, especially the Christian faith. Both humanism and deconstruction are predicated upon a "loss of faith," but Derrida claims to have overcome the nostalgia for the loss of meaning and the hope for the substitution for this loss in literary humanism. He claims to have overcome the despair of incomplete nihilism in metaphysical humanism.

Derrida offers a new alternative, another "break with a thinking of Being," which unlike Heidegger's thought, does not have "all the characteristics of a *relève* (*Aufhebung*) of humanism" (*M* 134). This break occurs not through a different conception of man, but through a meditation on language, on the "reduction of meaning":

> Rather, it is a question of determining the possibility of *meaning* on the basis of a "formal" organization which in itself has no meaning, which does not mean that it is either the non-sense or the anguishing absurdity which haunt metaphysical humanism. (*M* 134)

According to Derrida, this leads to a break with the phenomenologies of Hegel, Husserl, and Heidegger.

Derrida has uncovered "the principle of principles" of Husserl's phenomenology as the root of Heidegger's complicity with the metaphysics of presence. And Derrida's deconstruction of Husserl's transcendental idealism prepares the way for the deconstruction of the metaphysics of presence through a meditation on writing, for Derrida concludes that the subject is not constituted in self-presence but rather that "the subject (in its identity with itself, or eventually in its consciousness of its identity with itself, its self-consciousness) is inscribed in language, is a 'function' of language" (*M* 15).

CHAPTER 12

Deconstituting the subject

Moses said to God, "Suppose I go to the Israelites ... and they ask me, 'What is his name?' Then what shall I tell them?"

God said to Moses, "I am who I am. This is what you are to say to the Israelites: 'I AM has sent me to you.'"

Exodus 3:13–14

"You are not yet fifty years old," the Jews said to him, "and you have seen Abraham!"

"I tell you the truth," Jesus answered, "before Abraham was born, I am!"

John 8:57–58

The appearing of the *I* to itself in the *I am* is thus originally a relation with its own possible disappearance. Therefore, *I am* originally means *I am mortal. I am immortal* is an impossible proposition. We can even go further: as a linguistic statement "I am he who am" is the admission of a mortal.

Derrida, Speech and Phenomena

Your wisdom and your knowledge, they have deluded you; For you have said in your heart, "I am, and there is no one besides me."

Isaiah 47:10

The force of Derrida's move from man to language and from Being to writing comes from his deconstruction of the subject, of the self-presence of the conscious subject. This deconstruction emerges out of Derrida's encounter with Heidegger's predecessor and teacher, Edmund Husserl.[1] As John D. Caputo summarizes: "This rereading of Husserl is made possible ... by shifting the focus from consciousness to semiotics, from the subject to signs."[2] Derrida will deconstruct Husserl, demonstrating his complicity with the metaphysics of presence, not by taking Being as a clue, as Heidegger did in his rereading of Husserl, but by taking the sign as his clue. Instead of choosing Dasein as "the right entity for our example" (*BT* 26),

Derrida will begin with "the privileged example of the concept of the sign" (*SP* 5).

Through a deconstruction of Husserl's distinction between expression and indication, between the "spiritual" (*geistige*) ideality of a *Bedeutung* and the "bodily" reality of communication, Derrida will show that there is no pure internal sphere of self-consciousness and self-presence in which one expresses meaning to oneself without signs. Derrida's goal is to show that consciousness does not produce language, but rather that consciousness is produced by the structure, sign, and play of language; therefore, there is no inner sphere that is completely internal, completely "one's own." Consciousness is always already invaded by alterity.

The first alterity which accompanies the subject is the relation of self-consciousness to the object. Through an analysis of Husserl's formulation of this relation, Derrida will deconstruct the first meaning of presence, the presence of the object before the subject, thus demonstrating that "contrary to what phenomenology ... has tried to make us believe ... the thing itself always escapes" (*SP* 104).

In Husserl's theory expression does not mean that the subject expresses itself to another; rather, expression describes the way in which consciousness gives itself meaning about an object. According to Husserl, this process of expression is completely internal and completely free of the need for signs. But Derrida argues that the very process that allows for the distinction between the transcendental consciousness (in which expression occurs) and the empirical consciousness (in which expression is always intertwined with indication), i.e., the process of idealization, needs signs in order to be possible:

Since self-consciousness appears only in its relation to an object, whose presence it can keep and repeat, it is never perfectly foreign or anterior to the possibility of language. Husserl no doubt did want to maintain, as we shall see, an originally silent, "pre-expressive" stratum of experience. But since the possibility of constituting ideal objects belongs to the essence of consciousness, and since these ideal objects are historical products, only appearing thanks to acts of creation or intending, the element of consciousness and the element of language will be more and more difficult to discern. Will not their indiscernibility introduce nonpresence and difference (mediation, signs, referral back, etc.) in the heart of self-presence? (*SP* 15)

Signs are needed in order to constitute ideal objects because, according to Husserl, ideal objects are constituted by the ability of consciousness to repeat these objects (iterability). The only way the objects can be repeated within consciousness is in language, by replacing the object itself with signs.[3]

Husserl attempts to overcome this problem through positing a medium of expression which does not need signs, i.e., the phenomenological voice. According to Derrida, "Husserl will radicalize the necessary privilege of the *phone*, which is implied by the whole history of metaphysics" (*SP* 16). By privileging the voice in expression and excluding writing and indication from consciousness, Husserl "will necessarily confirm the classical metaphysics of presence" (*SP* 25). It is the voice which allows Husserl to constitute the second determination of presence, presence as a proximity to self in interiority.[4]

Husserl begins with a distinction between the sensory or bodily aspect of expression and its non-sensory or mental aspect. His goal in positing the phenomenological voice is to exclude the physical, sensory, and bodily aspect of language (indication) from the spiritual, non-sensory aspect of language (expression). Communication involves two exteriors which must be excluded from expression in order for it to be pure. In communication meaning is separated from pure intuition since the other, the listener, is separated from the lived experience of the speaker. And, in order to make this transfer, "the ideal content of the meaning and spirituality of expression [must be] here united to sensibility" (*SP* 22). Thus speaking in communication, Husserl's "indication," suffers the same "contamination" as writing, suffers the same "fall" into materiality and exteriority. In order to keep expression pure, free from the contamination involved in communication, Husserl must posit the phenomenological voice as "the unshaken purity of expression in a language without communication, in speech as monologue, in the completely muted voice of the 'solitary mental life'" (*SP* 22). This voice is free from a relation to the exteriority of the other and of the sensible signifier, and yet it still allows for the relationship of consciousness to the ideal object.

Thus, Husserl's theory of language, which makes possible the division between the transcendental and the worldly, is based upon a metaphysical dualism between the spiritual/ideal and the physical/sensible.

Pure expression will be the pure active intention (spirit, *psyche*, life, will) of an act of meaning (*bedeuten*) that animates a speech whose content (*Bedeutung*) is present. It is present not in nature, since only indication takes place in nature and across space, but in consciousness ... The meaning is therefore *present to the self* in the life of a present that has not yet gone forth from itself into the world, space, or nature. All these "goings-forth" effectively exile this life of self-presence in indications. We know now that indication ... is the process of death at work in signs. As soon as the other appears, indicative language – another name for the relation with death – can no longer be effaced. (*SP* 40)

Expression is characterized by all the privileged features of the spirit or soul, while indication is characterized by all the denigrated features of the body and death. Derrida argues that "the opposition between body and soul is not only at the center of this doctrine of signification, it is confirmed by it; and, as has always been at bottom the case in philosophy, it depends upon an interpretation of language" (*SP* 35). Therefore it is not the determination of man as body and soul, but rather the determination of language as signifier and signified which must first be deconstructed.

Derrida performs this deconstruction by finding a second alterity which precedes the self-presence of consciousness. In order for the phenomenological voice to express meaning to itself without signs, consciousness must precede the act of intending meaning, and it must be present at the moment of this act. Caputo gives a summary of how Husserl's theory of expression is grounded in the self-presence of consciousness in the now, and how Husserl himself provides the opening for the deconstruction of this theory:

The whole argument about the uselessness of signs stands or falls on the undividedness of the now. "Self-presence must be produced in the undivided unity of a temporal present so as to have nothing to reveal to itself by the agency of signs" (vPh 67/sp 60). But Husserl has himself shown that such absolute instantaneity is impossible for a consciousness embedded in the temporal "flux."[5]

Thus Derrida turns Husserl's own theory of internal time consciousness against him in order to show that absence and otherness are internal to presence. As Derrida explains Husserl's theory of time consciousness, "the presence of the perceived present can appear as such only inasmuch as it is *continuously compounded* with a nonpresence and nonperception, with primary memory and expectation (retention and protention)" (*SP* 64).

According to Derrida, retention, even if it is not identical with representation, has a common root in the trace:

[T]he possibility of re-petition in its most general form, that is, the constitution of a trace in the most universal sense – is a possibility which not only must inhabit the pure actuality of the now but must constitute it through the movement of differance it introduces. Such a trace is – if we can employ this language without immediately contradicting it or crossing it out as we proceed – more "primordial" than what is phenomenologically primordial. (*SP* 67)

This movement of the trace, this differance within the supposed pure internality of self-present consciousness, is not something that befalls the already constituted subject, according to Derrida. "This movement of differance is not something that happens to a transcendental subject; it produces the subject" (*SP* 82).

Thus Derrida deconstructs the metaphysical subject through demonstrating that it is written, in the sense of "protowriting."[6] This protowriting, which he also designates as writing in general and archi-writing, refers to the way in which both consciousness and its internal voice are "always already engaged in the 'movement' of the trace, that is, in the order of 'signification'" (*SP* 85). Whereas Heidegger objects to the metaphysical self, the Cartesian *cogito sum* in the name of Being, in that Descartes failed to determine the meaning of the Being of the *sum*, Derrida deconstructs the Cartesian "I am" in the name of writing, by showing that it has all the characteristics of writing, absence and death which Descartes sought to keep outside the *res cogitans*. "The appearing of the *I* to itself in the *I am* is thus originally a relation with its own possible disappearance. Therefore, *I am* originally means *I am mortal*. *I am immortal* is an impossible proposition" (*SP* 54). In order for the internal voice to speak the "I am," the "I" must become an ideal object, must be repeatable even in the absence of the object which in this case means the disappearance or death of the "I." While Descartes uses the ideality of the "I am" to "prove" the immortality of the soul, Derrida deconstructs this ideality to deny the possibility of an immortal I or soul. Derrida shows that the ideality of the "I am" can only be produced in signs and that the desire to exclude the need for signs from the interior monologue which says "I am" is the desire to exclude one's death.

For Derrida, the sign is the place of the interweaving of presence and absence, life and death, expression and indication, which

Husserl has tried to separate through his transcendental idealism. Through this idealism, Husserl reinstates all the values of a metaphysics of presence.

Beyond the opposition of "idealism" and "realism," "subjectivism" and "objectivism," etc., transcendental phenomenological idealism answers to the necessity of describing the *objectivity* of the *ob*ject (*Gegenstand*) and the *pre*sence of the present (*Gegenwart*) – and objectivity in presence – from the standpoint of "interiority," or rather from a self-proximity, an *ownness* (*Eigenheit*), which is not a simple *inside* but rather the intimate possibility of a relation to a beyond and to an outside in general. (*SP* 22)

Derrida calls this "the phenomenological project in its essence," and it leads to the same privileging of self-proximity and ownness as Heidegger's hermeneutic of Dasein.

Heidegger attempts to destroy the history of metaphysics by aiming to work out the question of the meaning of Being in general through a mediation on Dasein. This aim is made explicit at the end of *Being and Time*: "our way of exhibiting the constitution of Dasein's Being remains only *one way* which we may take. Our *aim* is to work out the question of Being in general." In a structurally similar move, Derrida deconstructs the metaphysics of presence through raising the question of the structure (not meaning) of the sign in general through a meditation on writing. Derrida indicates in a footnote that "the prime intention – and the ultimate scope – of the present essay" is to reintroduce "the difference involved in 'signs' at the core of what is 'primordial,'" that is, to reintroduce difference at the core of both speech, the presence of the subject, and of perception, the presence of the object. Whereas for Heidegger it is Being itself which alone escapes the instituting question of philosophy, "What is ...?," for Derrida the sign is "the sole 'thing' which, not being a thing, does not fall under the question 'what is'" (*SP* 25).

But does the deconstruction of consciousness, of humanity's self-presence, the ability to constitute meaning on one's "own," without signs, in short, the nonoriginality of the metaphysical subject, warrant such sweeping claims regarding the sign as the *sole* "thing" which escapes metaphysics' questioning of essence? Derrida believes that in deconstructing the ideal consciousness, all meaning and truth are shown to be the effects of signs, of différance. This is how Derrida differs from Husserl, as Caputo explains:

Husserl, wants to rescue the *arche* and *telos* [and one could add truth] by reinstating them as ideas in the Kantian sense, looming goals from which we are divided only by a kind of fall. Derrida on the other hand builds these limitations into the very structure of consciousness, treating them as structurally necessary, not as factual accidents which have somehow or another befallen the essence of pure consciousness.[7]

In *Of Grammatology*, Derrida writes that "all the metaphysical determinations of truth ... are more or less immediately inseparable from the instance of the logos, or of a reason thought within the lineage of the logos in whatever sense this is understood ... Within this logos, the original and essential link to the *phone* has never been broken" (*OG* 10). But does the deconstruction of the rationalist logos mean that all truth is the product of *différance*? Does the deconstruction of the transcendental consciousness mean that all transcendence has been destroyed?

Husserl himself makes a distinction between the transcendence of pure consciousness and the transcendence of God, although only to exclude the latter. Could this exclusion of the transcendence of God be in complicity with the exclusion of the need for signs, the dissimulation of death, in Husserl's attempt to purify the internal sphere of self-presence? Derrida takes for granted Husserl's exclusion of "another transcendence, which is not given like the pure Ego immediately united to consciousness in its reduced state, but comes to knowledge in a highly mediated form."[8] What about the possibility of a transcendent God, which would transcend Husserl's absolute Consciousness? And this God does not have to be the God of classical metaphysics. The concept of the trace may erase the self-presence of selfhood, but it doesn't erase the possibility of all presence, of a *parousia* to come.

Derrida fails to recognize the difference between the logos of rationalism and the logos of the Bible:

The trace is the erasure of selfhood, of one's own presence, and is constituted by the threat or anguish of its irremediable disappearance, of the disappearance of its disappearance. An unerasable trace is not a trace, it is a full presence, an immobile and uncorruptible substance, a son of God, a sign of parousia and not a seed, that is, a mortal germ. (*WD* 230)

Derrida has here only recognized the Johannine logos as it has been distorted through Greek and Hegelian conceptuality. Derrida leaps from "the erasure of selfhood" to a deconstruction of the "son of God" and his "parousia." Gasché describes how God, for Derrida, results from what Derrida calls "the theological trap,"[9] the

inevitable desire or "dream of an absolute erasure of the trace ...
Yet since a trace is only a trace if it is erasable – a nonerasable trace
would be a 'Son of God,' according to Derrida."[10] Because he reads
the "Son of God" as a transcendental signified, as a projection of the
desire for *parousia* in its Greek sense as "full presence," Derrida fails
to confront the biblical logos. The logos of the Bible does not found
the self-presence of the conscious subject, but unsettles this desire of
humanity to establish truth and meaning within a realm of one's
own.

The logos of the Bible, the person of Jesus Christ, is outside of a
Greek, metaphysical logic. What was "foolishness" and an "offense"
to the minds of the Greeks of the first century was the idea that the
Son of God could have died. The logos revealed in the Bible is not
what Derrida calls an "unerasable trace" because he is both the son
of God and a mortal germ, both divine and human. Jesus calls
himself a sign of the parousia of the kingdom of God, yet in speaking
of his death he compares himself to a seed, a mortal germ: "Truly,
truly, I say to you, unless a grain of wheat falls into the earth and
dies, it remains by itself alone; but if it dies, it bears much fruit"
(John 12:24). This biblical logos remains radically "other" to all
philosophical conceptions of the logos, despite the attempts from
Philo and the Alexandrian church fathers to Hegel, to equate the
two in an ontotheology.

In *Of Grammatology*, Derrida expands his deconstruction of
modern metaphysics into the deconstruction of the history of
Western ontotheology, but his project is flawed in that it fails to
distinguish between the logos of ontotheology and the logos of
biblical theology.

CHAPTER 13

Writing and metaphysics

[*T*]*he history of* (the only) *metaphysics*, which has, in spite of all differences, not only from Plato to Hegel (even including Leibniz) but also, beyond these apparent limits, from the pre-Socratics to Heidegger, always assigned the origin of truth in general to the logos: the history of truth, of the truth of truth, has always been – except for a metaphysical diversion that we shall have to explain – the debasement of writing, and its repression outside "full" speech.　　Derrida, *Of Grammatology*

Having deconstructed the subject of metaphysics through a medi-tation on the sign, Derrida next turns, in *Of Grammatology*, to the treatment of writing in metaphysics. According to Derrida, just as Husserl had tried to exclude from consciousness the need for signs, to exclude sensible signifiers from expression, so does the whole of metaphysics, from the pre-Socratics to Heidegger, exclude writing from the realm of truth. Metaphysics does this by debasing writing, making it a mere inscription of already present meaning and truth. Like the sign in his analysis of Husserl, "the treatment accorded to writing" is regarded as "a particularly revelatory symptom" (*Pos* 7).

In the first part of *Of Grammatology*, Derrida sets his deconstructive method and its results in its broadest context. In his own words: "The first part of this book, 'Writing before the Letter,' sketches in broad outlines a theoretical matrix. It indicates certain significant historical moments, and proposes certain critical concepts" (*OG* lxxxix). The scope of the book, the way it sketches out a theoretical matrix which Derrida develops in later essays, is similar to Heidegger's aim in *Being and Time*. The similarities do not end there, and they are not accidental.

Just as Heidegger sought to destroy ontotheology by reinterpreting man through a meditation on Being, so does Derrida rewrite this problematic while keeping its structure: "It is thus the idea of the sign that must be deconstructed through a mediation upon writing which would merge, as it must, with the undoing [*sollicitation*] of onto-theology, faithfully repeating it in its *totality* and *making* it *insecure* in its most assured evidences" (*OG* 73). The symptom or example given priority changes, but the goal is the same: the undoing of ontotheology. Heidegger's final aim in the project begun in *Being and Time* is not an existential analytic, but neither is it the achievement of a correct presentation of Being itself. Being itself is a clue in the loosening or shaking up of a hardened tradition: "We understand this task as one in which by taking *the question of Being as our clue*, we are to *destroy* the traditional content of ancient ontology" (Heidegger's emphases, *BT* 44). The goal of Heidegger's fundamental ontology is not to come up with the one, true meaning of Being, but rather to discover the hidden grounds of the tradition's previous answers to the question of Being, to repeat the tradition as a question. Although Derrida has learned the limits of any science, of any "-logy," from Heidegger's later abandonment of fundamental ontology[1] and although he acknowledges these limitations within *Of Grammatology*,[2] Derrida repeats this Heideggerian move by deconstructing the history of linguistics through a grammatology.

It is my belief that in both Heidegger and Derrida's thought the ultimate goal is a reworking of truth. Despite the appearance in philosophical texts of working towards truth, towards an understanding of truth, of the truth of truth, the decision, or better, the belief, about truth is made beforehand and guides all philosophical and hermeneutic inquiries. Heidegger wants to rethink truth as the truth of Being, as *aletheia*. Through all the permutations of Being, especially in Heidegger's investigation of the Greeks where Being appears under multiple names such as *logos*, *physis*, etc., and even when Heidegger moves "beyond" Being to *Ereignis*, the name and structure of *aletheia* is constant.[3] And Derrida wants to rewrite truth, "even the one beyond metaphysical ontotheology that Heidegger reminds us of," as an effect of *différance*, to erase truth while yet leaving it legible, while yet noting how the irrepressible lure of truth in the form of the transcendental signified operates in the history of metaphysics.

Both thinkers seek to uncover something that has been forgotten or repressed by the whole of metaphysics. Heidegger describes metaphysics as the forgetting of the question of Being, a forgetting of the ontological difference. Derrida takes yet another "step back" in order to capture Heidegger within a larger game, defining metaphysics as logocentrism, as the "forgetting" of writing (*OG* 8) in order to establish the presence of truth. Thus, in his "exergue" to *Of Grammatology*, Derrida rewrites Heidegger's preface to *Being and Time*, expanding the limits of metaphysics "from Plato to Hegel" to "beyond these apparent limits, from the pre-Socratics to Heidegger" (*OG* 3).

But, in characterizing the whole history of metaphysics by its logocentrism and subsequent debasement of writing, Derrida has defined ontotheology as a *whole*. Theology, as well as metaphysics, also takes on an all inclusive meaning. According to Derrida, theology is not limited to "an identifiable time and place," but rather is "a constitutive and permanent presupposition essential to the history of the West, therefore to metaphysics in its entirety, even when it professes to be atheist" (*OG* 323). Derrida, though privileging different examples, follows Heidegger in characterizing the whole of metaphysics as ontotheology, as the metaphysics of presence. But is this not a homogenization of both metaphysics and theology? That Derrida discovers a homogeneity in ontotheology, "in spite of all differences," is ironic, for Derrida argues in *Positions* that "the motif of homogeneity, the theological motif *par excellence*, is decidedly the one to be destroyed" (*Pos* 64). Although he does explore, or at least acknowledge, the differences between the premodern and modern,[4] the rabbinic and the poetic,[5] and the Jew and the Greek,[6] he still finds a common theme in the desire for a center, a transcendental signified, and the condemnation of fallen and finite writing as somehow disruptive of this center.[7]

It is my goal to question this homogenization of theology. In adopting Heidegger's formulation of ontotheology, Derrida inherits an historical blindness. Christian theology is always considered a minor variation of Greek metaphysics in Heidegger and Derrida's writing. It is my contention that there is a biblical theology which is "neither Greek, nor Jew," (though clearly in dialogue with both) and which escapes Derrida's deconstruction of ontotheology's dualist conception of the sign and its debasement of writing in favor of self-presence.

But, before attempting to define this other tradition, I must first give a commentary on Derrida's destruction of the sign. What

Derrida means by "destroying the concept of 'sign' and its entire logic" (*OG* 7) is that the splitting of the sign into signifier and signified, in which the signifier is contingent and secondary and the signified is free from all contingency and materiality, must be deconstructed. This traditional logic is stated succinctly and influentially in Aristotle's *De interpretatione*. "If, for Aristotle, for example, 'spoken words ... are the symbols of mental experience ... and written words are the symbols of spoken words' ... it is because the voice, producer of *the first symbols*, has a relationship of essential and immediate proximity with the mind" (*OG* 11). This logic is the root of the same phonocentrism Derrida deconstructed in Husserl's thought. The voice is closest to the signified, whether it be determined as thought or thing.

All signifiers, and first and foremost the written signifier, are derivative with regard to what would wed the voice indissolubly to the mind or to the thought of the signified sense, indeed to the thing itself (whether it is done in the Aristotelian manner that we have just indicated or in the manner of medieval theology, determining the *res* as a thing created from its *eidos*, from its sense thought in the logos or in the infinite understanding of God). (*OG* 11)

Derrida deconstructs this logic by first reversing the two related hierarchies involved. Instead of submitting the signifier to the logic of the signified, and writing to the voice, as in the metaphysics of presence, Derrida reverses this traditional hierarchy.

By claiming that not only writing but also the voice and even thinking involve signs, Derrida reverses the traditional logic of the sign. Writing is still the signifier of a signifier, but so are speaking and thinking. Consequently,

"signifier of the signifier" no longer defines accidental doubling and fallen secondarity. "Signifier of the signifier" describes on the contrary the movement of language ... The secondarity that it seemed possible to ascribe to writing alone affects all signifieds in general, affects them always already, the moment they *enter the game*. There is not a single signified that escapes, even if recaptured, the play of signifying references that constitute language. (*OG* 7)

This new formal and differential logic of language is formulated by Saussure, but the results of his linguistics were repressed in the name of phonocentrism. It is through a deconstruction of Saussure's linguistic theory that Derrida's deconstruction of the metaphysical

concept of consciousness becomes a deconstruction of the metaphysical concept of language.[8]

In some ways Saussure criticizes the tradition, making possible
the grammatological opening. As Derrida summarizes in his interview with Julia Kristeva:

> It has marked, against the tradition, that the signified is inseparable from
> the signifier, that the signified and signifier are the two sides of one and the
> same production. Saussure even purposely refused to have this opposition
> or this "two-sided unity" conform to a relationship between soul and body,
> as had always been done. (*Pos* 18)

But Derrida shows how this dualism returns as a result of Saussure's
decision to keep the traditional terminology for the sign, separating
it, *de jure* if not *de facto*, into *signans* and *signatum*. This division has the
same ground as Husserl's distinction between indication and expression, and Derrida takes it apart in the same way. He argues that this
division "leaves open the possibility of thinking a *concept signified in
and of itself*, a concept simply present for thought, independent of a
relationship to language, that is of a relationship to a system of
signifiers" (*Pos* 19). This possibility is opened up in Saussure as in
Husserl by a phonocentrism, by a privileging of speech over writing.
"Saussure, for essential, and essentially metaphysical, reasons had to
privilege speech, everything that links the sign to *phone*" (*Pos* 21).

Thus the dualism which Saussure sought to exclude in his definition of the sign returns with a vengeance as he holds on to the
distinction between signifier and signified. Derrida shows that semiology cannot cling to this Stoic and medieval distinction without
also retaining the other metaphysico-theological oppositions which
grow out of it:

> The semiological or, more specifically, linguistic "science" cannot there-
> fore hold on to the difference between signifier and signified – the very idea
> of the sign – without the difference between sensible and intelligible,
> certainly, but also not without retaining, more profoundly and more
> implicitly, and by the same token the reference to a signified able to "take
> place" in its intelligibility, before its "fall," before any expulsion into the
> exteriority of the sensible here below. (*OG* 13)

The distinction between signifier and signified, based on the difference between sensible and intelligible, is grounded in a Platonic
dualism, and the idea that the intelligible signified "falls" into a
sensible sign recalls the gnostic belief that the soul "falls" into the
prison of the body.

This dualism is made most clear in Saussure's treatment of writing. Writing is made the outside, the exterior of a language system which is defined by the unity of speech and thought. Writing merely transcribes this already constituted language; it plays no part in the formation of this system of signification. Writing is the image; speech-thought is the reality: Writing is representation; speech-thought is presence.

But this does not mean that a discussion of writing is simply absent from *The Course on General Linguistics*. In keeping with the underlying Platonic dualism, writing must be excluded as a danger and a threat.

Already in the *Phaedrus*, Plato says that the evil of writing comes from without (275a). The contamination by writing, the fact or the threat of it, are denounced in the accents of the moralist or preacher by the linguist from Geneva. The tone counts; it is as if, at the moment when the modern science of the logos would come into its autonomy and its scientificity, it became necessary again to attack a heresy. (*OG* 34)

Derrida's tone counts as well. He condemns the condemning tone of Saussure when he sounds like a Christian theologian such as Calvin, the preacher from Geneva. The Platonic dualism Derrida wishes to deconstruct is now identified as Christian as well. In this dualism, writing is considered not only as fallen and secondary but also as sin. "Thus incensed, Saussure's vehement argumentation aims at more than a theoretical error, more than a moral fault: at a sort of stain and primarily at a sin" (*OG* 34). Saussure will seek to recover language from this fall, from this "original sin of writing" (*OG* 35) in order to restore the "natural" relationship between speech and writing.

Derrida now turns to Enlightenment metaphysics in order to define sin and in order to bring together the speech/writing dualism and the mind/body dualism: "Sin has been defined often – among others by Malebranche and by Kant – as the inversion of the natural relationship between soul and body through passion." (Nietzsche, in his attacks on Christianity, reads this definition of sin into Paul and then attacks it vehemently, in the tone of a preacher, or at least a preacher's son.) "Saussure here points," continues Derrida, "at the inversion of the natural relationship between speech and writing. It is not a simple analogy: writing, the letter, the sensible inscription, has always been considered by Western tradition as the body and matter external to the spirit, to breath, to speech, and to the logos.

And the problem of soul and body is no doubt derived from the problem of writing from which it seems – conversely – to borrow its metaphors" (*OG* 34–35). Thus not only Platonism but also Christianity (as we see in the phrase, "has *always* been considered by *Western tradition*") is implicated in this dualism.

Although Derrida argues that throughout our entire epoch, "reading and writing, the production or interpretation of signs, the text in general as fabric of signs, allow themselves to be confined within secondariness" (*OG* 14), he does note what appears to be an exception, what he calls in his exergue "a metaphysical diversion that we shall have to explain" (*OG* 3). But this exception is based upon a metaphor which actually reinforces the logocentrism which has defined writing as external and fallen.

When it seems to go otherwise, it is because a metaphoric mediation has insinuated itself into the relationship and has simulated immediacy; the writing of truth in the soul, opposed by *Phaedrus* (278a) to bad writing (writing in the "literal" [*propre*] and ordinary sense, "sensible" writing "in space"), the book of Nature and God's writing, especially in the Middle Ages; all that functions as *metaphor* in these discourses confirms the privilege of the logos and founds the "literal" meaning then given to writing: a sign signifying a signifier itself signifying an eternal verity, eternally thought and spoken in the proximity of a present logos. (*OG* 15)

In this valorization of a certain metaphorical writing, the same dualism remains. Sensible, finite, literal writing is still condemned. The metaphorical writing which is praised is intelligible and non-temporal and therefore also privileges presence, but in the divine rather than the human logos. Added to the problematic is a dualism between human, finite, artificial writing and divine, eternal, natural writing. Privilege is still given to the presence of speech and thought. "There remains to be written," writes Derrida, "a history of this metaphor, a metaphor that systematically contrasts divine or natural writing and the human and laborious, finite and artificial inscription" (*OG* 15).

Derrida gives a list of quotations, including a rabbinic, rationalist, and existential author, in order to begin to sketch out the indices of such a history. But in *Of Grammatology*, Derrida works with three main indices. The first is Platonic, and the *Phaedrus* presents the paradigm by which other examples are implicated. The second is the medieval period through which Christianity is implicated. "As was the case with the Platonic writing of the truth in the soul, in the

Middle Ages too it is a writing understood in the metaphorical sense, that is to say a *natural*, eternal, and universal writing, the system of signified truth, which is recognized in its dignity. As in the *Phaedrus*, a certain fallen writing continues to be opposed to it" (*OG* 15). The final index, and the most important for Derrida in *Of Grammatology*, the one which he will trace fully in the second part of the book, is Rousseau.

Rousseau is here a representative of the Enlightenment, of "the great rationalisms of the seventeenth century" (*OG* 16). This "moment" marks a decisive separation for Derrida. "From then on, the condemnation of fallen and finite writing will take another form, within which we still live: it is non-self-presence that will be denounced" (*OG* 16–17). But the conception of writing, though not identical, remains the same:

> Rousseau repeats the Platonic gesture by referring to another model of presence: self-presence in the senses, in the sensible cogito, which simultaneously carries in itself the inscription of divine law. On the one hand, *representative*, fallen, secondary, instituted writing, writing in the literal and strict sense, is condemned in *The Essay on the Origin of Languages* ... Writing in the common sense is the dead letter, it is the carrier of death. It exhausts life. On the other hand, on the other face of the same proposition, writing in the metaphoric sense, natural, divine, and living writing, is venerated; it is equal in dignity to the origin of value, to the voice of conscience as divine law, to the heart, to sentiment, and so forth. (*OG* 17)

This summary of Rousseau's repetition of the Platonic gesture points out all the confusions between Greek and Christian discourse which occur in modern philosophy.

On the one hand, the metaphor used to separate good, metaphorical writing from fallen, literal writing is Pauline. The condemnation of the dead letter comes from Paul's statements in Romans and 2 Corinthians which we will examine in just a moment. The words Derrida uses to summarize the distinction are completely Pauline: "grammatological" vs. "pneumatological" writing (*OG* 17). But, on the other hand, this metaphor is used to justify a Greek conceptuality. The reference to "the voice of conscience as divine law" is based upon a Greek not a biblical conception of law (the same model which we saw Heidegger secularize in his analysis of conscience in *Being and Time*). That this model contradicts the Judaeo-Christian conception of law should be clear from the quotation from Rousseau which Derrida produces for us within his

preliminary analysis of Rousseau's place in this history of the valorization of metaphorical writing:

The Bible is the most sublime of all books ... but it is after all a book ... It
is not at all in a few sparse pages that one should look for God's law, but in
the human heart where His hand deigned to write (*Lettre a Vernes*). (*OG* 17)

The Bible as a limited revelation of God's law and the human heart
as the place of God's full revelation of his law is not Christian. It is
not Pauline; it is not "Scriptural." Derrida's deconstruction of the
logocentrism of ontotheology is limited by his lack of reflection upon
the differences between what is written in the Bible, in our example
Paul, about writing, and what is written in medieval and rationalist
onto-theologies about writing.

   Just as the medieval is historically located between original Christianity and Modernism, so does it tend to be in a middle position
conceptually. This is exemplified for us by Saint John Chrysostom,
discussed in Derrida's essay "Force and Signification." The passage
from Chrysostom quoted by Derrida is closer to a Romantic than it
is to a biblical conception of writing and Scripture: "'It were indeed
meet for us not at all to require the aid of the written Word, but to
exhibit a life so pure, that the grace of the spirit should be instead of
books to our souls, and that as these are inscribed with ink, even so
should our hearts be with the Spirit. But, since we have utterly put
away from us this grace, come let us at any rate embrace the second
best course'" (*WD* 11). In Chrysostom the written word is seen as
necessary due to human weakness and sin, but in Paul the writing of
the Spirit on our hearts *is* a grace which we can recover, and this
grace does not make Scripture superfluous. In Paul, this writing of
the Spirit on the heart has already occurred for the Christian, and
yet Scripture remains both necessary and holy.

CHAPTER 14

Reading the law: the Spirit and the letter

[T]he letter kills, but the Spirit gives life.

Paul, 2 Corinthians 3:6

[H]ow could Hebraism belittle the letter. . .?

Derrida, "Violence and Metaphysics"

In defending Paul against the Derridean deconstruction presented in *Of Grammatology*, I will also be defending the Bible's claim to be a distinctive revelation, different from the ontotheology deconstructed by Heidegger and Derrida. I will attempt in this chapter to distinguish the biblical opposition between the letter and Spirit from the metaphysical distinction between the sensible signifier and the ideal signified. In order to do this, we must also look both back to the Greek, Platonic conception of the opposition between the writing of divine laws on the heart and the writing of man's laws on stone or paper, and forward towards the appropriation of the Pauline distinction between letter and spirit in the metaphysical tradition, to the amalgamation of the Greek and biblical concepts in medieval and modern ontotheology.

The first distinction to be made is between Paul's opposition between letter and Spirit and the reading of this opposition by the idealist tradition (both in metaphysics and theology). That idealism is a central target in Derrida's deconstruction of the tradition is made clear in Derrida's interview with Houdebine and Scarpetta: "Logocentrism is *also*, fundamentally, an idealism. It is the matrix of idealism. Idealism is its most direct representative, the most constantly dominant force. And the dismantling of logocentrism is simultaneously – *a fortiori* – a deconstitution of idealism or spiritualism in all their variants" (*Pos* 51). Therefore my first task is to separate the biblical tradition from its idealist reinterpretation. But this is only the first step, for Derrida continues by remarking that "of course, logocentrism is a wider concept than idealism, for which it serves as a kind of overflowing foundation" (*Pos* 51).

Ernst Käsemann summarizes the idealist approach to the New Testament which reads the Pauline distinction between the letter and the Spirit as a Platonic dualism, the dualism which Derrida deconstructs in *Of Grammatology*:

> This tradition started from its concept of the spirit as the power of being aware of oneself and of being able to penetrate understandably the world which one encounters. Fastening on the doubtful and misleading translation *littera* for the Pauline word *gramma*, this tradition then understood the letter as the remaining external, contingent, arbitrary factor, as what cannot be ultimately assimilated into the spiritual life, as what is withdrawn from "inwardness" and moral life.[1]

This led to a reading of Paul as continuing the Greek tradition of the unwritten law, "written" on the heart, and therefore as disparaging the written letter of the law. "It is curious that these exegetes hardly ever gave any thought to the fact that the Jew simply could not brush aside the law as easily as this; and Paul, even as Christian, still remained Jewish enough to make the law one of the central problems of his theology, instead of viewing it as something entirely negligible."[2] In order to understand Paul's writings about the letter and Spirit, we must not look to an idealist tradition which began by giving the highest value to the self-presence of consciousness, the sphere of one's own. In reading Paul within the historical context of the early church, we will see that it is this very value which Paul wants to bring into question.

We must look to the historical context of the biblical writings in order to realize that Paul was trained in a Hebraic tradition (as a Pharisee under Gamaliel), and that his thought is fully immersed in this scriptural tradition. But we must also remember that Paul was educated as a Roman citizen and that he was familiar with Greek philosophy. Often his letters were warnings against gnostic, Hellenistic tendencies in the church or against legalistic Judaizers. Christian doctrine was produced not only as a continuation of the tradition of the Hebraic scriptures, but also in opposition to Greek philosophy and against some streams in the Jewish tradition, usually exemplified by the Pharisees. Keeping in mind this historical confluence of the West's most influential traditions, Jew, Greek, and Christian, in Paul's education, we now turn to the two epistles in which Paul refers to the law written on the heart.

The first appears in his letter to the church at Rome. The membership of the church was predominantly Gentile, but there are times in his letter when he addresses himself directly to the Jew. Paul's first reference to the law written on the heart concerns the Greek conception of the unwritten, divine law vs. the written human law. But the use of this division, the same one in Plato's *Phaedrus* which Derrida reads as a debasement of literal writing which must be deconstructed, must be seen as part of the argument with which Paul opens his letter (Romans 1:18 through 3:20). The point of the argument is to reveal humanity's sinful state and God's righteous judgment. This argument is directed for the most part towards Gentiles who have not had the law (*nomos*), i.e., the Hebrew scriptures. Paul is arguing that even apart from the law all people are sinners. God has revealed "his eternal power and divine nature" in creation as well as in Scripture; however, all people, Jew and Greek, "neither glorified him as God nor gave thanks to him, but their thinking became futile and their foolish hearts were darkened" (Rom. 1:21). Therefore God is righteous in pronouncing judgment on both Jew and Gentile. "There will be trouble and distress for every human being who does evil: first for the Jew, then for the Gentile; but glory, honor and peace for everyone who does good: first for the Jew, then for the Gentile" (2:9–10). God will not condemn a righteous person just because he or she does not have the law. "God 'will give to each person according to what he has done.' To those who by persistence in doing good seek glory, honor, and immortality, he will give eternal life. But for those who are self-seeking and who reject the truth and follow evil, there will be wrath and anger" (2:6–8).

It is in this context, in a parenthetical statement, that Paul refers to the Greek conception of the unwritten law:

(Indeed, when Gentiles, who do not have the law, do by nature things required by the law, they are a law for themselves, even though they do not have the law, since they show that the requirements of the law are written on their hearts, their consciences also bearing witness, and their thoughts now accusing, now even defending them.) (Romans 2:15)

It is clear within Paul's overall argument that the Gentile will not satisfy the law by listening to the inner voice of his or her conscience. Just as the Jew fails to keep the requirements of the written law, so does the Gentile fail to keep the requirements of the unwritten law. As he writes in the conclusion of his opening argument: "We have already made the charge that Jews and Gentiles alike are all under sin" (3:9). Paul now turns to the written law to prove his point: "As it is written: 'There is no one righteous, not even one; there is no one who understands, no one who seeks God'" (3:10–11). Paul is in no way elevating the unwritten law, the law written (only metaphorically) on the heart, over the written law.

Paul then turns to the Jew and his relation to the *nomos* or *Torah*. *Nomos* can refer to the Mosaic Torah (the Pentateuch, the first five books of the Hebrew scriptures), individual or collective commands of the Mosaic covenant, or the whole of Hebrew scriptures (or the "Old Testament"). Most often Paul uses the word to refer to all of the Holy Scriptures. Sometimes he uses the title, "the law and the prophets," to mean the same. *Nomos* is the Septuagint translation for Torah. Ricoeur finds this translation somewhat misleading. "The *Torah* of the Pharisees is certainly a book, the Law of Moses, the Pentateuch; but what makes the Law law is that it is an instruction from the Lord. Torah means teaching, instruction, and not law."[3]

Paul condemns the Jew who brags about his knowledge of the law and his circumcision. It is not the law that is condemned, but the Jew who while boasting in, resting in, and teaching the law to others, still breaks the law. Circumcision, the sign of the covenant between *El-Shaddai* (God Almighty) and Abraham (see Genesis 17), is of no value if the law is broken. "Circumcision has value if you observe the law, but if you break the law, you have become as though you had not been circumcised" (Romans 2:25). In Galatians, Paul shows how this conclusion comes from the law itself by quoting the Mosaic law from Deuteronomy: "Cursed is everyone who does not abide by all things written in the book of the law, to perform them" (Galatians 3:10).

Paul then refers to "those who are not circumcised" who "keep the law's requirements" (2:26). These are not the Greeks who have the unwritten law on their hearts, but rather Christians who have had their hearts circumcised by the Spirit. This is not a Greek conception but rather a Hebraic belief, based not on the unwritten law of the Greeks but the written law of the Hebrews: "The LORD [YHWH] your God will circumcise your hearts and the hearts of your descendants, so that you may love him with all your heart and with all your soul, and live" (Deuteronomy 30:6). This text comes from the Hebrew scriptures, from the law. "In explaining this ministry of the spirit ..., Paul ... straightway begins to cite and interpret

Scripture. This shows that Paul's rejection of *gramma* [the letter] is by no means a rejection of *Graphe* [writing, Scripture]."[4] That Paul bases his arguments here and throughout his epistles on the written Hebraic law should make us realize "(contrary to .the idealist tradition) that a thing does not become 'letter' because it is moulded by a tradition deposited in written documents."[5]

It is in this context that Paul describes the true Jew, the true inheritor of the promises of the Abrahamic covenant,[6] and it is here that Paul first introduces the distinction between letter and Spirit, between *gramma* and *pneuma*.

A man is not a Jew if he is only one outwardly [or apparently], nor is circumcision merely outward and physical. No, a man is a Jew if he is one inwardly [privately]; and circumcision is circumcision of the heart, in Spirit [*en pneumati*], not in letter [*en grammati*]. Such a man's praise is not from men, but from God. (Romans 2:28–29)

The translations "outwardly" and "inwardly" are probably not the best. At stake is not an idealist dualism but an attitude of the heart. Perhaps the best gloss on the meaning here would be Jesus' distinction in Matthew 6:1–18 between "practicing your righteousness before men to be noticed by them" and doing so "in secret." In both Jesus' statements and Paul's writing it is hypocrisy that is being condemned, not the outward and material in some kind of Platonic dualism.

Neither is the Spirit/letter division related to the Greek conception of the unwritten law. It rather marks a distinction between those who boast in the law, who think they have righteousness due to their own works, and those who boast in the Lord, who believe they have righteousness through grace, through the Spirit who gives power to keep the law. It is the same written law that must be obeyed, but it is a question of attempting to keep the law through one's own strength (which would be cause for boasting), or acknowledging the need for the Spirit.[7] Paul uses the word *gramma* to refer to this boasting in the law, to the belief that a person can be saved through his or her own efforts to keep the law. Ridderbos explains how this division is the basis for Paul's distinction between letter and Spirit:

Not only the transgressions of the law themselves ... make man guilty before God and prevent him from being righteous before God on the ground of the works of the law. The very attempt to maintain oneself before

God and to gain life on the ground of one's "own" works and merit makes such a seeking of righteousness a vain and reprehensible undertaking before God. We touch here the most profound and real aspect of this antithesis.[8]

The attitude of the "letter," this interpretation of the law, causes us to take the law into our own hands. Barth writes that, "What becomes of the law of God in our hands is that it is now the 'law of sin and death' (Rom. 8.2), the executor of the divine wrath (Rom. 4.15)."[9]

Just as Paul condemns the Jews for believing that they can be redeemed by obeying the law, so are the Greeks who boast in their unwritten law, in wisdom, also condemned. "Has not God made foolish the wisdom of the world. For since in the wisdom of God the world through its wisdom did not know him, God was pleased through the foolishness of what was preached to save those who believe" (1 Corinthians 1:20–21). This is the basis of Paul's, and Luther's after him, "destruction" of philosophy – "'I will destroy the wisdom of the wise'" (1 Corinthians 1:19).

Having concluded that no one is righteous through either works or wisdom, neither Jew nor Gentile, Paul then reveals the righteousness through faith available to both Jew and Gentile.

But now a righteousness from God, apart from law, has been made known, to which the Law and the Prophets testify. This righteousness from God comes through faith in Jesus Christ to all who believe. There is no difference, for all have sinned and fall short of the glory of God, and are justified freely by his grace through the redemption that came by Christ Jesus. (Romans 3:21–24)

But, in revealing a righteousness "apart from the law" through faith, does Paul do away with the law? "Do we then, nullify the law by this faith? Not at all! Rather, we uphold the law" (3:31). The law is upheld in that it is fulfilled by Jesus Christ, fulfilled in two senses: First, Jesus fulfills the law by keeping all its requirements and commandments. He was without sin. Second, Jesus also fulfills the Hebrew scriptures, "the Law and the Prophets," by realizing the prophecies of the coming Messiah. Jesus speaks of this clearly in Matthew, "'Do not think that I came to abolish the Law or the Prophets; I did not come to abolish, but to fulfill. For truly I say to you, until heaven and earth pass away, not the smallest letter or stroke shall pass away from the Law, until all is accomplished'" (Matthew 5:17–18).

This is one of many passages in which Jesus claims to be fulfilling prophecy from the Torah. In Luke's gospel, Jesus reads from the scroll (*biblion*) of Isaiah and then proclaims: "'Today this scripture is fulfilled in your hearing'" (Luke 4:21), and in John's gospel, Jesus, speaking to the Jews, claims to be the meaning of all of the holy scriptures: "You diligently study the Scriptures because you think that by them you possess eternal life. These are the Scriptures that testify about me" (John 6:39). Once again we see the basis of the Pauline division between two different ways of reading the scriptures, between the letter and the Spirit. This is hardly a disparagement of the law or a debasement of writing.[10]

Jesus, by keeping the requirements of the law and yet suffering the penalty of breaking the law, which is death, took our place, took our punishment upon himself. His death was an atonement for our sins, a propitiatory sacrifice. The law is fulfilled in Christ, and Christians are thereby set free from the power of sin and death. Through the baptism into Christ Jesus, into his death, the Christian is set free from the verdict of the law. For the law itself promised death for all those who did not keep its commands. Only through death can someone be set free from this "law of sin and death" (Romans 8:2). Thus, "by dying to what once bound us, we have been released from the law so that we serve in newness of spirit [*pneumatos*], and not in oldness of letter [*grammatos*]" (Romans 7:6).

Paul immediately makes it clear that this does not result in any condemnation of the written law: "So then, the law is holy, and the commandment is holy, righteous and good" (Romans 7:12). The problem lies not with the outward, written nature of the law, but with the inner recesses of the heart: "We know that the law is spiritual, but I am unspiritual" (Romans 7:14). The problem with the law is not that it is external, fallen, or secondary – not that it is written – but rather that anthropos has fallen into sin.

Richard B. Hays, in his fine study of Paul's use of Hebraic scripture, seems to fall into a phonocentric interpretation which condemns writing when he argues that "for Paul the problem with the old covenant lies precisely in its character as a written thing." But he continues to clarify this in a way which is much more in line with my own interpretation: "The problem with this old covenant is precisely that it is (only) written, lacking the power to effect the obedience that it demands. Since it has no power to transform the readers, it can only stand as a witness to their condemnation." Hays' language suggests at times that it is the written character of the old covenant which makes it deadly. But he also acknowledges the more fundamental difference between the old and new covenants in Paul: the old covenant "has no power to transform the readers." Hays can therefore reach a conclusion regarding the letter/Spirit distinction in Paul which separates it from the ontotheological tradition:

Thus, the Christian tradition's reading of the letter–spirit dichotomy as an antithesis between the outward and the inward, the manifest and the latent, the body and the soul, turns out to be a dramatic misreading, indeed a complete inversion. For Paul, the Spirit is – scandalously – identified precisely with the outward and palpable, the particular human community of the new covenant, putatively transformed by God's power so as to make Christ's message visible to all. The script [*gramma*], however, remains abstract and dead because it is not embodied.[11]

The problem with the law is that we are unable to obey it because of our sinful (sarxic) nature.

In what the law was powerless to do in that it was weakened by the flesh, God did by sending his own Son in the likeness of sinful flesh to be a sin offering. And so he condemned sin in the flesh, in order that the righteous requirements of the law might be fully met in us, who do not live according to the flesh but according to the Spirit. (Romans 8:3–4)

In Romans 7 and 8 we see the close relationship between the oppositions of *sarx/pneuma* and *gramma/pneuma*. In neither case are we dealing with a metaphysical dualism. Rather it is a question of whether one tries to establish truth and righteousness on one's own (*sarx, gramma*) or whether one relies upon the Spirit of God for salvation (*pneuma*): "Since they did not know the righteousness that comes from God and sought to establish *their own*, they did not submit to God's righteousness. Christ is the fulfillment of the law so that there may be righteousness for everyone who believes" (my emphasis, Romans 10:3–4).

The use of the *gramma/pneuma* opposition in 2 Corinthians is probably the most well known and the most misunderstood. Paul compares a writing on the heart by the Spirit to a writing on tablets of stone with ink. He concludes by stating that "the letter kills, but the Spirit gives life" (2 Corinthians 3:6). Is this not a return to the Greek tradition of the unwritten law? Not at all! There is another tradition of a writing on the heart, the same one which produced the idea of the circumcision of the heart. Paul is referring to the writings of Jeremiah in which both the circumcision of the heart (4:4) and the promise of a new covenant written on the heart are presented (31:33). These "themes" or promises are presented in many other places in the Hebrew scriptures, most notably in Deuteronomy and Ezekiel, but I will be concentrating on Jeremiah due to the centrality of this theme in his writings, and also with an eye towards Derrida's periodic references to Jeremiah.

Jeremiah prophesies, in the midst of an imminent disaster in Israel which he has predicted, that:

"The time is coming," declares the LORD, "when I will make a new covenant with the house of Israel and with the house of Judah. It will not be like the covenant I made with their forefathers when I took them by the hand to lead them out of Egypt, because they broke my covenant, though I was a husband to them," declares the LORD. "This is the covenant I will make with the house of Israel after that time," declares the LORD. "I will put my law in their minds and write it on their hearts. I will be their God, and they will be my people . . . For I will forgive their wickedness and will remember their sins no more." (Jeremiah 31:31-34)

This passage concerning the restoration of Israel (Jeremiah 30-33) contains numerous references to the coming Messiah and to the new aeon his coming will bring, and Paul applies this passage to the new covenant established by Jesus.

As in my discussion of the distinctions in the New Testament between this world and the world to come and between flesh and Spirit, so too here do we see Paul using not an ontotheological dualism, but rather a redemptive-eschatological division. Paul is not making a division between an old, written law and a new, unwritten law (or a law written only metaphorically on the heart). Rather, it is a question of fulfilling the one law. The new covenant will be unlike the Mosaic covenant not because a new, unwritten law is involved, but because the Mosaic law was disobeyed, "because they broke my covenant." The old covenant was based upon humanity's ability to obey the law; the new covenant is based upon God's gracious forgiveness of our sins. The new covenant does not present a new law, but rather is a promise that God will empower his people to obey the law and will forgive their transgressions. Therefore, "The Pauline antithesis is in no sense parallel to the Greek distinction between written law and *nomos agraphos* . . . In Paul, however, we have something unwritten, i.e., the Spirit, giving power to fulfill the innermost intentions of what is written."[12] The newness of the new covenant "is based on God's oath to enable his people's faithfulness to the covenant."[13]

Perhaps this can be made more clear by looking at a reference in an earlier passage in Jeremiah to another writing on the heart. This inward writing is not praised, but condemned. It is the writing of sin on the heart. "'Judah's sin is engraved with an iron tool, inscribed with a flint point, on the tablets of their hearts'" (Jeremiah 17:1). Jeremiah is alluding to the Mosaic law, the tablets of the law, for this is the law that the Israelites have broken in worshipping other gods (and the same command they broke when the LORD first inscribed these laws, causing Moses to literally break the stone tablets). But engraving with an iron tool on tablets also refers to the hardness, the stubbornness, of the Israelites' hearts which have turned away from God. It is not a division between a bad, literally written law and a good, metaphorically written law. It is a question of the attitude of the heart towards God, of the spiritual condition of humanity before God.

Just as in Paul, the division between letter and Spirit is presented in terms which are related to the separation between the flesh and the Spirit:

Cursed is the one who trusts in man, who depends on flesh for his strength ... But blessed is the man who trusts in the LORD, whose confidence is in him. (Jeremiah 17:5,7)

The first attitude is the way of the flesh and the letter; the second is the way of the Spirit. Just as in Paul, it is hypocrisy which is condemned, not the written. Those who boast in the law and yet disobey it are judged: "How can you say, 'We are wise, for we have the law of the LORD,' when actually the lying pen of the scribes has handled it falsely?" (Jeremiah 8:8). This division between the letter and the Spirit separates two different ways of fulfilling, of *living out* the law.

Paul is defending his way of interpreting the law in his second letter to the Corinthians. He is defending himself and his ministry against a group of "Judaizers" (Jewish Christians who sought to force Jewish practices, such as circumcision, upon Gentiles as a condition for salvation) who had passed through Corinth and attacked the validity of Paul's apostleship. These men had pointed out to the Corinthians that Paul had brought no letters of recommendation like they had. Paul writes back that the lives of the believers were his letter of recommendation: "You yourselves are our letter, written on our hearts, known and read by everybody. You show that you are a letter from Christ, the result of our ministry, written not with ink but with the Spirit of the living God, not on tablets of stone but on tablets of human hearts" (2 Corinthians 3:2–3).

Paul uses the controversy over the letters of recommendation to point out the differences between his gospel and the gospel of the false apostles they had recently received.

Such confidence as this is ours through Christ before God. Not that we are competent in ourselves to claim anything for ourselves, but our competence comes from God. He has made us competent as ministers of a new covenant – not of the letter but of the Spirit; for the letter kills, but the Spirit gives life. (2 Corinthains 3:4–6)

The new covenant, the one promised in Jeremiah, is not set apart as being unwritten, but rather is set apart as being based upon grace, not works. "The letter kills because it forces man into the service of his own righteousness ... Everything that forces us back on our own strength, ability and piety kills because it snatches the creature out of his creatureliness and thus away from the almighty power of grace, of which we are in constant need."[14] As in Jeremiah, it is a question of our attitude towards how we can fulfill the law; it is a question of where our confidence lies.

Paul uses a kind of neologism, *gramma*, in order to characterize this attitude of the heart, this way of interpreting and living out the law which perverts the divine intentions of the law. The word was normally used in the plural, and was even used to refer to the Holy Scriptures in John's writings, but Paul uses it in the singular, partly for the effectiveness of the antithesis created due to the similarity in sound between *gramma* and *pneuma*.[15] Paul uses *gramma* only in this negative sense, and uses the word *graphe* to refer to the holiness of Scripture when read with the right attitude of heart, when read with the Holy Spirit.

Paul constantly makes it clear that he is not setting up an antithesis between Scripture and Spirit. Nor is he describing a duality between the material body and immaterial spirit of Scripture. "Any suggestion is to be rejected which would have it that the spirit of Scripture is here opposed to its letter or its true or richer sense to the somatic body ... A related conception, no less incongruent with Paul, dominates the Platonic statements which would have it that what is written is an inadequate means to express spiritual insights."[16] Hays reaches the same conclusion: "When Paul contrasts Spirit to *gramma*, he is not opposing the basic intent of Scripture to its specific wording, as in our familiar distinction between 'the spirit and the letter of the law.' Nor is he thinking, like Philo or Origen, about a mystical latent sense concealed beneath the text's external form."[17]

Just as in the division between flesh and Spirit, the Pauline opposition between letter and Spirit is redemptive and eschatological, not metaphysical or Platonic. The Spirit as opposed to the letter represents the new covenant made available to the believer through the power which raised Jesus from the dead. The written law is not debased, but fulfilled.

In his commentary on Corinthians, Charles H. Talbert summarizes the opposition between letter and Spirit in terms of Paul's difference with the Pharisaic-rabbinic reading of the law. First in terms of eschatology: "The basic difference ... was eschatology. Paul believed the New Age had been inaugurated with the resurrection of Jesus and the resulting gift of the Spirit, which signals God's eschatological justification of the recipients."[18] This eschatology becomes the basis for two different views of the way of redemption, through the flesh, through man's own efforts or works, or through the Spirit, through faith in Jesus Christ. While Pharisaic Judaism taught that we could overcome our evil impulses, the evil *yetzer*, through disciplined obedience to the law, Paul teaches that because human nature is in bondage to sin, because of the weakness of our *sarx*, only God can deliver us from evil.[19]

Paul's division between letter and Spirit is thus to be separated from both Greek and Rabbinic thought. The separation of the letter and the Spirit divides two ways of interpreting the Holy Scriptures. Käsemann explains the hermeneutical basis of Paul's discussion:

The scripture must be read in the light of Christ and as preparation for him; then even the law regains its original divine intention and becomes a promise of a new, eschatological obedience. Here the spirit takes on a hermeneutical function ... For then two possibilities diverge – either to see the Old Testament under the veil of the Torah in its misunderstood character as a demand for good works; or to understand it in the light of the lifting of that veil through Christ ... The Christology that is interpreted through the doctrine of justification is the criterion which decides between spirit and letter, both of which can be derived from scriptures.[20]

Faith in Christ is presented as the way to overcome the heteronomous nature of the law without abolishing the law itself.

There is another way of overcoming the heteronomous nature of the law, an alternative which Derrida explores in his essay, "Edmond Jabès and the Question of the Book." I must note the need for a word of caution regarding the interpretation of this essay. We must be careful to differentiate between Derrida's commentary and his interpretation. Failure to notice this difference leads to Derrida's complaint about readings of his work in which "what I denounce is attributed to me, as if one were in less of a hurry to criticize or to discuss me, than first to put oneself in my place in order to do so" (*Pos* 53). For example, in "Edmond Jabès and the Question of the Book," the majority of the essay is devoted to a commentary on Jabès, and so, for example, it is not Derrida's belief that the "*difference* between speech and writing is sin . . . lost immediacy, work outside the garden" (*WD* 68). This rabbinic interpretation is the one Derrida wants to deconstruct.

The confusions resulting from failing to notice this difference can be seen in attempts to situate the relationship between Derrida and his Jewish background. Handelman's book, *The Slayers of Moses*, while dealing with a problematic very close to mine, makes in my view two radical mistakes in her reading of the relationship between postmodern critical theory and biblical hermeneutics. She first misreads Paul's division between letter and Spirit as being based entirely upon a Greek dualism. She then makes the unfounded conclusion that Paul used the letter/spirit opposition for "the task of discrediting Jewish law," of blaming the text, the written law for its inability to imitate the spiritual reality of Christianity.[21] In this reading, Paul becomes the target of Derrida's deconstruction of traditional sign theory. And Derrida becomes a rabbinic interpreter. That Derrida had different ideas about rabbinic interpretation and his relation to it is seen in his essays on Jabès.

This is also the point at which Shira Wolosky's essay, "Derrida, Jabès, Levinas: Sign-Theory as Ethical Discourse," breaks down. Wolosky confuses Derrida's commentary on Jabès with Derrida's own thoughts regarding the book, thereby seeing Derrida as supporting the Kabbalistic belief in the originality of the book. This leads Wolosky to misunderstand Derrida's critique of the center: "The withdrawal of the Godhead into itself as the original movement of creation, and the positing of an unnameable and still center from which proceeds writing as world, concurs in Derrida, in Jabès, and in the Lurianic Kabbalah."[22]

Like Handelman, Wolosky writes from a Jewish perspective which is unsympathetic to the Pauline writings. Both writers elaborate on the connection between Derrida's deconstruction of sign theory and the Pauline distinction between letter and Spirit. But both writers, as Derrida apparently does too, offer a blatantly unhistorical misreading of Paul's distinction between the letter and Spirit. Wolosky writes, much as did Handelman, that Derrida's thematic of the trace "abolishes the Pauline distinction between spirit and letter. An internal, 'spiritual,' and therefore significant communion from which a fallen materiality is excluded" is deconstructed by Derrida.[23]

Derrida contrasts a rabbinic and poetic reading of the law of Moses not in order to valorize the rabbinic or the poetic, but rather in order to represent "two interpretations of interpretation."[24] Jabès, though writing on the relationship of the Jew to writing and the letter, represents the poet's way of interpreting the law, the poet's way of freedom from the law. "The wisdom of the poet thus culminates its freedom in the passion of translating obedience to the law of the word into autonomy" (*WD* 66). But the poet must oppose the rabbis in order to write of or within this autonomy: "Autonomous too, as we said. Which assumes that the poet does not simply receive his speech and his law from God. Judaic heteronomy has no need of a poet's intercession. Poetry is to prophecy what the idol is to truth" (*WD* 67). Thus the poet overcomes the heteronomous law by becoming his own law (auto-nomous). Therefore this "Poetic autonomy, comparable to none other, presupposes broken Tables" (*WD* 67).

These are the same broken tables which Nietzsche's Zarathustra celebrates (quoted by Derrida at the end of his essay "Force and Signification").[25] Zarathustra, though he is ashamed that he still plays this role, is yet a poet (*Z* 197). And, like Jabès, he depends upon the fact that the old law tables are broken. Moses was the first to break the tablets of the law, not as a way of overcoming the demands of the law, but in anger at seeing the Israelites breaking the law.

Moses turned and went down the mountain with the two tablets of the Testimony in his hands. They were inscribed on both sides, front and back. The tablets were the work of God; the writing was the writing of God, engraved on the tablets ...
When Moses approached the camp and saw the calf and the dancing, his

anger burned and he threw the tablets out of his hands, breaking them to pieces at the foot of the mountain. (Exodus 32:19)

Nietzsche mimics this scene in order to set up Zarathustra as a new Moses bringing new law tablets:

Like the sun, Zarathustra also wants to go under; now he sits here and waits, surrounded by broken old tablets and new tablets half covered with writing.

Behold, here is a new tablet; but where are my brothers to carry it down with me to the valley and into hearts of flesh? (𝑍 198–199)

The tables are half-written because Zarathustra waits for the Jeremian fulfillment of his new law, for his new law table to be written on the heart. Nietzsche is echoing the Old Testament (for example, Ezekiel 36:26) when he refers to "hearts of flesh" ("fleshy hearts" in Hollingdale's translation).[26]

Paul also claims a relationship to Moses while setting himself apart from him, but not by breaking the tablets of the law. Rather Paul writes that Christians are able to remove Moses' veil which he wore after the stone tablets were restored, reinscribed. "We are not like Moses, who would put a veil over his face to keep the Israelites from gazing at it while the radiance was fading away. But their minds were made dull, for to this day the same veil remains when the old covenant is read. It has not been removed, because only in Christ is it taken away ... whenever anyone turns to the Lord, the veil is taken away. Now the Lord is the Spirit, and where the Spirit of the Lord is, there is freedom" (2 Corinthians 3:13–17).

Christ's role in overcoming the heteronomous quality of the law can be seen in John 8:1–11. "The teachers of the law and the Pharisees brought in a woman caught in adultery." They want to stone the woman to death in fulfillment of the law which was "inscribed by the finger of God" (Exodus 31:18). "But Jesus bent down and started to write on the ground with his finger." With this writing by his finger, Jesus introduces forgiveness into the law inscribed by the finger of God. " 'If any one of you is without sin, let him be the first to throw a stone at her.' Again he stooped down and wrote on the ground. At this, those who heard began to go away one at a time."[27] Only Jesus, who fulfilled the law by being without sin, could forgive sins against the law.

Unlike the Christian who finds freedom in the gift of the Spirit made available through the fulfillment of the law in Jesus Christ, the poet finds his freedom in the cracks of the broken law, cracks in which the poet's words can grow like weeds. "The Law then becomes Question ... The book of man is a book of question" (*WD* 67). Jabès, the poet, finds these broken tables in a Cabalistic reading of the law or Book, for the rabbi sees the written Torah as subordinate to an eternal oral Torah, an unwritten Torah.

This subordination of the written word to oral tradition is the basis for most of Jesus' attacks against the Pharisees. "And thus you nullify the word of God for the sake of your tradition" (Matthew 15:6).

Now, what they [the Pharisees] tried to set up is exactly the opposite of a monument to literalism; since the great thing, according to them, is to "fulfill" the Law and the Prophets, it is not possible to cling to the Scriptures – that is to say, to the written Torah – as a relic of the past ... they aimed to raise the oral tradition to the rank of Torah – which they called unwritten Torah.[28]

Thus it is oral traditions which cause the written law to become "the letter."

Derrida comments upon Jabès' anti-rabbinical, poetic, exegesis:

In *Exodus* God repented and said so at least twice, before the first and before the new Tables, between origin and repetition (*Exodus* 32:14; 33:17). Writing is, thus, originally hermetic and secondary. Our writing, certainly, but already His, which starts with the stifling of his voice and the dissimulation of his Face. This difference, this negativity in God is our freedom. (*WD* 67)

But in founding his freedom on broken tables, Jabès stays within the metaphysics of presence which makes writing secondary to the voice. In Jabès, the poet's freedom is based upon God's silence: "God no longer speaks to us ... we must take words upon ourselves. We must ... entrust ourselves to traces, must become men of vision because we have ceased hearing the voice from within the immediate proximity of the garden ... The *difference* between speech and writing is sin" (*WD* 68).

According to Derrida, the book of man is as phono-logo-centric as the Book of the Law, as God's Book. As Derrida writes, "the act of faith in the book can precede, as we know, belief in the Bible. And can also survive it" (*WD* 76). Instead of trying to recapture a lost meaning like a premodern saint, the modernist poet tries to constitute meaning, but both poet and rabbi share a desire for a center, and live the lack of a center as exile. "The necessity of commentary, like the poetic necessity, is the very form of exiled speech" (*WD* 67). Both poet and rabbi still believe "that the world is in all its parts a cryptogram to be constituted or reconstituted through poetic inscription or deciphering; that the book is original, that everything *belongs to the book* before being and in order to come into the world; that any thing can be born only by *approaching* the book, can die only by failing *in sight of* the book; and that always the impassible shore of the book is *first*" (*WD* 76–77).

Derrida wants to deconstruct this belief in the originality of the book, to replace it with an "original" illegibility. "Original illegibility is not simply a moment interior to the book, to reason or to logos; nor is it any more their opposite, having no relationship of symmetry to them, being incommensurable with them. Prior to the book (in the nonchronological sense), original illegibility is therefore the very possibility of the book" (*WD* 77). Derrida will soon place the originality of this illegibility *sous rature*, but the desire to deconstruct the book, the truth of the book, will remain. In order to perform this "destruction of the book," to destroy "the encyclopedic protection of theology and of logocentrism against the disruption of writing," it will not be necessary for Derrida to shatter the law tables, to create cracks which his words can fill. Rather he will develop a new concept of writing, not by "confiding new writings to the envelope of a book," but rather by "beginning to write without the line" and "finally reading what wrote itself between the lines in the volumes" (*OG* 86).

In order to inaugurate this new writing, Derrida will set up a dichotomy of his own. Instead of a division between the letter and the Spirit as in Paul, Derrida will posit a division between the book and the text. First Derrida defines "the book":

The idea of the book is the idea of a totality, finite or infinite, of the signifier; this totality of the signifier cannot be a totality, unless a totality constituted by the signified preexists it, supervises its inscriptions and its signs, and is independent of it in its ideality. (*OG* 18)

Aside from the metaphysical diction which could cause confusion in relating this passage to the Christian's relation to the Bible ("the Book"), this definition seems to fit the Christian's belief in the Bible as the Word of God. The Bible is seen as the revelation of Jesus Christ as the Son of God, as the Word of God, and that both Jesus and the Bible are referred to as the Word of God is purposeful, since both reveal the Father. Jesus is regarded, and regards himself (see for example, John 5:39), as, to borrow Derrida's phraseology for a moment, the "transcendental signified" of the Bible. He existed before the written Scriptures and is in that sense "independent" of them, though his relationship to the written word, to the law and the prophets, is much closer than the phrase "independent of it in its ideality" would suggest. Although Derrida is reading Christian hermeneutics through Hegelian idealism, the contrast between the Christian belief in the Bible, the Book of Scriptures, and Derrida's conception of writing as centerless text should be clear. "The idea of the book ... is profoundly alien to the sense of writing ... If I distinguish the text from the book, I shall say that the destruction of the book, as it is now under way in all domains, denudes the surface of the text" (*OG* 18).

But we must be careful not to read into this opposition to the Book a Nietzschean breaking of the law (though the results will be in my mind indistinguishable). This is made most clear in "Ellipsis," Derrida's return to Jabès at the end of *Writing and Difference*. Although Derrida writes that the "question of writing could be opened only if the book was closed" (*WD* 294), he makes it clear here and elsewhere that this does not mean that the book comes to an end. When Derrida writes of "the text" he is referring to a hermeneutical or perhaps I should say meta-hermeneutical principle.

Just as the reading of the law from a Christocentric position does not abolish the law, so does a Derridean reading of the book as a centerless text not abolish the book. Reading writing as text is dependent upon a repetition of the book, but this repetition is in no way a fulfillment: "Pure repetition, were it to change neither thing nor sign, carries with it an unlimited power of perversion and subversion" (*WD* 296). In repeating the book, the center is brought into play, a play that Derrida agrees with Nietzsche should be affirmed, not nostalgically mourned. But once the center is brought into play, the idea of the book is undone: "The return of the book is then the abandoning of the book" (*WD* 295). The repetition of the book, which Derrida repeatedly refers to as "the scroll" (recalling the use of the terms *ciphrah* and *biblios*, both of which are translated as "scroll" in the Bible to refer to sacred Scripture), is intended to undo the Book of Scripture (along with the Book of Man) in favor of the text of *écriture*.

CHAPTER 15

Scripture or écriture: the limitations of Derrida's deconstruction of ontotheology

> That the logos is first imprinted and that that imprint is the writing-resource of language, signifies, to be sure, that the logos is not a creative activity, the continuous full element of the divine word, etc.
>
> Derrida, *Of Grammatology*

> In the beginning was the *logos*, and the *logos* was with God, and the *logos* was God. He was in the beginning with God. All things came into being through Him, and without Him not even one thing came into being that has come into being.
>
> John 1:1–4

Like Nietzsche and Heidegger before him, Derrida attempts to perform a de(con)struction of the ontotheological character of metaphysics through an overcoming of the founding, metaphysical dualisms of Western thought. But none of these thinkers gives sufficient attention to an understanding of Judaeo-Christian thought before it is synthesized with Greek and modern rationalisms; therefore, when these philosophers claim to have performed a de(con)-struction of the whole of Western thought, their projects are severely limited by being blind to one of the most powerful influences on this thought. I want to demonstrate here that Derrida's deconstruction of the logocentrism of Western thought undermines only the human *logos* of Greek and modern rationalism, not the divine *logos* of biblical, Christian theology.

In an interview transcribed in *Positions*, Derrida describes "a kind of *general strategy of deconstruction*," composed of two movements by which he deconstructs metaphysical dualisms.

> On the one hand, we must traverse a phase of *overturning*. To do justice to this necessity is to recognize that in a classical philosophical opposition we are not dealing with the peaceful coexistence of a *vis-à-vis*, but rather with a violent hierarchy. One of the two terms governs the other (axiologically,

logically, etc.), or has the upper hand. To deconstruct the opposition, first of all, is to overturn the hierarchy at a given moment . . .

That being said – and on the other hand – to remain in this phase is still to operate on the terrain of and from within the deconstructed system. By means of this double, and precisely stratified, dislodged and dislodging, writing, we must also mark the interval between inversion, which brings low what was high, and the irruptive emergence of a new "concept," a concept that can no longer be, and never could be, included in the previous regime. (*Pos* 41–42)

Derrida is trying to avoid Heidegger's charge against Nietzsche, that by merely inverting Platonism he remained entrenched within the same metaphysical regime. In doing so, Derrida's description of the strategy of deconstruction sounds very much like Heidegger's early interpretation of Nietzsche's overturning of metaphysics (when Heidegger still believed that Nietzsche was successful not only in reversing Platonism, the first move of deconstruction, but also in overcoming Platonism, the second move). According to Heidegger, in Nietzsche's revaluation the "new hierarchy does not simply wish to reverse matters within the old structural order, now reverencing the sensuous and scorning the nonsensuous . . . A new hierarchy and new valuation means that the ordering *structure* must be changed. To that extent, overturning Platonism must become a twisting free of it" (*N* I 209).

In this chapter I want to examine the theological implications not of the first move of deconstruction, the overturning of the existing hierarchy, but rather the atheistic presuppositions of the second move, the discovery of a new "concept" which produces and upsets the traditional hierarchy (*Pos* 42–43). In the case of the privileged example of the sign and the revelatory symptom of writing, "it is not a question of resorting to the same concept of writing and of simply inverting the dissymmetry that now has become problematical. It is a question, rather, of producing a new concept of writing" (*Pos* 26). Derrida calls this new concept of writing "*gramme*" or "*différance*."

The *gramme* is a neologism like *différance*. It is based upon the Greek word for letter or writing, *gramma*, which we saw Paul use in his epistles as a sort of neologism to describe a way of reading and living out the Law. Derrida's *gramme* is similar to Paul's use of *gramma*, since Derrida is also describing a new way of reading, a new way of reading metaphysics. It is also related to the Greek "*gramme*" (line), but it is defined more in opposition to this Greek term than in collocation with it, for it is the concept of a linear writing that Derrida wants to deconstruct.

Derrida's *gramme* means a way of rereading writing through a deconstruction of the privileging of speech over writing in Western thought. It is the basic element of Derrida's new concept of writing, similar to the way in which the *phonie* is the basic unit of phonetic writing and the *graphie* is the simplest unit of the traditional concept of writing. But of course there is a difference. It is an element which is not a simple, discrete unit of a linguistic system, but rather an element or structure which produces every semiotic system. "The gram [*gramme*], then, is the most general concept of semiology – which thus becomes grammatology – and it covers not only the field of writing in the restricted sense, but also the field of linguistics" (*Pos* 26).

This new concept of a general or arche-writing comes out of a deconstructive reading of Saussure. Derrida uses Saussure's insights into "the *differential* and *formal* characteristics of semiological functioning" (*Pos* 18) to deconstruct Saussure's phono-logocentric presuppositions and conclusions. These formal and differential characteristics of language introduce into all linguistic systems, including thought and speech, the same characteristics of writing which phonocentric metaphysics desires to exclude through the debasement of writing outside of full speech. All linguistic systems, not only writing, are secondary, but if all are secondary then none is primary or original, and so the logic of the system deconstructs itself.

The key to Derrida's analysis is Saussure's thesis of the "arbitrariness" of the sign. Derrida laments the choice of the term for the concept ("so grossly misnamed"), but finds in this concept the lever with which to deconstruct phonocentrism. That the sign is "arbitrary" means that there is not a natural relationship between either sign and thing or signifier and signified.

Now from the moment that one considers the totality of determined signs, spoken, and a fortiori written, as unmotivated institutions, one must exclude any relationship of natural subordination, any natural hierarchy among signifiers or order of signifiers. (*OG* 44)

The sign is "instituted," Derrida's replacement for the term "arbitrary," and therefore does not have meaning in itself, but only in relation to other signs.

Each signifier only signifies in being distinguished from the other signifiers in the sign chain. The "natural" relationship between speech and thought, the premise of phonocentrism, is broken; consequently, "writing in general," rather than speaking, becomes the elementary structure of linguistic signs.

Thus all language and all sign systems are writing, a generalized writing, but this "presupposes a modification of the concept of writing" (*OG* 55).

This arche-writing would be at work not only in the form and substance of graphic expression but also in those of non-graphic expression. It would constitute not only the pattern uniting form to all substance, graphic or otherwise, but the movement of the *sign-function* linking a content to an expression, whether it be graphic or not. (*OG* 60)

General writing determines the common root of both spoken and written signs. The word "writing" is kept in order to overturn the hierarchy of phonocentrism, and because "within the work of historical repression, writing was, by its situation, destined to signify the most formidable difference" (*OG* 56). The term arche-writing designates the way in which this movement of *différance*, the structure of the trace, characterizes all sign systems.

. The structure of the trace is used to deconstruct traditional sign-theory in much the same way that it was used to deconstruct the subject in Derrida's reading of Husserl. I have described how in *Speech and Phenomenon* Derrida demonstrates that consciousness can express meaning only through reference to the past and the future in the process of retention and protention. Self-presence is thus constituted only through being continually compounded with non-presence, only through the movement of the trace (*SP* 64). In *Of Grammatology*, Derrida now argues that linguistic meaning in general, like the expression of consciousness, is constituted through the formal play of differences, of traces. A sign can only function, express meaning, by referring to another sign which is not present; the sign is constituted by the trace "within" it of other signs with which it differs. Thus arche-writing, the movement of *différance*, opens "in one and the same possibility, temporalization as well as relationship with the other and language" (*OG* 60).

The trace names the process whereby both the signified and the thing itself are infinitely deferred from absolute presence. Traditional semiotics has always defined the sign as the absence of the thing, the signifier as the absence of the signified, but it presupposed that the sign was conceivable only on the basis of the deferred presence which would be reappropriated in the logos. But in Derrida, the "play of differences supposes, in effect, syntheses and referrals which forbid at any moment, or in any sense, that a simple element be *present* in and of itself, referring only to itself" (*Pos* 26). Derrida concludes that the sign can no longer be defined by presence but rather by the trace.

The word "sign" is therefore replaced by the term *"gramme"* which resists the Platonic division which the sign was subjected to: "the *gram* is neither a signifier nor a signified, neither a sign nor a thing, neither a presence nor an absence, neither a position nor a negation" (*Pos* 43). "These oppositions have meaning only *after* the possibility of the trace" (*OG* 47).

But the metaphysical tradition which determines the meaning of the sign as presence (*OG* 18) tries to arrest the play of differences through the concept of the transcendental signified. This desire for the transcendental signified produces the metaphysical dualisms which the trace makes possible, and yet the trace also makes possible their deconstruction:

The presence–absence of the trace ... its play ... carries in itself the problems of the letter and the spirit, of body and soul ... All dualisms, all theories of the immortality of the soul or of the spirit ... are the unique theme of a metaphysics whose entire history was compelled to strive toward the reduction of the trace. The subordination of the trace to the full presence summed up in the logos, the humbling of writing beneath a speech dreaming of its plenitude, such are the gestures required by an onto-theology determining the archeological and eschatological meaning of being as presence, as parousia, as life without différance. (*OG* 71)

The play of the trace makes these dualisms possible in that it opens the relation between the inside and the outside, between the self and the other. And metaphysics requires these dualisms in order to expel absence, death, non-self-presence into a secondary, fallen realm (writing, body, etc.) which in turn enables metaphysics to separate a realm (of the logos, the spirit, etc.) unstained by fallen secondarity.

In Husserl this transcendental signified takes the form of meaning which is a spiritual ideality, which is free from the process of signification and *différance*. This realm is based on a dualism "between the signifying (sensible) aspect, whose originality he recognizes, but which he excludes from his logico-grammatical problematic, and the aspect of signified meaning (which is intelligible, ideal, 'spiritual')" (*Pos* 30).

Even Heidegger "would reinstate rather than destroy the instance of the logos and of the truth of being as 'primum signatum': the 'transcendental signified'" (*OG* 20). At times, especially in the early Heidegger, Being is treated as "'the originary word' ('*Urwort*'), the transcendental word assuring the possibility of being-word to all other words" (*OG* 20). We can confirm this through a citation which Derrida does not note, but which describes Being as the transcendental signified. Even as late as "The Letter on Humanism," Heidegger asks rhetorically if we can be absolved of "the responsibility of thinking of that which primarily remains to-be-thought and, as Being, remains *the guarantee and truth prior to every being*?" (my emphasis, LH 295).

But it is also Heidegger who more than any other thinker opens up the possibility of a deconstruction of the transcendental signified. In repeating metaphysics as the *question* of Being, Heidegger opens up the possibility of questioning the metaphysical determination of the meaning of Being, the truth of Being, as presence. "To question the origin of that domination does not amount to hypostatizing a transcendental signified, but to a questioning of what constitutes our history and what produced transcendentality itself" (*OG* 23).

Heidegger goes so far as to determine Being as a trace, as never present in metaphysics, only leaving the trace of its absence, but Derrida takes another step back and shows that the trace is more "originary" than Being itself.

If Being, according to the Greek forgetting which would have been the very form of its advent, has never meant anything except beings, then perhaps difference is older than Being itself ... Beyond Being and beings, this difference, ceaselessly differing from and deferring (itself), would trace (itself) (by itself) – this *différance* would be the first or last trace if one still could speak, here, of origin and end. (*M* 67)

Just as Heidegger claimed that "the destiny of Being" is "more essential and older ... than the lack of God" (*N* IV 248), so now does Derrida claim that *différance*" is older than Being itself."

But différance can never act as a transcendental signified in the way that God and Being have in ontotheology. There is no trace itself, and all attempts to name the trace, to name its essence or origin, would belong to the metaphysical desire to recapture it in presence.

These deconstructions of Husserl and Heidegger are important for Derrida in that they allow his results to apply to not only a finite, created being such as man, but also to a transcendental or ideal consciousness and even to Being itself. "To think play radically the ontological and transcendental problematics must first be seriously *exhausted*; the question of the meaning of being, the being of the entity and of the transcendental origin of the world – of the world-ness of the world – must be patiently and rigorously worked through, the critical movement of the Husserlian and Heideggerian questions must be effectively followed to the very end *and their effectiveness and legibility must be conserved*" (final emphasis mine; *OG* 50). The deconstruction of Husserl shows that we "*think only in signs*" (*OG* 50) and that "*The thing itself is a sign*" (*OG* 49). The reading of Heidegger demonstrates that "fundamentally nothing escapes the movement of the signifier" (*OG* 23).

Thus Derrida can write of an "originary" trace, but only by crossing out (the later Heidegger's method) or by placing *sous rature* (Derrida's translation) the word "origin."

The trace is not only the disappearance of origin – within the discourse that we sustain and according to the path that we follow it means that the origin did not even disappear, that it was never constituted except reciprocally by a nonorigin, the trace, which thus becomes the origin of the origin. From then on, to wrench the concept of the trace from the classical scheme, which would derive it from a presence or from an originary nontrace and which would make of it an empirical mark, one must indeed speak of an originary trace or arche-trace. Yet we know that that concept destroys its name and that, if all begins with the trace, there is above all no originary trace. (*OG* 61)

By tracing back toward the supposed origin of writing, from writing to speech to thought to perception, Derrida shows that each step toward the "origin" is based upon the same play of differences, the same play of presence and absence, as writing. Derrida calls *différance* this concept of the "originary" trace which erases all concepts of the origin. "*The (pure) trace is différance*" (*OG* 62).

In his reading of Husserl, Derrida deconstructs self-presence, of consciousness and ideal meaning, that is based on the interior voice. This realm of expression, in Husserl's terms, was shown to be constituted by the movement of the trace and therefore not on presence. But Derrida will go further to deconstruct the concept of presence as the ground for even the pre-expressive, i.e., prelinguistic or presemiotic, the realm of pure meaning or perception in the logos. Thus logocentrism as well as phonocentrism is deconstructed.

Derrida refers to Saussure's distinction between the signified as "psychic imprint" and the material, physical event or object which produced that psychic imprint. In Saussure's example, there is a difference between the sound heard and the being-heard of the sound, the psychic imprint of the sound. Using Husserl, Derrida makes it clear that the psychic imprint is not "an internal reality copying an external one" (*OG* 64). In Husserl's reduction, the psychic imprint is ideal. Through the Husserlian correction, Saussure's difference becomes a difference between the appearing and the lived appearing.

The unheard difference between the appearing and the appearance (between the "world" and "lived experience") is the condition of all other differences, of all other traces, and *it is already a trace*. (*OG* 65)

That this difference is already a trace is developed mostly out of a Freudian framework which marks a difference between the psychic imprint and perception. "This impression has left behind a laborious trace which has never been *perceived*, whose meaning has never been lived in the present, i.e., has never been lived consciously" (*WD* 214). Consciousness has access only to the trace left by the psychic imprint; therefore, the trace refers to "an always-already-there that no reactivation of the origin could fully master and awaken to presence" (*OG* 66). Derrida names this an "absolute past," a past which was never present (to consciousness) and which can never be brought to presence (in consciousness). Therefore, "Writing supplements perception before perception even appears to itself [is conscious of itself] ... The 'perceived' may be read only in the past, beneath perception and after it" (*WD* 224).

The deconstruction of the self-presence of consciousness, of its inner monologue and even its perception, has led to the deconstruction of the logos.

That the logos is first imprinted and that that imprint is the writing-resource of language, signifies, to be sure, that the logos is not a creative activity, the continuous full element of the divine word, etc. (*OG* 68)

But is there not a leap here, a "leap of unfaith," which jumps from the deconstruction of human consciousness, whether it be transcendental or not, to the claims of undoing "the *divine* word?" Derrida takes the word "trace," the concept which he uses to deconstruct the logos, in part from Levinas (*OG* 70), who in turn took the term from Exodus. Shira Wolosky explains: "He derives the term 'trace' from Exodus, where Moses, in beholding God's glory, could not sustain the sight of the divine face but only its back as the divine glory passed by. Of the biblical text, Levinas writes: 'The revealed God ... conserves all the infinity of his absence. He does not show himself except by his trace, as in Exodus 33.'"[1] In Derrida's thought of the trace, however, there is no origin of the trace. The trace means there is no origin, or in the case of Exodus 33, there is no God.

Derrida would justify this move by claiming that the divine logos is only the way in which ontotheology reduces the play of *différance* in order to satisfy its desire for presence.

Thus, within this epoch, reading and writing, the production or interpretation of signs, the text in general as fabric of signs, allow themselves to be confined within secondariness. They are preceded by a truth, or a meaning already constituted by and within the element of the logos. Even when the thing, the "referent," is not immediately related to the logos of a creator God where it began by being spoken/thought sense, the signified has at any rate an immediate relationship with the logos in general (finite or infinite). (*OG* 14–15)

But Derrida's rhetoric here, his way of writing that "*Even when* the thing, the 'referent,' *is not* immediately related to the logos of a creator God," begs a question. Where is the deconstruction of this logos of a creator God (which would certainly include the Johannine logos)? The undoing of the logos of a creator God, the Johannine, biblical logos, occurred in rationalist/idealist philosophy, in the very philosophy which Derrida deconstructs. Derrida deconstructs the very ground of the modernist metaphysical attack on Christianity, the assertion of the self-present, autonomous self, yet he takes the modern critique of Christianity and theism for granted.

Derrida has deconstructed only the human logos, and only "the name of God ... *as it is pronounced in classic rationalism*" (*OG* 71), only the god who acts as a metaphysical ground for the operations of the independent and autonomous ego. Derrida recognizes the role played by the rationalists' god:

The infinite alterity of the divine substance does not interpose itself as an element of mediation or opacity in the transparence of self-relationship and the purity of auto-affection. God is the name and element of that which makes possible an absolutely pure and absolutely self-present self-knowledge. From Descartes to Hegel and in spite of all the differences that separate the different places and moments in the structure of that epoch, God's infinite understanding is the other name for the logos as self-presence. (*OG* 98)

I fully agree with this analysis of the god of rationalist metaphysics, but the God written about in the Bible is completely different from this man-made god. The God revealed in the Bible does not make possible, but rather makes impossible, an absolutely pure and absolutely self-present self-knowledge. The God of the Bible destroys humanity's pretensions to a realm and life of one's "own" and labels any efforts to claim one's life as one's own sin. From Descartes to Hegel, rationalist philosophers worked to replace the God of the Bible with the god of ontotheology, a god which is only "that which makes possible an absolutely pure and absolutely self-present self-knowledge."

Yet Derrida will claim that his theory of *différance* applies to any logos, "and not only for a finite and created spirit" (*OG* 73). He claims that the movement of *différance* upsets "all theology" (*M* 67), not only onto-theology or the infinitist theologies of rationalism.

Biblicists will note that in all of this the agent of persistent and recurrent illusion is logocentrism, the constant return, wittingly or not, to the metaphysics of the classical *logos* ... Obviously this is not the Christian *logos*: but Derrida repudiates that too.[2]

What the work of deconstruction has not accomplished, denial will supplement.

In his essay "Différance," Derrida gives a reading of his previous text, a work of clarification and denial of misreadings much like that which Heidegger performs in his "Letter on Humanism." And the denial of the theological is no less persistent in Derrida's text than it is in Heidegger's. Just as Heidegger insists repeatedly that "It would undoubtedly be the greatest error" to interpret his analysis of the ex-sistence of *Dasein* as a secularized translation of Christian anthropology, so does Derrida stress that, "those aspects of *différance* which are thereby delineated are not theological, not even in the order of the most negative theologies, which are always concerned with disengaging a superessentiality beyond the finite categories of essence and existence, that is, of presence, of existence, only in order to acknowledge his superior, inconceivable, and ineffable mode of being" (*M* 6).

But this separation of *différance* from the theological then becomes a denial of the theological.

First consequence: *différance* is not. It is not a present being, however excellent, unique, principal, or transcendent. It governs nothing, reigns over nothing, and nowhere exercises any authority ... Not only is there not a kingdom of *différance*, but *différance* instigates the subversion of every kingdom. Which makes it obviously threatening and infallibly dreaded by everything within us that desires a kingdom, the past or future presence of a kingdom. (*OG* 21–22)

Apparently the kingdom of God announced in the Bible is included. Derrida has set *différance* up as a subversive force against the kingdom of God and its *parousia*[3] (which it should be noted is not a presence controllable by a self-present consciousness, but rather a coming which will come like a thief in the night). In contrast to the word of the Bible: "There is nothing kerygmatic about this 'word' [*différance*]" (*M* 27).

Through *différance*, Derrida names God as an illusion, just like the two atheistic thinkers who most influenced him: Freud and Nietzsche. In a lecture given at Jerusalem in which he expands upon the difference between his thought of *différance* and (negative) theology, Derrida presents God as an illusion which satisfies our desire for presence and truth. *Différance* is not kerygmatic, does not proclaim or call to man, it contains no "prophetic annunciation." But according to Derrida, neither does God call humanity; rather, humanity calls to God. Instead of the Logos calling humanity into being, humanity calls God into being: "it is always possible to call on God, to call this assumed origin of all speech by the name of God, its required cause ... It is for speech, or for the best silence, a request, a demand, or a desire, if you wish, for what one equally well calls meaning, the referent, truth. *This is what God's name always names*" (D 98). I emphasize the final phrase to demonstrate that it is not just the God of classical philosophy which Derrida claims to have deconstructed. Derrida repeats here the same move as Nietzsche, Marx, and Freud, a move originated by Feuerbach in *The Essence of Christianity*. God is seen as the projection of humanity, as an illusory projection in which humanity places and reifies all its desires.

At the conclusion of this argument, Derrida writes: "Language has started without us, in us and before us. This is what theology calls God" (D 99). Some theologians, most influentially Mark C.

Taylor, have tried to incorporate this linguistic twist on Feuerbach into a "new" theology. Taylor writes that "The death of God is the birth of the Word."[4] Taylor is not alone in attempting to appropriate Derridean thought into a new theology.[5] Raschke calls deconstruction "*the death of God put into writing.*"[6] But these attempts to appropriate Derrida's thought for use in theological discourse represent a misreading of Derrida, who in his essay "How to Avoid Speaking: Denials" makes it clear that "If the movement of this reappropriation [of deconstruction by theology] appears in fact irrepressible, its ultimate failure is no less necessary" (D 79).

Derrida's *différance*, the thought of the trace, does not take the place of God, but rather excludes God and anything that would take his place. His thought is a denial of any God, and any son of God, of any thought of the logos, including the logos of John's prologue. But the work of deconstruction only breaks the false logos of rationalism. In breaking the Enlightenment faith in reason, of our concept of truth as residing in self-presence, as our own, Derrida can be useful for Christian thinkers. But Derrida takes apart only the logocentrism of rationalism and idealism and yet claims to have deconstructed the thought of any presence before or outside semiological difference.

Jeremiah writes God's lament:

> My people have committed two sins:
> They have forsaken me,
>   the spring of living water,
> and they have dug their own cisterns,
>   broken cisterns that cannot hold water. (Jeremiah 2:13)

Derrida has deconstructed the metaphysical belief in a truth proceeding from and present in our own consciousness, our "own cisterns." He has shown the cracks in this cistern, that it cannot hold water. But although humanity's cistern has been broken, the water of life, the spring of living water, remains untasted, forgotten.

Conclusion: ontotheology, negative theology, and the theology of the cross

Christian theology must think of God's being in suffering and dying and finally in the death of Jesus, if it is not to surrender itself and lose its identity . . . the controversy between Christian theology and the philosophical concept of God must now be taken further . . . the time has finally come for differentiating the Father of Jesus Christ from the God of the pagans and the philosophers (Pascal) in the interest of Christian faith.

Moltmann, *The Crucified God: The Cross of Christ as the Foundation and Criticism of Christian Theology*

DENIALS: NEGATING/NEGATIVE THEOLOGY

God encounters the soul as "either-or"; and this involves acceptance or rejection, affirmation or denial. (Karl Barth, *The Epistle to the Romans*)

It is clear that Nietzsche, Heidegger, and Derrida all reject metaphysical theology. I have tried to show that this rejection of metaphysical theology, or ontotheology, implies for each of these thinkers a similar rejection of Christian theology. I have also attempted to demonstrate that biblical theology – Christian theology based upon the revelation of Jesus Christ and articulated through the conceptuality of the Hebraic scriptures – should be distinguished from the Christian theology which these thinkers claim to have revalued, destroyed or deconstructed. Biblical theology can and should be disengaged from ancient and modern ontotheologies.

Kevin Hart, in his recent work on deconstruction and theology, *The Trespass of the Sign*, argues that negative theology is the only theological discourse which resists deconstruction. His thesis is that "negative theology, properly understood, *is* that theology . . . which works at once inside and outside onto-theology, submitting its images of God to deconstruction. My position is not that deconstruction is a form of negative theology but that negative theology is a

form of deconstruction."[1] Hart thus acknowledges Derrida's assertions that he is not writing a negative theology. "No, what I write is
not 'negative theology'" (D 77). But he disagrees with Derrida's
claim that in negative theology the "negative movement of the
discourse on God is only a phase of positive ontotheology" (*WD* 337,
note 37).

I want to use Derrida's own assessment of the relationship
between negative theology and ontotheology to criticize Hart's
thesis. Derrida argues that although negative theology "seems to
exceed the alternative of a theism or an atheism," since it does not
argue about the "existence" of God who is considered "beyond"
Being or even "without" Being,[2] negative theology nevertheless
remains tied to ontotheology in an essential way, since it "seems to
reserve, beyond all positive predication, beyond all negation, even
beyond Being, some hyperessentiality, a being beyond Being"
(D 77). Negative theology still appeals to an essence, even if only to
a hyper-essentiality "outside" of or "beyond" *différance*.

Hart wants to formulate a "general negative theology" which
would resist this critique. He argues that Derrida only considers
negative theology formulated "as part of a *dialectic* with positive
theology."[3] Hart proposes, in opposition to such a "restricted negative theology," a "general" negative theology which would resist
and deconstruct all positive theology. "However, if we add the
Derridean problematic to theology what results is a general negative
theology, one which ... provides us with an account of the only
possible way in which a theology can resist the illusions of metaphysics."[4] But negative theology does not escape the illusions of
ontotheology.

Historically, negative theology has represented a departure from
biblical theology. Raoul Mortley, in his two-volume study of negative theology, argues that the "absence of the *via negativa* in Christian
thought can be explained by the fact that the nature of God is
scarcely an issue in Christianity." Rather, it is Greek thought which
raises the ontological question, "What is God?" – in the same way
that Heidegger writes that we must begin "from the truth of Being"
in order to be able to understand "what the word 'God' is to signify"
(LH 294). It is only "with the progressive Hellenization of Christianity that questions about the essence of reality come to the fore,
and the nature of God becomes an issue."[5]

Despite the desire of negative theology to divorce God from Being, this approach to God is still an ontotheology because it uses a Greek conceptuality, especially Platonic and Neoplatonic philosophy, to claim that God is not Being. Derrida questions whether "a certain Platonism – or Neoplatonism – is indispensable" in negative theology.[6] And this synthesis of Christianity and Neoplatonism, this ontotheology, leads, as always, to a subordination of biblical revelation:

the apophatic design is anxious to render itself independent of revelation, of all the literal language of New Testament eventness ... of the coming of Christ, of the Passion ... An immediate but intuitionless mysticism, a sort of abstract kenosis, frees this language from all authority, all narrative, all dogma, all belief – and at the limit from all faith.[7]

This often leads to the forgetting of the biblical division between God and humanity, as the mystic claims "I am (as) God," and also to a forgetting of the biblical division between this age and the age to come, as the mystic seeks to free him or herself from the material world in order to achieve an intellectual or at least noncorporeal vision of God.

That negative theology remains tied to ontotheology can also be seen by looking back to Feuerbach, who describes how negative theology is an essential part of ontotheology:

God as God, that is, as a being not finite, not human, not materially conditioned, not phenomenal, is only an object of thought. He is the incorporeal, formless, incomprehensible – the abstract, negative being: he is known, *i.e.*, becomes an object, only by abstraction and negation (*via negationis*) ... God, said the schoolmen, the Christian fathers, and long before them the heathen philosophers, – God is immaterial essence, intelligence, spirit, pure understanding.

What sets the biblical God apart from the god of ontotheology and negative theology is that the God of the Bible has revealed himself in human history. The God revealed in the Bible, revealed in Jesus, is not simply the negation of the finite, the human and the material. "His attributes cannot be expressed by negation of the sphere of the earthly, human, mortal and transient, but only in recalling and recounting the history of his promise."[8]

The view of God as the negation of the world, time and becoming is what Nietzsche criticizes in his attack upon the Christian God. However, the God of the Bible does not negate, but rather creates,

sustains, and redeems the world. This God brings about a revaluation of metaphysical thought even more radical than Nietzsche's:

With the Christian message of the cross of Christ, something new and
strange has entered the metaphysical world. For this faith must understand
the deity of God from the event of the suffering and death of the Son of God
and thus bring about a fundamental change in the orders of being of
metaphysical thought and the value tables of religious feeling.[9]

Christianity, as testified to in the Bible, overturned the meta-
physical-moral god long before Nietzsche's repudiation of the
transcendental world. But Christianity does not simply negate idols;
rather, biblical revelation destroys all man-made gods, all the gods
of ontotheology, to reveal the true and living God.

Heidegger develops his thesis that Nietzsche remained entrenched
in ontotheology by calling his repudiation of the Christian view of
the world a negative theology. He argues that Nietzsche's conception of the world as chaos represents a kind of negative theology
which refuses to make assertions about being as a whole:

What Nietzsche is practicing here with regard to the world totality is a kind
of "negative theology," which tries to grasp the Absolute as purely as
possible by holding at a distance all "relative" determinations, that is, all
those that relate to human beings. Except that Nietzsche's determination of
the world as a whole [as chaos] is a negative theology without the Christian
God. (*N* II 95)

But, rather than describe Nietzsche's cosmology as "a negative
theology without the Christian God," I have argued that
Nietzsche's cosmology is better described as a *negation* of Christian
theology. In describing the cosmos as chaos, Nietzsche denies it the
predicates given it by theology: order, meaning, purpose, goal. But
Nietzsche is not only rejecting the god of metaphysics who guaran-
tees man's understanding of the world. He also denies the Christian
belief that the world has a Creator.

Heidegger also excludes belief in a Creator. Although at times he
pays lip-service to the distinction between a Christian theology
which responds in faith to revelation and a theiology which relies
upon metaphysics, Heidegger nevertheless clearly rejects the biblical answer to his question of Being:

Anyone for whom the Bible is divine revelation and truth has the answer to
the question "Why are there essents rather than nothing?" even before it is
asked: everything that is, except God himself, has been created by Him.
God himself, the increate creator, "is" ...

What we have said about security in faith as one position in regard to the truth does not imply that the biblical "In the beginning God created heaven and earth" is an answer to our question ... they [for whom the Bible is divine revelation] can supply no answer to our question because they are in no way related to it. (*IM* 7)

Like Nietzsche, Heidegger rejects the Christian conception of the cosmos, of beings, as created. Though once again the biblical and Greek paradigms are not considered separately, Heidegger rejects the Christian account of beings because its account is metaphysical. "The Christian idea of the causation of all beings through a first cause is metaphysical, especially the version of the creation story of the Old Testament as rehearsed in Greek metaphysics" (*N* III 7). But what about the Christian account of creation as narrated in the Hebraic scriptures, before Philo turned it into an allegory of Platonism?

In the same passage from *The Introduction to Metaphysics*, Heidegger rejects "'Christian philosophy' [as] a round square and a misunderstanding" (*IM* 7).[10] Heidegger has to reject the idea of a Christian philosophy not because it is metaphysical, but because he sees that Christian faith negates his entire project: "'If faith summoned me in this manner, I would close down shop'" (as quoted in D 130). Heidegger's question of Being, his shop, is based upon the absence, the denial, of the Christian faith. Similarly, Nietzsche laments, "what could one create if gods existed?" (*Z* 87).

As we see in his *Der Spiegel* interview, "Only a God Can Save Us," Heidegger can await a god, but not the God of the Bible.[11] Heidegger awaits a new revelation of the divine, a god who would follow and replace the presencing "of the divine in the world of the Greeks, in prophetic Judaism, in the preaching of Jesus" (*PLT* 184). Hart criticizes the quietism of Heidegger's promised theology: "Heidegger offers the possibility of a divine God being revealed to us, though one that is far removed from the God of biblical revelation, and about whom we cannot say anything at all" (94). This call to await a god who will save us, a god which we have no way of knowing how to recognize, is potentially more dangerous than quietism.[12] Nietzsche would criticize this theology as irrelevant: Heidegger's unknown god is "not consoling, redeeming, or obligating: how could something unknown obligate us?" (*TI* 485). Heidegger can say nothing about this god, even whether it will arrive or not, so it is Heidegger, not Nietzsche, who practices a kind of negative theology.

Just as Heidegger describes his precursor's (Nietzsche's) writings as a negative theology, so does Derrida describe the writings of his precursor, Heidegger, in a similar manner. In his lecture on negative theology delivered at Jerusalem, Derrida finds that Heidegger's discussions of the relation between his philosophy and theology are in collusion with negative theology. Although Derrida refers to Heidegger's negation of Christian theology, his denial of the possibility of a Christian philosophy, Derrida is more interested in Heidegger's discussion of his temptation to write a theology.

Responding to students at the University of Zurich in 1951, Heidegger recalls that Being and God are not identical, and that he would always avoid thinking God's essence by means of Being. He makes this more precise ... : "if I *were* yet to *write* a theology, as I am sometimes tempted to do, the word 'being' *ought* not to appear there [take place there, occur, figure, or happen there]." (Derrida's emphases and gloss; D 126–27)

Derrida notes that this denial of the word Being is quite different from Heidegger's crossing out of the word Being in *The Question of Being*. There Heidegger crosses through Being not to avoid speaking of Being, but rather in order to bring out the meaning of Being, as the gathering of the fourfold which the cross over the word "Being" represents (*QB* 81ff.). But in the saying which fascinates Derrida, "the point is, rather, not to allow the word *being* to occur, on the subject of God" (D 126).

Derrida hints, correctly I think, that Heidegger nevertheless does speak of a relation between Being and God, between God's revelation and the revelation of Being. Just as in his explanations of the relationship between fundamental ontology and Christian existence, the thought of Being, banished from theology, returns as a prerequisite for thinking about God. "Although God is not and need not be thought from Being as His essence or foundation, the *dimension of Being* opens up access to the advent, the experience, the encounter with this God who nevertheless is not" (D 127). In Heidegger's own words:

Only from the truth of Being can the essence of the holy be thought. Only from the essence of the holy can the essence of divinity be thought. Only in the light of the essence of divinity can it be thought and said what the word "God" is to signify. Or must we not first be able to understand and hear these words carefully if we as men, i.e., as exsisting beings, are to have the privilege of experiencing a relation of God to man? (LH 294)

Thus according to Heidegger it is through a *gnosis*, an understanding of the esoteric "truth of Being," that we gain the "privilege" of thinking and speaking about "God."

Derrida plays with Heidegger's two denials of Being, his crossing out of Being in his own thought and his expulsion of the word "Being" from theological discourse, showing that perhaps they are the same. Perhaps the theology he wanted to write which would not have the word Being in it is the same as his crossing out of Being in his later texts.

In fact, since Being is not (a being) and in truth is nothing (that is), what difference is there between writing *Being*, this Being which is not, and writing *God*, this God of whom Heidegger also says that He is not? Indeed Heidegger does not merely say that God is not a being; he specifies that He "has nothing to do here with Being" ... But since he recognizes that God announces Himself to experience in the "dimension of Being," what difference is there between writing a theology and writing on Being, of Being, as Heidegger never ceases doing? Most of all, when he writes the word *being* under and in the place (*Ort*) of the cancellation in the form of a cross. Hasn't Heidegger written what he says he would have liked to write, a theology *without* the word *being*? But didn't he also write what he says should not be written, what he should not have written, namely a theology that is opened, dominated, and invaded by the word *being*? (D 128)

Although Derrida refuses to answer his own rhetorical questions, I think he is correct in implying that Heidegger wrote what he said he should not write, a theology dominated by his own philosophy of Being. Derrida implies that Heidegger is writing a sort of negative theology in which God is considered under the sign of the cross which covers over Being.

But the sign of the cross over Being should not be read as an allusion to the theology of the cross. Although Heidegger's critique of ontotheology came out of Luther's theology of the cross,[13] Heidegger concludes that philosophy has nothing to learn, should have nothing to do, with a theology built upon faith in biblical revelation.

In writing an imaginary dialogue between Heidegger and Christian theologians (who are intent upon appropriating Heidegger's thought), Derrida has Heidegger respond that his thought about spirit, about the holy and the divine, "without being opposed to Christianity, would be foreign to it, and even at the origin of Christianity" (*OS* 107). Although this accurately portrays Heidegger's oft repeated standpoint, I have tried to show that while

Heidegger's thought about the gods certainly is "foreign" to Christian theology, it is, despite Heidegger's denials, "opposed" to Christian theology.

Heidegger contradicts himself concerning the relationship between his thinking of Being and Christian faith in both his early and later writings. Although he argues that Christian theology should follow Luther in writing a theology in which faith is primary (a theology which does not rely upon philosophical concepts), in making his own philosophy an exception to this rule, Heidegger "forgets" the insight he learned from Paul, Luther and Kierkegaard. Heidegger writes what he accuses Nietzsche of writing: "a negative theology without the Christian God." Although there are echoes of the Christian concept of grace in Heidegger's later obscure theological remarks, Heidegger, like earlier ontotheologies, makes God the end point of human thinking about Being.

Caputo gives an excellent summary of the ways in which Heidegger secularizes the Christian *Heilsgeschichte* in his later writings. "[I]t is clear to everyone but Heidegger's most fanatic disciples that he is clearly Hellenizing and secularizing a fundamentally biblical conception of the history of salvation – a ruse both compounded and betrayed by the radicality with which he tries to exclude the biblical provenance of these operations."[14] Caputo's most recent work focuses on a critique of Heidegger's "remythologizing" tendencies in his writings after *Being and Time*, while I have concentrated upon a critique of Heidegger's "demythologizing," or better "detheologizing," of biblical theology in his writings up to and including *Being and Time*. As a result of this analysis I have concluded that we should not, as Caputo and van Buren have argued, celebrate the early Heidegger, using his early writings to "demythologize" the later writings.

Both Nietzsche and Heidegger do create a kind of mythology in their later writings, Nietzsche in his doctrine of the eternal return and Heidegger in his awaiting of the divine God. Just as Nietzsche asserts that nihilism "might be a divine way of thinking," so does Heidegger turn his methodological atheism into the "piety of thought."

Only Derrida seems to break completely with religious tradition. Although Derrida follows Nietzsche and Heidegger in criticizing the metaphysics of presence, he avoids, no doubt as a result of the fact that unlike Nietzsche and Heidegger he was not raised in a Christian tradition, importing secularized Christian concepts into his philosophy. But while Derrida avoids writing a *negative* theology, he does not avoid the atheistic gesture of *negating* theology.

Sheehan argues that Derrida's rejection of eschatology, whether it be biblical, secular or metaphysical, marks his innovation over against Heidegger's destruction of ontotheology.

> If he does make an advance beyond Heidegger, or the Heideggerians, that step might well consist in his indictment of eschatology as the final form of decidability ... Derrida is remarking the closure of eschatology in *all* its forms, from Zoroaster, where the notion seems to emerge, down through Daniel and Jesus and Augustine and Hegel and perhaps even Heidegger ... The utter silencing of theology – not only of revealed theology but also of philosophical ontotheology and even of negative ontotheology – might well be a contemporary echo of the suggestion made in 1843 [by Marx] that "the critique of religion is the premise of all [other] critique."[15]

This seems to me to be a clear and accurate assessment of Derrida's relationship to theology. His work does follow Nietzsche, Marx, and Freud in criticizing the truth claims of theology in all its forms, and one of his most important strategies for doing this, for deconstructing ontotheology, negative theology and biblical theology all at once, is to attack the concept of the *eschaton*.

In an interview with Richard Kearney, Derrida makes the provocative statement that his interrogation of "the idea of an *eschaton* or *telos* in the absolute formulations of classical philosophy ... does not mean I dismiss all forms of Messianic or prophetic eschatology."[16] But although he may not "dismiss" Messianic and prophetic eschatology, he does deconstruct its claims to reveal the end. Schneidau is clearly right in asserting that Derrida claims to deconstruct Christian eschatology as well as ontotheological teleology:

> he is fond of playfully linking *parousia* with *ousia*, millenarianism with substantialism; within our epoch, he says, all "histories" are those "whose origin may always be revealed or whose end may be anticipated in the form of presence" ... We have no trouble recognizing this as a swipe at Christianity from *arche* to *telos*.[17]

But many critics have had a great deal of trouble recognizing not only Derrida's, but also Heidegger's and even Nietzsche's "swipe at Christianity."

In his reading of the book of Revelation, Derrida deconstructs Christian eschatology to announce an "apocalypse without apocalypse, an apocalypse without vision, without truth, without revelation ... without last judgment, without any other eschatology than the tone of the 'Come' itself, its very difference, an apocalypse beyond good and evil" (OAT 66). Rapaport asserts that "Such statements are not, to the contrary of what some Christian readers will suspect, expressions of a deep-seated atheism."[18] I would argue that although they may not be expressions of a "deep-seated" atheism, they are yet the expressions of a superficial anti-Christianity, as the allusion to Nietzsche's atheistic philosophy would suggest. Derrida cannot think the difference between the Greek *parousia* of presence and the Judaeo-Christian *parousia* of advent without a prior, Nietzschean rejection of every philosophy and theology "that knows some *finale*, some final state of some sort, every predominantly aesthetic or religious craving for some Apart, Beyond, Outside, Above" (*GS* "Preface" 2).

Taylor has used this deconstruction of the *eschaton* in Derrida to rewrite Christian eschatology. "The trace of this erasure is the deferral of the Parousia – a deferral, which, as infinite, marks and remarks the timelessness of time itself."[19] Thus Taylor calls upon us to "draw near the sacred by patiently awaiting what never arrives."[20] The central expectation of the Bible, the *parousia* of the Messiah, is thus explicitly denied. Taylor also criticizes what he calls "christo-logic" in which "crucifixion harbors resurrection," arguing that, "The empty tomb can ... be understood in at least two ways: as a sign of the reality of resurrection or as a sign of the impossibility of resurrection."[21] Taylor, in using Derrida to articulate his atheology, denies the redemptive–eschatological hope of the Bible.

Caputo, after his recent disaffection with Heidegger in the light of his Nazi activities, makes the latest attempt to use Derrida's postmodern theory to revitalize theology. He argues that Derrida allows us to recover a "jewgreek" conception of justice. But, in using Derrida to perform this retrieval, Caputo de-eschatologizes the biblical redemption history, arguing that "the myth of justice is betrayed by locating a chosen people (the Jews), or the people of God (the Christians), as if some people were and some people were not God's, as if God prefers Jews to Egyptians, Christians to Jews, Europeans to non-Westerners, and so on. The whole idea behind justice is not to exclude anyone from the kingdom, which means the kingdom is nowhere in particular."[22] But to equate the redemption history revealed in the Bible with Euro-centrism and racism is to violently misconstrue the Christian history of redemption. In biblical revelation, the Jews are the chosen people, and only through Christ is salvation achieved, but in the kingdom of God "there is neither Jew nor Greek ... neither slave nor free ... neither male nor female" (Galatians 3:28).

Derrida may consider his own thought, "paradoxically, as neither Greek nor Jew,"[23] but this does not mean that his discourse can be aligned with Paul's gospel of the kingdom of God in which believers are "neither Jew or Greek," but rather fellow "heirs according to the promise" (Galatians 3:28–29). For Derrida's deconstruction is driven by his "discovery of the genealogical and genetic critique of Nietzsche and Freud,"[24] both of which were developed in opposition to the promise of Christianity.

Just as Heidegger at times makes a distinction between a theology based upon faith and ontotheology, so does Derrida begin to question the homogeneity of ontotheology in some of his later writings. In a letter to John Leavey, Jr., Derrida writes that

in effect I believe that what is called "negative theology" (a rich and very diverse corpus) does not let itself be easily assembled under the general category of "onto-theology-to-be-deconstructed." Undoubtedly there are also the places of "positive" theology, about which as much could be said – and the very unity, in any case the assembled homogeneity, of an onto-theology always seems to me problematic and today more than ever.[25]

I have tried to argue that biblical theology is a "place" of "positive theology" which does not fall under the category "ontotheology-to-be-deconstructed." But this is not to equate Derrida's deconstruction with Jewish or biblical theology.

Derrida may now admit that "what we know as Christian and Jewish theology today is a cultural ensemble which has already been largely 'Hellenized,'"[26] and he may even criticize Heidegger for presupposing "that there is one single site, unique and univocal, for THE metaphysics and THE Christianity."[27] Nevertheless, in his early work, when he is articulating the critique of ontotheology which underlies his entire project, Derrida, as much as Nietzsche and Heidegger, assumes that both metaphysics and Christianity can be deconstructed under the single concept of ontotheology. In questioning the unity of Western metaphysics, Derrida is using Nietzsche against Heidegger to question "the axiomatic structure of metaphysics, inasmuch as *metaphysics itself* desires, or dreams, or imagines its own unity."[28] Derrida is criticizing the ontotheological desire for unity, not opening up the possibility of a non-metaphysical theology.

All attempts to use the latest trends in philosophy to articulate Christian theology lead to the creation of an ontotheology. Heidegger draws upon Luther, who echoes Paul, to assert that Christian theology should not use metaphysical concepts to articulate its faith.

Only epochs which no longer fully believe in the true greatness of the task of theology arrive at the disastrous notion that philosophy can help to provide a refurbished theology if not a substitute for theology, which will satisfy the needs and tastes of the time. (*IM* 7)

I want to place this quotation as an epigraph (or better yet an epitaph!) over the attempts to use the postmodern theories of Nietzsche, Heidegger, and Derrida to refurbish theology, or to write a substitute for theology, which satisfies the fashions of the present age.

Heidegger goes on to allude to Paul's rejection of "worldly" philosophy: "For the original Christian faith philosophy is foolishness" (*IM* 7). Although Heidegger turns Paul's pronouncement around to criticize Christian philosophy, Paul's indictment of the wisdom of this world and his call to remain faithful to the *kerygma* of ·Jesus Christ were intended as a model for a Christian destruction of both atheism and ontotheology.

For the message of the cross is foolishness to those who are perishing, but to us who are being saved it is the power of God. For it is written:

> "I will destroy the wisdom of the wise; the intelligence of the intelligent I will frustrate."

Where is the wise man? Where is the scholar? Where is the philosopher of this age? Has not God made foolish the wisdom of the world? For since in the wisdom of God the world through its wisdom did not know him, God was pleased through the foolishness of what was preached to save those who believe ... we preach Christ crucified: a stumbling block to Jews and foolishness to the Gentiles, but to those whom God has called, both Jews and Greeks, Christ the power of God and the wisdom of God. (1 Corinthians 1: 18–24)

This description of a Christian destruction of philosophy, the original inspiration for Heidegger's destruction of metaphysics, is not a call to anti-intellectualism, for Paul does "speak a message of wisdom" for those with ears to hear (1 Corinthians 2:6–8), a wisdom based upon God's revelation through Jesus Christ (1 Corinthians 2:9–10). This revelation destroys all the pretensions of human wisdom, especially ontotheology in which humanity attempts to think its way to God, and its antithesis, atheism, which claims to be able to know that there is no God.

FROM ONTOTHEOLOGY TO THE THEOLOGY OF THE CROSS

[I]n articles of faith one must have recourse to another dialectic and philosophy, which is called the word of God and faith. (Luther)

a new organ has been assumed here: faith ... and a new teacher: the god in time. (Kierkegaard)

Nietzsche valorizes the world of becoming over the permanently present world of being. Heidegger destroys the history of Being through a critique of the thought of Being as presence. Derrida's deconstruction of logocentrism is a critique of presence as the foundation of consciousness and truth. Thus by deconstructing the metaphysics of presence, these thinkers all claim to have deconstructed ontotheology, both Greek metaphysics and Christian theology. But the logos of biblical theology is radically different from the logos of Greek philosophy and modern rationalism. Moltmann, in his *Theology of Hope*, works to disengage Christian theology from its synthesis with Greek philosophy by contrasting Parmenides' God of presence with the biblical God of the promise.[29]

[T]he God who reveals himself in Jesus must be thought of as the God of the Old Testament, as the God of the exodus and promise, as the God with "future as his essential nature," and therefore must not be identified with the Greek view of God, with Parmenides' "eternal present" of Being, with Plato's highest Idea and with the Unmoved Mover of Aristotle, not even in his attributes ... The God of the exodus and of the resurrection "is" not eternal presence, but he promises his presence and nearness to him who follows the path on which he is sent into the future.[30]

Moltmann admits that "Parmenides' concept of God has thrust its way deeply indeed into Christian theology," but he also asserts that this God of Parmenides, the eternal present of Being, is alien to the biblical representation of God.

Nietzsche, Heidegger and Derrida all attack the God of Greek metaphysics, but they only discuss the Christian God after His image has been perverted by Greek conceptuality. Both metaphysics and post-structuralist thought "beyond" metaphysics have forgotten the God of the Bible and have remembered only the god of metaphysics.

I am in many ways indebted to the work of Paul Ricoeur in the formulation of my project of recovering the biblical *kerygma* which has been "forgotten" in ontotheology. Ricoeur has argued that in the hermeneutics of suspicion, "only one path has been decisively closed off, that of an ontotheology."[31] He has emphasized the "positive good [of] the critique of ethics and religion that has been undertaken by the school of suspicion,"[32] arguing that we must pass through the modern hermeneutics of suspicion in order to formulate a hermeneutics of recovery, in order to recover the biblical proclamation. Similarly, I recognize the value of working through the postmodern critique of ontotheology, for my confrontation with postmodern theory has helped me to disengage biblical theology from ontotheology.

A similar confrontation of biblical theology with Marxism, and even more pressing at this time, feminism, is needed. Just as my confrontation with postmodern theory has helped me to disengage biblical theology from ontotheologies, so will a confrontation with Marxism lead to a disengagement of biblical theology from ideologies of individualism and self-reliance (and especially in America this will help us to differentiate between Christianity and conservative politics). A confrontation with feminism will lead to a disengagement of biblical theology from sexist ideologies which forget that in the kingdom of God there is "neither male nor female" (Galatians 3:28). Moltmann defines one of the tasks of a Christian critical theory as "the critical disestablishment of Christianity from bourgeois religions of the particular societies in which that theism has predominated."[33] However, as in our confrontation with postmodern theory, we must show not only the validity but also the limits of Marxist and feminist critiques of religion, in so far as these critiques are informed by modern, Enlightenment and postmodern, post-structuralist rejections of theology.

Christian thought must not let postmodern theory guide its critique: it should be guided by a hermeneutics of faith, which in turn must be guided by biblical revelation. A Christian critical theory must not only confront the hermeneutics of suspicion articulated by the "masters of suspicion." It must also turn its own hermeneutics of suspicion upon these "masters." Ricoeur has called for this critique as well, arguing that in the turning-point from deconstruction to reinterpretation, there "is again a destruction, but a destruction of what destroys, a de-construction of the assurances of modern man."[34] In order to turn to the positive task of a hermeneutics of faith, the hermeneutics of suspicion must be directed not only against Christianity, but also against the modern and postmodern masters of suspicion.

While I am greatly indebted to Ricoeur's example in his attempt to formulate a hermeneutics of recovery of the biblical *kerygma*, I believe Ricoeur grants too much power to the atheistic critique of religion in his confrontation with modern philosophy. In "Religion, Atheism, and Faith," Ricoeur argues that the Christian philosopher must go through atheism in order to achieve a "postreligious faith." While I agree that atheistic philosophy can be used as a tool in differentiating religion and faith, it is not atheism which "makes possible" a postreligious faith.[35] Only a hermeneutics that begins with faith can use the atheistic critique of religion as a means to recover a biblical faith. And, as Ricoeur himself notes elsewhere, the critique of religion in Nietzsche, Marx, and Freud is anticipated in the prophetic teachings of the Bible.[36] Why not draw upon this prophetic critique of religion rather than the modern, atheistic critique of religion?

Ricoeur writes that atheism must mediate between religion and faith in his work because he, as a philosopher "remains suspended between atheism and faith."[37] Ricoeur is accepting Heidegger's version of the separation between philosophy and theology. He admits that the philosopher (not only the Christian philosopher) shouldn't/can't bracket "what he believes, for how could he philosophize in such a state of abstraction with respect to what is essential?" Nevertheless, he believes that, as a philosopher, he must work "within the limits of reason alone."[38] But to accept this Kantian limitation is in my view a grave mistake. Christian thought should make use of biblical revelation and faith in the articulation of a Christian critical theory.

While Ricoeur argues persuasively that faith must be based upon a "renewed interpretation of the sign-events reported by Scripture, such as the Exodus in the Old Testament and the Resurrection in the New Testament," he believes that the philosopher must take the "long detour" through Heidegger's "'fundamental analysis of Dasein.'"[39] Against this view I reiterate that Heidegger's *Holzwege*, his pathways in the forest, are a dead-end which leave one lost in the woods.

Despite my disagreement with him on his use of Heidegger, Ricoeur is nevertheless right to call for the "preacher" (even if he denies this to the philosopher) to follow the biblical iconoclasts who destroy idols in "the expectation and hearing of a kerygma."[40] This is what is missing from postmodern theory. When questioned whether his work is in some way "prophetic in its attempt to deconstruct philosophy," Derrida responds:

Unfortunately, I do not feel inspired by any sort of hope which would permit me to presume that my work of deconstruction has a prophetic function ... The fact that I declare it "unfortunate" that I do not personally feel inspired may be a signal that deep down I still hope. It means that I am in fact still looking for something.[41]

It is unfortunate that Derrida is not inspired by any hope but only by the gay affirmation of Nietzsche's atheism; nevertheless, it is hopeful that Derrida, if only for a moment, feels a lack, considers the possibility that he is, we are, still looking for something.

I have tried to begin to seek the God of the Bible, as He is expressed in the biblical revelation of the cross of Christ, and also as the theology of the cross is recovered in the great tradition of theology represented by thinkers such as Luther, Pascal, Kierkegaard, Barth, and Moltmann. These thinkers have attempted to recover a faith in the biblical God through a reversal of the direction of ontotheology. Luther effected this reversal in his destruction of Scholastic theology built upon Aristotle's philosophy; Kierkegaard effected this reversal in his critique of speculative theology built upon the idealism of Hegel; and Barth effected this reversal against the liberal, existential theology of his age. Barth describes the abiding concern of his theological project:

my thinking ... is unchanged in this, that *not* so-called "religion" is its object, its source, and its criterion, but rather, as far as it can be my intention, *the Word of God* ... The Word of God which is the mystery of God in his relation to man and not, as the term "religion" seems to imply, the mystery of man in his relation to God. I hope that I have been able to faithfully testify to the possibility and hope of such a reversal.[42]

Only through a return to this insight, this reversal, will Christian theology be revitalized while remaining faithful to its source. Only in this way will the distinctiveness of the Judaeo-Christian revelation be preserved and will Christianity have a voice with which to confront and criticize its own theology and the philosophy of the age.

In my introduction I defined ontotheology as theology based upon human imaginings about God. Thus ontotheology is the result of our attempt to formulate an understanding of god rather than the result of God's revelation toward us. But, as Paul told the philosophers at Athens, "we should not think that the divine being is . . . an image made by man's design or skill" (Acts 17:29).

Atheism, the denial of god, is built upon the same presupposition as ontotheology, that we are able of ourselves to know about God, even if we only know that he is nothing but an illusion. But Christian theology which remains faithful to biblical revelation "completely reverses the direction of that theology: it is not the ascent of man to God but the revelation of God in his self-emptying in the crucified Christ"[43] which is the "essence of Christianity." We *should*, therefore, vanquish god's shadow, the shadow god created by human reason and imagination, that we might seek the revelation of the living God in the cross of Christ.

The theology of the cross pronounces an either/or: either biblical revelation or philosophical speculation. The same either/or must be proclaimed to the present age: either biblical theology or postmodern theory. Only as a theology of the cross will Christianity recover its prophetic voice. Only then will Ricoeur's hope for a "prophetic preacher," who "would be able to make a radical return to the origins of Jewish and Christian faith, and, at the same time, make of this return an event which speaks to our own time," begin to be realized.[44]

Notes

INTRODUCTION: POSTMODERNISM, ONTOTHEOLOGY, AND
CHRISTIANITY

1 Jean-François Lyotard, *The Postmodern Condition: A Report on Knowledge*,
trans. Geoff Bennington and Brian Massumi (Minneapolis: University
of Minnesota Press, 1984).
2 Eric Auerbach, *Mimesis*, trans. Willard R. Trask (Princeton University
Press, 1974) 15.
3 *Ibid*. 15–16.
4 Hans Frei, *The Eclipse of Biblical Narrative* (New Haven: Yale University
Press, 1974) 6.
5 René Descartes, *Meditations on First Philosophy*, trans. Donald A. Cress
(Indianapolis: Hackett Publishing Company, 1979) 1.
6 Ludwig Feuerbach, *The Essence of Christianity*, trans. George Eliot (New
York: Harper & Row, 1957) 38.
7 *Ibid*. 26.
8 I take this well-known terminology from Paul Ricoeur. See "The
Critique of Religion," *The Philosophy of Paul Ricoeur*, ed. Charles E.
Reagan and David Stewart (Boston, Massachusetts: Beacon Press,
1978) 213–222.
9 Feuerbach, *The Essence of Christianity* 35.
10 *Ibid*. 38.
11 Jürgen Moltmann, *Theology of Hope*, trans. James W. Leitch (1975; New
York: HarperCollins Publishers, 1991) 171.
12 Karl Barth, *The Christian Life*, trans. Geoffrey W. Bromiley (Grand
Rapids, Michigan: William B. Eerdmans Publishing Company, 1981)
128.
13 Roland Barthes, "The Death of the Author," *Image-Music-Text*, trans.
Stephen Heath (New York: Hill and Wang, 1977) 147.
14 Michel Foucault, "What Is an Author?" *Language, Counter-Memory,
Practice*, trans. Donald F. Bouchard and Sherry Simon, ed. Donald F.
Bouchard, (Ithaca, New York: Cornell University Press, 1986) 120.
15 Kevin Hart's assertion, in his preface to *The Trespass of the Sign* (Cambridge University Press, 1989), that "deconstruction is not an attack

against theology" is therefore not correct. In postmodern theory, it is not only mysticism "which must at all costs be excluded from philosophical discourse," but any sort of theology, including negative theology. Hart is right in asserting that "deconstruction's target is metaphysics," but theology is regarded in postmodern theory as part and parcel of ontotheological metaphysics.

16 Richard Kearney, *Dialogues with Contemporary Continental Thinkers* (Manchester University Press, 1984) 117.

17 See Kevin Hart, *The Trespass of the Sign* 96–104. Here Hart discusses the possibilities of "non-metaphysical theologies." He argues that there are "two principal ways in which a theology can be non-metaphysical: by claiming a decisive rift between the God of metaphysics and the God of faith; and by elaborating a theology which works between them." Hart takes the latter course and in these passages criticizes the tradition which I am following, a tradition he identifies with the works of St. Paul, Tertullian, St. Augustine, Luther, Pascal, Kierkegaard, and Barth.

Mark C. Taylor, in his *Tears*, (New York: SUNY Press, 1990) 75, identifies a similar division between Hegel and Kierkegaard who "represent the two poles between which the most creative philosophical and theological thinking throughout this century has oscillated." He sees Kierkegaard's tradition continuing in the twentieth century with Karl Barth and Hegel's tradition continuing in Altizer. Taylor claims to "stake out a position *between* these two major figures" by turning to the writings of Derrida.

In this study I seek to defend the tradition rejected by two of the best recent commentators on the relation between postmodern theory and theology, the tradition which posits a rift between Christian theology and Western philosophy, rather than trying to accommodate the former to the latter.

18 Karl Barth, *Die christliche Dogmatik in Entwurf*, I, *Die Lehre vom Worte Gottes, Prolegomena zur christlichen Dogmatik* (Munich: Chr. Kaiser Verlag, 1927) 403, as quoted in David L. Mueller, *Karl Barth* (Peabody, Massachusetts: Hendrickson Publishers, 1972) 35–36.

19 We do not, despite our inability to completely separate biblical theology from ontotheology, need to opt for a postmodern conception of the "jewgreek," as John D. Caputo calls for in his recent work, *Demythologizing Heidegger* (Bloomington: Indiana University Press, 1993). This is merely to create a postmodern ontotheology.

1 THE DEATH OF GOD: LOSS OF BELIEF IN THE CHRISTIAN GOD AS THE CAUSE OF NIHILISM

1 Henry L. Mencken, *The Philosophy of Friedrich Nietzsche* (Boston: Luce and Company, 1908) 128.

2 René Girard, "Dionysus versus the Crucified," *Modern Language Notes* 99.4 (September 1984): 816.

3 G. Wilson Knight, *Christ and Nietzsche* (London: Staples Press, 1970) 215.

4 Thomas J. J. Altizer, *The Gospel of Christian Atheism* (Philadelphia: The Westminster Press, 1966). See especially 55–61 and 147–157.

5 *Ibid.* 61.

6 *Ibid.* 151.

7 Karl Jaspers, *Nietzsche and Christianity*, trans. E. B. Ashton (Henry Regnery Company, 1967) viii.

8 *Ibid.* 7.

9 I am alluding here to *Thus Spoke Zarathustra* where Zarathustra asserts that Jesus "died too early" and that "he himself would have recanted his teaching had he reached my age" (Z "On Free Death" 73). See also "The Voluntary Beggar" in part IV of *Zarathustra* where Jesus, "the sermonizer on the mount," "kissed the hands of the man to whom he was talking [Zarathustra] and his eyes welled over, and he behaved exactly as one to whom a precious gift and treasure falls unexpectedly from the sky" (Z 269).

10 Karl Löwith, *From Hegel to Nietzsche*, trans. David E. Green (New York: Holt, Rinehart and Winston, 1964) 179.

11 Hans-Georg Gadamer, "The Drama of Zarathustra," trans. Thomas Heilke, *Nietzsche's New Seas*, ed. Michael Gillespie and Tracy Strong (University of Chicago Press, 1988) 221.

12 Jaspers, *Nietzsche and Christianity* 97–99.

13 Walter Kaufmann, *Nietzsche: Philosopher, Psychologist, Antichrist* (1950; Princeton University Press, 1968) xv.

14 *Ibid.* 231.

15 *Ibid.* 270.

16 *Ibid.* 270.

17 *Ibid.* 270.

18 "Nietzsche's repudiation of Christ cannot be understood – any more than Kierkegaard's *Attack on Christendom* – unless one distinguishes between contemporary Christianity and the original gospel" (*Ibid.* 337).

19 *Ibid.* 363–364.

20 Girard, "Dionysius versus the Crucified" 816.

21 *Ibid.* 817.

22 Heidegger concludes this sentence by stating that Nietzsche's attack on Christendom is not an attack upon what is Christian "any more than a critique of theology is necessarily a critique of faith, whose interpretation theology is said to be." Heidegger is here denying that his own project, in which he is critical of theology, is an attack upon Christian faith. The accuracy of this self-assessment will be questioned in part two of my study.

23 See Heidegger (*N* I 159–160).

24 Compare this reading with Eugene Biser's which interprets this passage as an attack on the ontological argument for God's existence. He reads the madman as "a counterpart to the 'fool' in Anselm's argument in the *Prosologion*." "Nietzsche: Critic in the Grand Style," trans. Timothy F. Sellner, *Studies in Nietzsche and the Judaeo-Christian Tradition*, ed. James C. O'Flaherty, Timothy F. Sellner, and Robert M. Helm (Chapel Hill: The University of North Carolina Press, 1985) 24.

25 Eric von der Luft, "Sources of Nietzsche's 'God is Dead!' and Its Meaning for Heidegger," *Journal of History of Ideas* 45.2 (April–June 1984): 263.

26 Hans Küng, *Does God Exist?*, trans. Edward Quinn (Garden City, New York: Doubleday & Company, 1980) 371.

27 See for example Eugene Biser, "The Critical Imitator of Jesus," trans. Timothy F. Sellner, *Studies in Nietzsche and the Judaeo-Christian Tradition* 92–93. It seems clear that Nietzsche, like Heidegger, fell away from an early faith in Christianity. A year after writing a poem in which he writes of God calling him to Himself and his desire to "come gladly" in response, Nietzsche writes a satirical poem "Before the Crucifix" in which he, in Biser's words, "challenges the Crucified One half-mockingly, half-pityingly to climb down from His 'martyr's-stake' in order together with him to come 'down to earth.'" Here we see the beginning of Nietzsche's critique of Christianity's belief in a true, transcendent realm.

Küng traces a similar loss of faith in Nietzsche, also through an analysis of a youthful poem. Küng, *Does God Exist?* 352–355.

28 See numbers 4–7 in Nietzsche's outline in the first note of *The Will To Power* for one of his many critiques of this secularization of the Christian-moral interpretation.

29 Jürgen Moltmann, *Theology of Hope* 170.

30 But Plato's philosopher-ruler, after being compelled to leave the dark of the cave for the light of the fire and then the sun, is then compelled to return to the cave in order to distinguish between shadows and reality for those still trapped in the cave. No such humanitarian impulse appears to guide Nietzsche's overmen.

2 VANQUISHING GOD'S REALM: NIETZSCHE'S ABOLITION OF THE TRUE WORLD

1 See *WP* 4 for Nietzsche's summary of "the advantages of the Christian moral hypothesis."

2 See especially volume IV of Heidegger's *Nietzsche* on nihilism.

3 See Girard, "Dionysus versus the Crucified" 18: "Now that we are no longer limited to the excerpts carefully selected and organized by Nietzsche's sister, and we can read all of the formerly unpublished writing, we cannot doubt that the closer we get to the end the more

obsessive the Christian theme becomes with Nietzsche. The number and importance of the fragments dealing with the subject increase." The same can be said of Nietzsche's published works, especially *The Antichrist* and *Ecce Homo*. In the latter work, Nietzsche tends to read his entire œuvre as a repudiation of Christianity.

4 Bernd Magnus, *Nietzsche's Existential Imperative* (Bloomington: Indiana University Press, 1978) 9.

5 Magnus, *Nietzsche's Existential Imperative* 9.

6 Note how Nietzsche's vision of the ideal society is similar to Plato's. Both exalt a noble class over the lower classes whose only function is to serve this higher class.

7 Notice, however, that the logic of the unmasking of the true world as an error begins only after the secularization of the idea in Kant. Only after Kant's reduction of the true world to an "unknown *x*" can Nietzsche begin to write "consequently" in describing the progressive refutation of the idea. Thus, while Nietzsche claims to have abolished all true worlds, he gives reasons for abolishing only the true world of modern metaphysics.

8 Maudemarie Clark, *Nietzsche On Truth and Philosophy* (Cambridge University Press, 1990) 97.

9 Jaspers, *Nietzsche and Christianity* 6.

3 NIETZSCHE ON THE JUDAEO–CHRISTIAN DENIAL OF THE WORLD

1 Feuerbach, *The Essence of Christianity* xl.

2 *Ibid.* 26.

3 *Harrap's New Collegiate French and English Dictionary*, ed. Peter Collin, et al. (London: Harrap, 1982).

4 Küng, *Does God Exist?* 403.

5 See Feuerbach, *The Essence of Christianity* 13. "But when religion – consciousness of God – is designated as the self-consciousness of man, this is not to be understood as affirming that the religious man is directly aware of this identity; for, on the contrary, ignorance of it is fundamental to the peculiar nature of religion."

6 *Ibid.* 13.

7 Jürgen Moltmann, *The Crucified God*, trans. R. A. Wilson and John Bowden (1974; New York: SCM Press; New York: HarperCollins Publishers, 1991) 251.

8 I have referred above to Heidegger and Biser's interpretations of the madman's proclamation as referring to the god of ontotheology. Ricoeur makes the same claim in "Religion, Atheism, and Faith," trans. Charles Freilich, *The Conflict of Interpretations*, ed. Don Ihde (Evanston, Illinois: Northwestern University Press, 1974) 445:

Which god is dead? We can now reply: the god of metaphysics and also the god of theology, insofar as theology rests on the metaphysics of the first cause, necessary being, and the prime mover, conceived as the source of values and as the absolute good. Let us say the god of onto-theology, to use the expression that was coined by Heidegger, following Kant.

9 Küng, *Does God Exist?* 372.
10 Feuerbach, *The Essence of Christianity* 21.
11 Nietzsche either ignores other passages from the gospels which view the kingdom of God as the coming reign of God on earth or misreads them as the expression of the disciples' *ressentiment*. See the following section on New Testament eschatology.
12 Nietzsche's allusion to Constantine's call to conquer *"in hoc signo"* is doubly ironic when it is recalled that this can be considered the moment when "master" or worldly power took over the sign of the cross for its own purposes. Nietzsche reads this moment as the triumph of slave morality over master morality or the triumph of Judea over Rome, but it is actually the appropriation of Christian morality by a worldly, political power or the triumph of Rome over Judeao-Christianity.
13 Arthur Schopenhauer, "On Affirmation and Denial of the Will to Live," *Arthur Schopenhauer: Essays and Aphorisms*, trans. and ed. R. J. Hollingdale (Middlesex, England: Penguin Books Ltd., 1970) 63.
14 Schopenhauer, "On the Suffering of the World," *Essays and Aphorisms* 49.
15 *Ibid.* 49.
16 Schopenhauer, "On Religion," *Essays and Aphorisms* 191.
17 Schopenhauer, *The World as Will and Representation*, trans. E. F. J. Payne (New York: Dover Publications, Inc., 1969) 412.
18 Schopenhauer, "On Affirmation and Denial of the Will to Live," *Essays and Aphorisms* 62.
19 Feuerbach, *The Essence of Christianity* xxxvi.
20 *Ibid.* 161.
21 *Ibid.* 162.
22 *Ibid.* 308.
23 *Ibid.* 309.
24 *Ibid.* 310.
25 Reinhold Niebuhr, *Beyond Tragedy: Essays on the Christian Interpretation of History* (New York: Charles Scribner's Sons, 1937) 188.
26 Schopenhauer, "On the Suffering of the World," *Essays and Aphorisms* 48.
27 Schopenhauer, "On Religion," *Essays and Aphorisms* 190–191.
28 George Eldon Ladd, *The Pattern of New Testament Truth* (Grand Rapids, Michigan: William B. Eerdmans Publishing Company, 1968) 14.

4 THE REDEMPTIVE–ESCHATOLOGICAL SEPARATION BETWEEN
THE PRESENT WORLD AND THE WORLD TO COME IN THE NEW
TESTAMENT

1 Küng, *Does God Exist?* 405.
2 This note is also instructive to those who too quickly absolve Nietzsche of anti-Semitism. Nietzsche blames the baseness and mendaciousness of the New Testament on the fact that it was written by Jews.
3 Walter Kaufmann, preface, *The Antichrist* in *The Portable Nietzsche* (New York: Penguin Books, 1982) 568.
4 Niebuhr, *Beyond Tragedy* 21–22.
5 Schopenhauer, "On Religion," *Essays and Aphorisms* 184.
6 *Ibid.* 186.
7 I refer here to Jesus' teaching as recorded in the gospels. Despite the numerous attempts, including Nietzsche's, to discover the "historical" or "psychological type of the redeemer" behind the gospels, the gospels remain our only source concerning the person, life, teachings, and self-representation of Jesus of Nazareth. All attempts to go "behind" the gospels, to cut through the supposed reinterpretation of Jesus by his disciples, are based upon unfounded speculation. Either the gospels present a reliable witness of Jesus or Jesus has been lost to us.
8 See Rudolf Bultmann, *Theology of the New Testament*, I, trans. Kendrick Grobel (New York: Charles Scribner's Sons, 1951) 254.
9 See Max Scheler, *Ressentiment*, trans. William W. Holdheim, ed. Lewis A. Coser (New York: Free Press of Glencoe, 1961) 94, and Moltmann, *The Crucified God* 267–290, for elaborations of the distinction between the Greek view of God as apathetic and the biblical view of God as personal and capable of feelings toward his creation.
10 H. Sasse, "World," *Theological Dictionary of the New Testament*, trans. and abridged Geoffrey W. Bromiley, ed. Gerhard Kittel and Gerhard Friedrich (Grand Rapids, Michigan: William B. Eerdmans Publishing Company, 1985) 463.
11 Karl Barth, *Witness to the Word: A Commentary on John 1*, trans. Geoffrey W. Bromiley, ed. Walter Furst (Grand Rapids, Michigan: William B. Eerdmans Publishing Company, 1986) 62.
12 For a further discussion of gnostic dualism see Hans Conzelmann and Andreas Lindemann, *Interpreting the New Testament: An Introduction to the Principles and Methods of N.T. Exegesis*, trans. Siegfried S. Schatzmann (Peabody, Massachusetts: Hendrickson Publishers, 1988) 149–157 and Hans Jonas, *The Gnostic Religion: The Message of the Alien God and the Beginnings of Christianity* (Boston, Massachusetts: Beacon Press, 1963) 42–46.
13 C. F. D. Moule, *Essays in New Testament Interpretation* (Cambridge University Press, 1982) 201.
14 For a study of the Hebraic term *'olam* in the OT and its influence on

Paul, see Geerhardus Vos, *The Pauline Eschatology* (Grand Rapids, Michigan: Baker Book House, 1979) 17.

15 Bultmann, *Theology of the New Testament*, I: 256.

16 Oscar Cullman, *Christ and Time: The Primitive Christian Conception of Time and History*, trans. Floyd V. Filson (Philadelphia: Westminster Press, 1964) 47.

17 Everett Ferguson, "The Kingdom of God in Early Patristic Literature," in *The Kingdom of God in 20th-Century Interpretation*, ed. Wendell Willis (Peabody, Massachusetts: Hendrickson Publishers, 1987) 192 and 200.

18 Cullman, *Christ and Time* 54.

19 Sasse, "World" 464.

20 *Ibid.* 464.

21 Although there is a debate over whether Paul is the (sole) author of the later epistles, that these letters are "Pauline" is sufficient for my purposes.

22 J. Christiaan Beker, *Paul the Apostle: The Triumph of God in Life and Thought* (Philadelphia: Fortress Press, 1984) 149.

23 Andrew T. Lincoln, *Paradise Now and Not Yet: Studies in the Role of the Heavenly Dimension in Paul's Thought with Special Reference to His Eschatology* (Grand Rapids, Michigan: Baker Book House, 1991) 5.

24 Lincoln cites F. C. Porter, C. H. Dodd, and T. Boman as examples of this type of interpretation. See *Paradise Now and Not Yet* 181. See also Hans Conzelmann, *An Outline of the Theology of the New Testament* (New York: Harper & Row Publishers, 1969) 310.

25 Lincoln, *Paradise Now and Not Yet* 174.

26 For a summary of the debate see F. F. Bruce, *New International Biblical Commentary: Philippians*, XI, ed. W. Ward Gasque (Peabody, Massachusetts: Hendrickson Publishers, 1989) 131.

27 *Ibid.* 130.

28 Homer A. Kent, Jr., "Philippians," *The Expositor's Bible Commentary*, XI (Ephesians–Philemon), ed. Frank E. Gaebelein (Grand Rapids, Michigan: Zondervan Publishing House, 1978) 147.

29 Lincoln, *Paradise Now and Not Yet* 96.

30 *Ibid.* 97.

31 This is why it can be misleading to use the term "fall" to describe the Genesis narrative of humanity's alienation from God. The Old Testament uses the term "fall" in a moral rather than a cosmological sense, so the term can be used with caution to describe the biblical understanding of the origin of humanity's sinful existence.

32 Kent, "Philippians" 148.

33 Bruce, *Philippians* 133 and Kent, "Philippians" 147.

34 See Pheme Perkins, "Philippians: Theology for the Heavenly Politeuma," *Pauline Theology*, I: *Thessalonians, Philippians, Galatians, Philemon*, ed. Jouette M. Bassler (Minneapolis: Fortress Press, 1991) 102.

35 Beker, *Paul the Apostle* 255.
36 Lincoln, *Paradise Now and Not Yet* 7.
37 See Arthur G. Patzia, *New International Biblical Commentary: Ephesians, Colossians, Philemon*, x: 4–7, for a summary of the elements in the syncretistic religious system which Paul opposes in Colossians.
38 Curtis Vaughan, "Colossians," *The Expositor's Bible Commentary*, xi: 167.
39 *Ibid.* 167.
40 Lincoln, *Paradise Now and Not Yet* 120.
41 *Ibid.* 193.
42 *Ibid.* 127.
43 Plato, "Phaedo," *The Dialogues of Plato*, trans. R. S. Bluck (New York: Bantam Books, 1986) 93.
44 Rudolf Bultmann, *Primitive Christianity in Its Contemporary Setting*, trans. Reverend R. H. Fuller (1956; New York: New American Library, 1974) 197. See Donald Guthrie, *New Testament Theology* (Grand Rapids, Michigan: Intervarsity Press, 1981) 130–134 for a critique of Bultmann's view and a summary of the debate.
45 Barth, *Witness to the Word* 65.
46 Dodd, *The Interpretation of the Fourth Gospel* 295.
47 George Eldon Ladd, *A Theology of the New Testament* (Grand Rapids, Michigan: William B. Eerdmans, 1991) 232.
48 Dodd, *The Interpretation of the Fourth Gospel* 146.
49 Ladd, *The Pattern of New Testament Truth* 67.
50 Dodd, *The Interpretation of the Fourth Gospel* 74.
51 Bultmann, *Theology of the New Testament*, ii: 6.
52 Dodd, *The Interpretation of the Fourth Gospel* 98.
53 Bultmann, *Primitive Christianity* 196ff.
54 *Ibid.* 178.
55 *Ibid.* 194–195.
56 Rudolf Bultmann, "New Testament and Mythology: The Problem of Demythologizing the New Testament Proclamation," *New Testament and Mythology*, trans. and ed. Schubert M. Ogden (Philadelphia: Fortress Press, 1984) 16.
57 Bultmann, *Primitive Christianity* 196.
58 Gerhard von Rad, *Old Testament Theology*, ii, *The Theology of Israel's Prophetic Traditions*, trans. D. M. G. Stalker (New York: Harper and Row Publishers, 1965) 353–354.
59 Bultmann, *Primitive Christianity* 186.
60 Hans Blumenberg, *The Legitimacy of the Modern Age*, trans. Robert M. Wallace (Cambridge, Massachusetts: The MIT Press, 1983) 41.
61 Bultmann, *New Testament and Mythology* 20.
62 Cullman, *Christ and Time* 27.
63 Paul Ricoeur, "Freedom in the Light of Hope," *The Conflict of Interpretations* 407.
64 Amos N. Wilder, *Eschatology and Ethics in the Teaching of Jesus* (1939; Westport, Connecticut: Greenwood Press Publishers, 1950) 9.

65 Bultmann, *New Testament and Mythology* 5.
66 Wendell Willis, "The Discovery of the Eschatological Kingdom: Johannes Weiss and Albert Schweitzer," *The Kingdom of God in 20th-Century Interpretation* 2.
67 *Ibid.* 3.
68 Richard H. Hiers, Jr., "Pivotal Reactions to the Eschatological Interpretations: Rudolf Bultmann and C. H. Dodd," *The Kingdom of God in 20th-Century Interpretation* 32.
69 E. Earle Ellis, *Paul and His Recent Interpreters* (Grand Rapids, Michigan: William B. Eerdmans Publishing Company. 1961) 31.
70 Beker, *Paul the Apostle* 157–58.
71 Werner Georg Kümmel, *Promise and Fulfillment: The Eschatological Message of Jesus* (London: SCM Press, 1961) 148.
72 George Eldon Ladd, *The Presence of the Future: The Eschatology of Biblical Realism* (Grand Rapids, Michigan: William B. Eerdmans Publishing Company, 1981) 218.
73 Niebuhr, *Beyond Tragedy* 4.
74 *Ibid.* 4.
75 Moltmann, *The Theology of Hope* 16.
76 Jürgen Moltmann *Theology Today*, trans. John Bowden (Philadelphia: Trinity Press International, 1988) 23.
77 Dietrich Bonhoeffer, *Letters and Papers from Prison*, ed. Eberhard Bethge (1953; New York: SCM Press, 1972) 336.

5 ON REDEMPTION: THE ETERNAL RETURN OR BIBLICAL ESCHATOLOGY

1 Kathleen Higgins, *Nietzsche's* Zarathustra (Philadelphia: Temple University Press, 1987) 100.
2 Laurence Lampert, *Nietzsche's Teaching: An Interpretation of* Thus Spoke Zarathustra (New Haven: Yale University Press, 1986) 248. See also Higgins, *Nietzsche's* Zarathustra 73. Despite my objection to Lampert's emphasis, I am nevertheless indebted to his fine study of *Thus Spoke Zarathustra*.
3 For treatments of this question in German see Fritz Martini, *Das Wagnis der Sprache* (Stuttgart: Klett, 1954) 33–34 and Johannes Klein, *Die Dichtung Nietzsches* (München: Beck, 1936) 112 (as noted in Donald F. Nelson, "Nietzsche, Zarathustra, and *Jesus Redivivus*: The Unholy Trinity," *The Germanic Review* 48 (1973): 175.)
4 Nietzsche's call for a method of "breeding and selection" of which "races ... are chosen to rule" (*WP* 1053) should no longer be exonerated as "metaphorical" and unrelated to its use in Nazi propaganda. See Bruce Detweiler, *Nietzsche and the Politics of Aristocratic Radicalism* (University of Chicago Press, 1990) for an excellent and long overdue critique of this aspect of Nietzsche's thought.

5 On the *Heilsgeschichte* of the Bible and on Christ as the midpoint of this history see Cullman, *Christ and Time*, especially 27 and 107.

6 Both Laurence Hatab, *Nietzsche and Eternal Recurrence: The Redemption of Time and Becoming* (Washington, D.C.: University Press of America, 1978), and Karl Löwith, *Meaning in History* (University of Chicago Press, 1949), agree that Nietzsche combines elements from the linear view of time with his cyclical view of time. Hatab sees Nietzsche's "valuing of the moment as such, i.e. *this* moment, and not merely the cyclic repetition, the 'copying' of an archetypal past" as the result of a "'synthesis' of the cyclic and linear views of time" in Nietzsche's thought (127). Löwith sees Nietzsche's continued reliance on the biblical view of history and biblical eschatology in his emphasis upon "the thought of the *future* and the *will* to create it" (221).

7 Löwith, *Meaning in History* 220. Heidegger makes similar arguments about Nietzsche's project. For example in a commentary on *WP* 916, Heidegger objects to Nietzsche's description of his own philosophy as paganism, for "anything 'pagan' is always still something Christian – the counter-Christian" (*N* I 5).

8 Magnus, *Nietzsche's Existential Imperative* 159.

9 Löwith, *Meaning in History* 217.

10 Magnus, *Nietzsche's Existential Imperative* 142.

11 For the emphasis upon this interpretation, see, in addition to Magnus, Alexander Nehamas, *Nietzsche: Life as Literature* (Cambridge, Massachusetts: Harvard University Press, 1985).

12 Magnus, *Nietzsche's Existential Imperative* xiv.

13 *Ibid.* 213, note 9.

14 Recall my use of Niebuhr's statement, in the previous chapter, that, in Christianity, "Salvation lies at the end of history and not in some realm of eternity above history."

On the meaning of "eternal" in the Bible, as opposed to Greek metaphysics, as "endless time" see Cullman, *Christ and Time*: "eternity whenever it is taken into consideration [in the Bible], is not to be interpreted in the Platonic and modern philosophical sense ... it does not signify cessation of time or timelessness. It means rather endless time and therefore an ongoing of time incomprehensible to men ... Thus in the New Testament field it is not time and eternity that stand opposed, but limited time and unlimited, endless time" (46–47).

15 Lampert, *Nietzsche's Teaching* 257.

16 Ironically, it is the cyclical view of time which led to the devaluation of time and becoming in Greek philosophy: "Redemption in Hellenism can consist only in the fact that we are transferred from existence in this world, an existence bound to the circular course of time, into that Beyond which is removed from time and is already and always available. The Greek conception of blessedness is thus spatial; it is determined by the contrast between this world and the timeless Beyond" (Cullman, *Christ and Time* 52).

17 Hatab, *Nietzsche and Eternal Recurrence* 126–127.

18 Nietzsche explains how willing the future redeems the past in a couple of passages: "I taught them to work on the future and to redeem with their creation all that *has been*. To redeem what is past in man and to re-create all 'it was' until the will says, 'Thus I willed it! Thus I shall will it!' – that I called redemption and this alone I taught them to call redemption" (*Z* 198). "In your children you shall make up for being the children of your fathers; thus you shall redeem all that is past" (*Z* 204).

19 Higgins, *Nietzsche's* Zarathustra 174.

20 Lampert, *Nietzsche's Teaching* 3.

21 *Ibid.* 212.

22 "By naming the last chapter of the last part 'The Seven Seals,' Nietzsche ends his own sixty-six chapters by invoking the sixty-sixth and final book of the Bible, thereby signaling the passing of what was once a new testament ... The eschatological symbolism of the Bible is also reflected in the marriage that ends *Zarathustra*, for the final event in the book of *Revelation* is the marriage of the victorious, imperial Christ to the purified Church, the New Jerusalem" (*Ibid.* 240–241).

23 For this type of celebration of postmodernism, see Zygmunt Bauman, "Postmodernity, or Living with Ambivalence," in *A Postmodern Reader*, ed. Joseph Natoli and Linda Hutcheon (New York: SUNY Press, 1993).

24 And is Nietzsche's philosophy, which calls for a recovery of the natural instinct "to be master over all men," so far removed from the Nazi appropriation of his thought?

25 On this contrast see also Higgins, "Eternal Recurrence Versus the Doctrine of Sin," *Nietzsche's* Zarathustra 159–202.

6 FROM THE DEATH OF GOD TO THE FORGETTING OF BEING

1 Laurence Lampert, "Heidegger's Nietzsche Interpretation," *Man and World* 7 (1974): 357.

2 Hans-Georg Gadamer, *Heidegger's Ways*, trans. John W. Stanley (Albany: SUNY Press, 1994) 164 and 167. Gadamer goes on to write that "it is a completely different question to ask whether the claims made on Heidegger by Christian theology are justified – even though half a century has already passed in which Christian theologians have been turning to Heidegger's thought" (167). I want to emphasize that the claims made *by* Heidegger *on* Christianity are *not* justified.

3 Martin Heidegger, *History of the Concept of Time, Prolegomena*, trans. Theodore Kisiel (Bloomington: Indiana University Press, 1985) 80.

4 Cf. section 58 of Husserl's *Ideas: General Introduction to Phenomenology*, trans. W. R. Boyce Gibson (New York: Collier Books, 1962) where Husserl excludes the transcendence of God from phenomenological consideration.

5 Heidegger refers to Nietzsche only three times in *Being and Time*. See Bernd Magnus, *Heidegger's Metahistory of Philosophy: Amor Fati, Being and Truth* (The Hague: Martinus Nijhoff, 1970) 59, for a list of the three references. See Jacques Taminiaux, *Heidegger and the Project of Fundamental Ontology*, trans. Michael Gendre (New York: SUNY Press, 1991) for a detailed discussion of two of these references. I will be exploring one of the references in my discussion of Heidegger's concept of authentic being-towards-death below.

6 David Farrell Krell, *Intimations of Mortality: Time, Truth, and Finitude in Heidegger's Thinking of Being* (University Park: The Pennsylvania State University Press, 1986) 128–129. See also Lampert, "Heidegger's Nietzsche Interpretation" 372 and Joseph P. Lawrence, "Nietzsche and Heidegger," *History of European Ideas* 11 (1989): 712, for the influence of Nietzsche on *Being and Time*.

7 Robert B. Pippin, "Nietzsche, Heidegger, and the Metaphysics of Modernity," in *Nietzsche and Modern German Thought*, ed. Keith Ansell-Pearson (New York: Routledge, 1991) 295.

8 Hannah Arendt, *The Life of the Mind.* 2 vols. (New York: Harcourt Brace Jovanovich, 1977–78) II: 172–194.

9 See Joan Stambaugh, "Nihilism and the End of Philosophy," *Research in Phenomenology* XV (1985): 79–97, for an analysis of Heidegger's critique of Nietzsche's concept of nihilism.

10 Pippin, "Nietzsche, Heidegger" 299. Pippin cites Michael Haar's criticism of Heidegger's Nietzsche interpretation on this same basis, in "La Critique nietzscheenne de la subjectivité," *Nietzsche-Studien* 12 (1983): 86ff.

11 Descartes, *Meditations on First Philosophy* 1.

12 The death of God is perpetrated by humanity in Nietzsche, but the withdrawal of Being is caused by Being itself, a point the later Heidegger insists upon. However at the same time this withdrawal of Being causes man to omit the thought of Being itself.

7 HEIDEGGER'S THEOLOGICAL ORIGINS: FROM BIBLICAL THEOLOGY TO FUNDAMENTAL ONTOLOGY

1 Quoted in Hans-Georg Gadamer, "Being, Spirit, God," in *Heidegger Memorial Lectures*, trans. Steven W. Davis, ed. Werner Marx (Pittsburgh: Duquesne University Press, 1982) 56. See Theodore Kisiel, *The Genesis of Heidegger's* Being and Time (Berkeley: University of California Press, 1993) 78–80 for a detailed reading of Heidegger's letter to Löwith.

2 See especially Otto Pöggeler, *Martin Heidegger's Path of Thinking*, trans. Daniel Magurshak and Sigmund Barber (Atlantic Highlands, New Jersey: Humanities Press International, Inc., 1990); Thomas J. Sheehan, "Heidegger's 'Introduction to the Phenomenology of

Religion,' 1920–1921," in *A Companion to Martin Heidegger's 'Being and Time'*, ed. Joseph J. Kockelmans (Washington, D.C.: University Press of America, 1986); Theodore J. Kisiel, *The Genesis of Heidegger's* Being and Time (1993); and John van Buren, *The Young Heidegger*, forthcoming from Indiana University Press.

3 Victor Farias, *Heidegger and Nazism*, trans. Paul Burrell, ed. Joseph Margolis and Tom Rockmore (Philadelphia: Temple University Press, 1989); Hugo Ott, *Martin Heidegger: A Political Life*, trans. Allan Blunden (New York: Basic Books, 1993); and Caputo, *Demythologizing Heidegger* (1993). See also Theodore Kisiel's helpful review of Farias and Ott in "Heidegger's Apology: Biography as Philosophy and Ideology," in *The Heidegger Case: On Philosophy and Politics*, ed. Tom Rockmore and Joseph Margolis (Philadelphia: Temple University Press, 1992).

4 Ott, *Martin Heidegger* 37.

5 This analysis will have important implications concerning the failure of Heidegger's rectorship, but I can only hint at these implications in this work.

6 John Macquarrie, *An Existentialist Theology: A Comparison of Heidegger and Bultmann* (New York: Harper and Row, 1965) 240.

7 See note 2 above.

8 On Heidegger's Catholic background, see especially Ott's chapter "'The Struggle with the Faith of my Birth,'" in *Martin Heidegger* 39–121.

9 Ott, *Martin Heidegger* 97–98 and 116–119.

10 Kisiel, *The Genesis* 80.

11 From Heidegger's letter to the Freiburg theologian Krebs when resigning responsibility for the philosophical instruction for Catholic theologians. Quoted in Pöggeler, *Martin Heidegger's Path of Thinking* 265.

12 Kisiel, *The Genesis* 19.

13 Husserl's letter to Rudolf Otto as quoted in Kisiel, *The Genesis* 73.

14 See Kisiel, *The Genesis* 72–74 and 89–93, on the importance of Schleiermacher, often called "the father of liberal theology," on Heidegger's early thought.

15 Thomas J. Sheehan, "Heidegger's 'Introduction to the Phenomenology of Religion'" 40.

16 *Ibid.* 46.

17 Pöggeler, *Martin Heidegger's Path of Thinking* 25–26.

18 Kisiel, *The Genesis* 100–105.

19 Sheehan, "Heidegger's 'Introduction to the Phenomenology of Religion'" 55.

20 *Ibid.* 56–57.

21 *Ibid.* 58.

22 Søren Kierkegaard, *The Concept of Anxiety*, trans. Reidar Thomte (Princeton University Press, 1980) 82–93. I am indebted to Caputo, *Demythologizing Heidegger* 181, for this reference.

23 Michael E. Zimmerman, *The Eclipse of the Self: The Development of Heidegger's Concept of Authenticity* (Athens: Ohio University Press, 1981) 136. See also Caputo, *Demythologizing Heidegger* 181.

24 Zimmerman, *The Eclipse of the Self* 136.

25 Sheehan, "Heidegger's 'Introduction to the Phenomenology of Religion'" 57–58.

26 Caputo, *Demythologizing Heidegger* 4. Caputo is summarizing Kisiel's argument in *The Genesis* here.

27 Ricoeur, "Freedom in the Light of Hope," *The Conflict of Interpretations* 407.

28 Sheehan, "Heidegger's 'Introduction to the Phenomenology of Religion,'" 56. See also Kisiel, *The Genesis* 184–189.

29 Bruce Ballard, *The Role of Mood in Heidegger's Ontology* (New York: University Press of America, 1990) 108.

30 Sheehan, "Heidegger's 'Introduction to the Phenomenology of Religion'" 57.

31 Kisiel, *The Genesis* 186.

32 Sheehan, "Heidegger's 'Introduction to the Phenomenology of Religion'" 57.

33 Theodore Kisiel, "The Missing Link in the Early Heidegger," in *Hermeneutic Phenomenology: Lectures and Essays*, ed. Joseph J. Kockelmans (Washington, D.C.: University Press of America, 1988) 40.

34 *Ibid.* 40.

35 Kisiel, *The Genesis* 172.

36 Caputo, *Demythologizing Heidegger* 4.

37 Kisiel, *The Genesis* 219.

38 George Kovacs, *The Question of God in Heidegger's Phenomenology* (Evanston, Illinois: Northwestern University Press, 1990) 41ff. and Zimmerman, *The Eclipse of the Self* xxii.

39 Zimmerman, *ibid.* xxii and 47.

40 *Ibid.* 17.

41 *Ibid.* 61.

42 See for example *ibid.* 59.

43 Kovacs, *The Question of God* 50 and 87.

44 *Ibid.* 95.

45 *Ibid.* 269.

46 Derrida uses this term to characterize Heidegger's modification of the word *geistlich* (*OS* 29).

47 Quoted in Zimmerman, *The Eclipse of the Self* 278.

48 See especially Hans-Georg Gadamer's essay, "The Religious Dimension," in *Heidegger's Ways* 177.

49 See Hugo Ott, *Martin Heidegger* and Nicolas Tertulian, "The History of Being and Political Revolution," in *The Heidegger Case* 208–227 on Heidegger's opposition to Christianity during this period.

50 Theodore Kisiel, "Heidegger's Apology: Biography as Philosophy and Ideology," in *The Heidegger Case* 34. Kisiel goes on to argue that it is Heidegger's "antireligious attitude ... that sweeps Heidegger into National Socialism, with all the romantic fervor of another religious conversion" (34).

8 THE REDEMPTIVE–ESCHATOLOGICAL SEPARATION OF FLESH AND SPIRIT IN THE EPISTLES OF THE APOSTLE PAUL

1 (*N* III 217–218). Heidegger supports this interpretation by quoting from "On the Despiser's of the Body" in *Thus Spoke Zarathustra*, a passage which is clearly directed against Christian conceptions of human being. See also *WCT* 57–73 on Heidegger's analysis of the relation between Nietzsche's overman and the metaphysical conception of human being as *animal rationale*.

2 Heidegger's term for human beings in their unique relationship with Being. This term will be used hereafter, without italics, to refer to Heidegger's original use of the term.

3 The Greek term used in the New Testament for human being. This word will be used hereafter, without italics, to refer to the biblical understanding of humanity.

4 Martin Heidegger, "The Way Back Into the Ground of Metaphysics," in *Existentialism from Dostoevsky to Sartre*, ed. Walter Kaufmann (Cleveland: Meridian Books, 1956) 215.

5 This is also reminiscent of the opening of Augustine's *Confessions*, which may have been a more direct source for Heidegger's work. But the source of Augustine's imagery here is in large part the New Testament.

6 Both Pöggeler, *Martin Heidegger's Path of Thinking* 27–28 and John van Buren, for example in "Young Heidegger, Aristotle, Ethics," in *Ethics and Danger: Essays on Heidegger and Continental Thought*, ed. Arleen B. Dallery and Charles E. Scott (Albany: SUNY Press, 1992) 170, stress how Heidegger, in his call for a destruction of ontotheology, is borrowing from Luther's Heidelberg Disputation where he calls for a destroying of Greek philosophy and scholasticism through a biblical "theology of the cross." On the "theology of the cross," see my conclusion.

7 In his later writings, Heidegger will describe Dasein's transcendence as a gift of Being.

8 These Greek terms will no longer be italicized (except in quotations).

9 Werner Georg Kümmel, *Man in the New Testament*, trans. John J. Vincent. (Philadelphia: The Westminster Press, 1963) 38.

10 Johannes Behm, *"kardia," Theological Dictionary of the New Testament*, trans. Geoffrey W. Bromiley, ed. Gerhard Kittel and Gerhard W. Friedrich, 10 vols. (Grand Rapids, Michigan: William B. Eerdmans, 1985) III: 611.

11 Herman Ridderbos, *Paul: An Outline of His Theology*, trans. John Richard de Witt (Grand Rapids, Michigan: William. B. Eerdmans, 1975) 120–121.

12 See Eduard Schweizer, "*psyche*," *Theological Dictionary of the New Testament*, abridged, 1349 and his article on "*pneuma*," in the same work, 891.

13 Ridderbos, *Paul* 115.

14 Kümmel, *Man in the New Testament* 38.

15 Ridderbos, *Paul* 115.

16 *Ibid.* 66.

17 Kümmel, *Man in the New Testament* 41.

18 *Ibid.* 61.

19 Ridderbos, *Paul* 94.

20 Karl Barth, *The Epistle to the Romans*, trans. from sixth edition by Edwyn C. Hoskyns (1933; London: Oxford University Press, 1968) 99.

21 Ernst Käsemann, *Perspectives on Paul*, trans. Margaret Kohl (Philadelphia: Fortress Press, 1971) 9.

22 Eduard Schweizer, in his article on *sarx* in *The Theological Dictionary of the New Testament*, calls the resurrection of the body "a bulwark against Hellenistic dualism" (1007).

23 Ridderbos, *Paul* 104 and 116.

24 Schweizer, "*pneuma*" 436.

25 Käsemann, *Perspectives on Paul* 28.

26 *Ibid.* 31.

27 Thomas J. Altizer, "Paul and the Birth of Self-Consciousness," in *History as Apocalypse* (Albany: State University of New York Press, 1985) 65.

28 Kümmel, *Man in the New Testament* 71.

9 INAUTHENTICITY AND THE FLESH

1 Rudolf Bultmann, "New Testament and Mythology," in *Kerygma and Myth: A Theological Debate*, ed. Hans Werner Bartsch (New York: Harper and Brothers, 1961) 24.

2 See note 18 below.

3 Hans Jonas, "Heidegger and Theology," *Review of Metaphysics*, 18 (December 1964): 212.

4 Kisiel, *The Genesis* 191.

5 It is difficult to assess whether this statement applies to Nietzsche, Heidegger, or both.

6 See PT 112–119.

7 Martin Heidegger, *Hegel's Concept of Experience* (New York: Harper and Row, 1970) 135.

8 See Caputo, *Demythologizing Heidegger* 179–181 for a summary of the influence of Heidegger on Christian theology.

9 The best works in English to consult on this subject remain George

Steiner's *Martin Heidegger* (Great Britain: Harvester Press, 1978), Michael E. Zimmerman's *Eclipse of the Self*, and John Macquarrie's *An Existentialist Theology*.

10 Hubert L. Dreyfus and Jane Rubin, "Kierkegaard, Division II, and Later Heidegger," an appendix to Hubert L. Dreyfus, *Being-in-the-World: A Commentary on Heidegger's* Being and Time, *Division I* (Cambridge, Massachusetts: The MIT Press, 1991) 314. Dreyfus and Rubin write that the "repudiation of the Christian-dogmatic side of Kierkegaard's thought we call Heidegger's secularization of Kierkegaard" (299). I applaud this use of the term "secularization" to describe Heidegger's relation to Christian philosophical theology. Of course Heidegger prefers to call Christian theology "ontic" in order to separate it from his own "ontological" analyses, but I believe that this rhetoric covers over Heidegger's true relation to Christian theology.

On Heidegger's relation to Kierkegaard, see also Calvin O. Schrag, *Existence and Freedom: Toward an Ontology of Human Finitude* (Evanston: Northwestern University Press, 1961), George J. Stack, *Kierkegaard's Existential Ethics* (The University of Alabama Press, 1977), and Michael Wyschogrod, *Kierkegaard and Heidegger: Ontology of Existence* (New York: Humanities Press, 1969).

11 Hans-Georg Gadamer, "Heidegger's Later Philosophy," *Philosophical Hermeneutics*, trans. David E. Linge (Berkeley: University of California Press, 1977) 217.

12 See especially Heidegger's footnote references to Paul, Augustine, Luther, Pascal, and Kierkegaard. I will analyze these notes below.

13 Heidegger traces this positive use of the term "world" to Kant. But Heidegger makes a further distinction between his existential use of the term to refer to Dasein's Being (his ex-sistence or transcendence) and Kant's existentiell use of the term to mean "*Dasein's relationship to being in its totality*" (*ER* 83).

14 "And even if we succeeded in doing the impossible, if we succeeded in proving rationally that man is a created being, the characterization of man as an *ens creatum* would only point up the fact of his finitude without clarifying its essence and without showing how this essence constitutes the fundamental nature of the essence of man." Martin Heidegger, *Kant and the Problem of Metaphysics*, trans. James S. Churchill (Bloomington: Indiana University Press, 1965) 227. From a biblical perspective, I would merely turn this objection back upon Heidegger, for in describing man's finitude with his concept of "thrownness," Heidegger does not clarify how this finitude constitutes the fundamental nature of the essence of man. For Christianity, createdness *is* the fundamental nature of man's finitude.

15 Steiner, *Martin Heidegger* 97.

16 Cf. Dreyfus and Rubin, *Being-in-the-World* 313. "It helps in understanding Heidegger here to realize that he can be read as again secularizing

Kierkegaard, in this case Kierkegaard's interpretation of the Christian doctrine of the fall ... Kierkegaard in his psychological account of the Fall calls the distraction and denial built into our everyday practices *sinfulness*; Heidegger, secularizing Kierkegaard, calls the cover-up that is always already in the one [*das Man*], *fallenness*."

In a footnote to this passage, Dreyfus and Rubin explore Heidegger's denial of the theological sources and implications of his doctrine of Dasein's fallenness: "On this point Heidegger does not even include the usual reference to Kierkegaard as having seen an important phenomenon but only in a religious context. Not only does Heidegger fail to thank Kierkegaard in *Being and Time*, in his lectures *he protests with strange vehemence* against any idea that what he says about fallenness has religious or psychological associations" (my emphasis, 360).

17 Karl Barth, *Church Dogmatics* III/2, ed. G. W. Bromiley and T. F. Torrance (Edinburgh: T. & T. Clark, 1968) 346.

18 Heidegger's claims regarding the relation between his phenomenological analysis and Christian theology are virtually repeated by Bultmann in his defense of his use of Heidegger to conceptualize his theology. See Bultmann's "The Historicity of Man and Faith," in *Existence and Faith*, trans. Schubert M. Ogden (New York: Living Age Books, 1960) 92–110. In this essay Bultmann agrees with Heidegger that Christian theology is a "positive science" which must look to philosophy's understanding of Being in order to conceptualize its analysis of Christian faith. With Heidegger, Bultmann believes that theology must look to philosophy's existential structures in order to articulate the existentiell possibilities of faithful existence. Bultmann argues that the only way that the theologian would have a case against Heidegger would be to show that a particular ontic phenomenon of faithful existence cannot be understood on the basis of Heidegger's ontological structure: "He would have a case against Heidegger only by showing that love [an ontic phenomenon of faithful existence] cannot be understood as a phenomenon of human existence on the basis of the 'care' structure [an existential of Heidegger's ontological analysis]" (305). I agree. And I intend in the following pages to show that the Christian conception of sin cannot be understood on the basis of Heidegger's ontological analysis of guilt.

19 Paul Ricoeur, *The Symbolism of Evil*, trans. Emerson Buchanan (New York: Harper and Row, 1967) 101. I would substitute "*spiritual* basis" for Ricoeur's "*ontological* moment."

20 W. Grundmann, "*hamartano ... hamartema ... hamartia*," *Theological Dictionary of the New Testament*, abridged, 48.

21 Ricoeur, *The Symbolism of Evil* 104.

10 THE *EIGENTLICH SELBST* OR THE *PNEUMATIKOS ANTHROPOS*

1 On the influence of Augustine and Luther, see especially Kisiel's discussion of Heidegger's 1921 course, "Augustine and Platonism," in *The Genesis* 192–217.

2 For the influence of Kierkegaard's analysis of anxiety on Heidegger, see especially Dreyfus and Rubin, *Being-in-the-World* 299–304. After making the comparison between Kierkegaard and Heidegger, however, these authors reach a wrong conclusion regarding the role of anxiety in Heidegger's analysis. They write that in Heidegger, "Anxiety reveals that the self has no possibilities of its own, and so Dasein's response to anxiety cannot be to find some resource in *itself*" (304). But anxiety does exactly the opposite. It shows Dasein that it has possibilities of its own and teaches it to look to its self, its authentic self, for its possibilities.

3 I am indebted to Dreyfus and Rubin, *ibid.* 297, for pointing out this quotation.

4 Even this change from the New Testament paradigm is based upon Heidegger's reading of Paul's eschatology in 1 Thessalonians. See the analysis above in my chapter, "Heidegger's theological origins."

5 In his defense of the compatibility of Heidegger's hermeneutic of Dasein and the biblical revelation of man, Bultmann begins to make ·this connection. See "The Historicity of Man and Faith," *Existence and Faith* 110.

6 Zimmerman, *The Eclipse of the Self* 139.

7 Kovacs, *The Question of God* 107.

8 Taminiaux, "The Presence of Nietzsche in *Sein und Zeit*," *Heidegger and the Project of Fundamental Ontology* 179.

9 *Ibid.* 181.

10 The quotation of Nietzsche occurs immediately afterwards:

> When, by anticipation, one becomes free *for* one's own death, one is liberated from one's lostness ... In anticipation, Dasein guards against falling back behind itself, or behind the potentiality-for-Being which it has understood. It guards itself against "becoming too old for its victories" (Nietzsche). (*BT* 308)

11 As I argued in my chapter "The redemptive-eschatological division between this world and the world to come," according to the Bible, the gift of eternal life is a "this-worldly" event, not an "other-worldly" event, so Heidegger's distinction is inadequate from a biblical viewpoint.

12 Kovacs, *The Question of God* 52.

13 W. D. Davies, "Conscience and Its Use in the New Testament," in *Jewish and Pauline Studies* (Philadelphia: Fortress Press, 1984) 243.

14 *Ibid.* 254.

15 Nevertheless, the later Heidegger will claim that it is "Being" which calls Dasein, but of course Heidegger denies that Being is "some entity."

16 On the meaning of the *Augenblick* in Heidegger see also Macquarrie, *An Existentialist Theology* 194 and Kovacs, *The Question of God* 111. Kovacs explains how the "'now' as the present of authentic temporality is based on the ontology of There-being; it is an ectasis, a moment or instant (*Augenblick*) of re-solve."

17 See the gloss on this term in Dreyfus, *Being-in-the-World* x.

18 On a comparison of Heidegger's understanding of the *Augenblick* and Kierkegaard's conception of the *Oieblik*, see Dreyfus and Rubin, *Being-in-the-World* 321–322.

19 Kierkegaard develops his analysis of the Moment out of this passage from Paul. See *The Concept of Anxiety* 88.

20 See also *N* II 56–57.

21 Taminiaux, *Heidegger and the Project of Fundamental Ontology* 188.

22 On Heidegger's use of his term "resoluteness" (*Entschlossenheit*) to interpret Nietzsche's conception of will to power, see Pippin, "Nietzsche, Heidegger" 295.

23 Jonas, "Heidegger and Theology" 220.

24 Martin Heidegger, *The Basic Problems of Phenomenology*, trans. Albert Hofstadter (Bloomington: Indiana University Press, 1988) 297.

·25 Although the Christian church's response to Nazism was mixed, the cases of Barth and Bonhoeffer demonstrate that the Christian's submission to Christ does not necessarily lead to a submission to worldly powers. In contrast, Heidegger's "ontic" decision to submit to the Führer was apparently not precluded by his fundamental ontology. Also, while National Socialists violently opposed Judaeo-Christianity (as did Heidegger during his Nazi period), Nietzsche's will to power was appropriated by Nazi writers, and Heidegger felt his own philosophy was compatible with National Socialism. Of course this topic needs to be developed in a separate study.

26 Immanuel Kant, "What is Enlightenment?," *Foundations of the Metaphysics of Morals and What is Enlightenment?*, trans. Lewis White Beck (New York: Bobbs-Merrill, 1959) 85.

11 FROM THE ENDS OF MAN TO THE BEGINNINGS OF WRITING

1 Because of my focus on Heidegger's hermeneutic of Dasein, I have attempted to defend my own reading of Heidegger from a similar charge. See the introduction to my chapter "Inauthenticity and the flesh," above.

2 See Jacques Derrida, *Limited Inc* (Evanston, Illinois: Northwestern University Press, 1988) 146 for his defense against this misconception of deconstruction.

3 Hans-Georg Gadamer, "*Destruktion* and Deconstruction," *Dialogue and Deconstruction: The Gadamer–Derrida Encounter*, ed. Diane P. Michelfelder and Richard E. Palmer (Albany: SUNY Press, 1989) 113. For a helpful reading of this debate between Gadamer and Derrida, see, in addition to the essays collected in *Dialogue and Deconstruction*, Ernst Behler's chapter, "Deconstruction and Hermeneutics," in his *Confrontations: Derrida/Heidegger/Nietzsche*, trans. Steven Taubeneck (Stanford University Press, 1991) 137–157.

4 Hans-Georg Gadamer, "Hermeneutics and Logocentrism," *Dialogue and Deconstruction* 115.

5 Hans-Georg Gadamer, "Letter to Dallmayr," *ibid.* 97.

6 Paul Ricoeur follows this problematic in Heidegger beyond the *Kehre* in "Heidegger and the Question of the Subject," *The Conflict of Interpretations* 223–235. "A problem now arises from the coincidence between the two definitions of Dasein: as the one who inquires and as the one who has to be its own being and has it as its own" (230).

7 See Hans Jonas, *Philosophical Essays: From Ancient Creed to Philosophical Man* (Englewood Cliffs, New Jersey: Prentice Hall, 1974).

8 In Gabriel Marcel, *Tragic Wisdom and Beyond*, trans. Stephen Jolin and Peter McCormick (Evanston, Illinois: Northwestern University Press, 1973) 242.

9 Jacques Derrida, "Afterword," *Limited Inc* 146.

10 For a critique of deconstruction from a humanistic perspective, see Colin Falck, *Myth, Truth and Literature: Towards a True Post-Modernism* (Cambridge University Press, 1994) and George Steiner, *Real Presences* (The University of Chicago Press, 1989).

11 Murray Krieger, "Literature and *Ecriture*: Constructions and Deconstructions in Recent Literary Theory," *Studies in the Literary Imagination* 12 (Spring 1979): 5 and 12.

12 DECONSTITUTING THE SUBJECT

1 I will be focusing on how Derrida develops his own philosophy in his confrontation with Husserl. For a critique of the accuracy of Derrida's reading of Husserl, see Joseph Claude Evans, *Strategies of Deconstruction: Derrida and the Myth of the Voice* (Minneapolis: University of Minnesota Press, 1991).

2 John D. Caputo, *Radical Hermeneutics: Repetition, Deconstruction, and the Hermeneutic Project* (Indianapolis: Indiana University Press, 1987) 120.

3 Derrida further points out that the distinction between the transcendental and the empirical consciousness does not in fact exist. The difference occurs only *in language* (*SP* 14).

4 See *SP* 75 for Derrida's summary of Husserl's (and metaphysics') two determinations of presence. This privileging of presence in the subject/object relation is often stressed in Heidegger as well.

5 Caputo, *Radical Hermeneutics* 133.
6 Derrida reaches the same conclusion in "Freud and the Scene of Writing." He reaches this aim mostly "with" Freud, whereas he achieves this conclusion in *SP* mostly "against" Husserl. But this movement of "with" or "against" predecessors' texts is never pure in Derrida.
7 Caputo, *Radical Hermeneutics* 129.
8 Edmund Husserl, *Ideas* 157–158.
9 Jacques Derrida, *Dissemination*, trans. Barbara Johnson (The University of Chicago Press, 1981) 258.
10 Rodolphe Gasché, "God, for Example," *Inventions of Difference: On Jacques Derrida* (Cambridge, Massachusetts: Harvard University Press, 1994) 161.

13 WRITING AND METAPHYSICS

1 See Heidegger's "The Way Back into the Ground of Metaphysics," in *Existentialism from Dostoevsky to Sartre*, especially 219 where Heidegger explains his abandonment of the phrase, "fundamental ontology."
2 See section three of part one of *OG*, "Of Grammatology as a Positive Science," especially 73–74. On the question of the aim of Heidegger's fundamental ontology and its relation to Derrida's project, see Caputo's section entitled "Heidegger Demythologized" in *Radical Hermeneutics* 171–186.
3 See for example the final page of Heidegger's "On Time and Being," in *On Time and Being*, trans. Joan Stambaugh (New York: Harper & Row, 1972) 24: "But what if we take what was said and adopt it unceasingly as the guide for our thinking, and consider that this Same is not even anything new, but the oldest of the old in Western thought: that ancient something which conceals itself in *a-letheia*?"
4 After a list of citations from Rabbi Eliezer to Jaspers, Derrida writes: "Above all, the profound differences distinguishing all these treatments of the same metaphor must not be ignored. In the history of this treatment, the most decisive separation appears at the moment when, at the same time as the science of nature, the determination of the absolute presence is constituted as self-presence, as subjectivity. It is the moment of the great rationalisms of the seventeenth century. From then on, the condemnation of fallen or finite writing will take another form, within which we still live: it is non-self-presence that will be denounced" (*OG* 16–17). For another description of this historical change see *OG* 97.
  Note that, while acknowledging the "profound differences distinguishing all these treatments of the same metaphor," Derrida still finds a common element in the condemnation of fallen or finite writing.

5 We will explore this difference when we turn to Derrida's essay, "Edmond Jabès and the Question of the Book" (*WD* 64–78).

6 See especially "Violence and Metaphysics: An Essay on the Thought of Emmanuel Levinas" (*WD* 79–153).

7 Later, writing in the 1980s, Derrida will begin to question this unified characterization of ontotheology. See my conclusion for a discussion.

8 As in my reading of Derrida's Husserl interpretation, I am not concerned here with the accuracy of Derrida's interpretation of Saussure. For a critique of Derrida's reading of Saussure see Robert M. Strozier, *Derrida, and the Metaphysics of Subjectivity* (New York: Mouton de Gruyter, 1988) and Evans, *Strategies of Deconstruction*.

14 READING THE LAW: THE SPIRIT AND THE LETTER

1 Ernst Käsemann, "The Spirit and the Letter," *Perspectives on Paul* 139.

2 *Ibid.* 145.

3 Paul Ricoeur, *The Symbolism of Evil* 123.

4 Richard B. Hays, *Echoes of Scripture in the Letters of Paul* (New Haven: Yale University Press, 1989) 151.

5 Käsemann, *Perspectives on Paul* 159.

6 In opening up the promise of salvation to the Gentiles, Paul refers to God's promise to Abraham rather than the Mosaic covenant of obligation as the covenant which applies to the Gentiles, and this promise was given before the command of circumcision and long before the Mosaic commands. Like the new covenant prophesied by Jeremiah and other prophets, which Paul sees fulfilled in the death and resurrection of Jesus Christ, the covenant with Abraham was based not on works, but on belief in God's ability to keep his promise.

Paul finds the same dichotomy between letter and Spirit in Abraham's story. Paul allegorizes the biblical account of Abraham in order to see Ishmael as representative of the old covenant and Isaac as representative of the new. Ishmael was the son of his wife's maid or servant. He represents humanity's efforts to gain salvation, to fulfill the promise, through its own efforts. Isaac was born of Abraham's aging wife, demonstrating that it is by God's power that the promise will be fulfilled.

7 Paul is reinscribing the law's distinction between righteousness and self-righteousness.

8 Ridderbos, *Paul* 138–139.

9 Karl Barth, "Gospel and Law," *God, Grace and Gospel*, trans. James McNab (London: Oliver and Boyd, 1959) 22.

10 It should be noted that this discussion of the hermeneutical principles of reading the law, the "Old Testament," by Christianity is the basis of the structure of modern and postmodern attempts to overcome, end, or close philosophy in order to open a new age or aeon. Hegel's conception

of the transformation of religion into philosophy came out of a reading
of the transformation of Judaism by Christianity. See Hegel's *The Spirit
of Christianity and its Fate* in *Early Theological Writings*, trans. T. M. Knox
(Philadelphia: University of Pennsylvania Press, 1985) 182–301, and
Derrida's reading of this text in *Glas*, trans. John P. Leavey, Jr. and
Richard Rand (Lincoln: University of Nebraska Press, 1986). See
especially 58–63 of *Glas* where Derrida comments on Hegel's reading in
The Spirit of Christianity of Christ as the fulfillment of the law.

11 Hays, *Echoes of Scripture* 131.
12 G. Schrenk, "*Grapho, graphe, gramma*," *Theological Dictionary of the New
Testament* 1: 768.
13 Charles H. Talbert, *Reading Corinthians: A Literary and Theological Commentary on 1 and 2 Corinthians* (New York: Crossroad, 1987) 146.
14 Käsemann, *Perspectives on Paul* 150.
15 Schrenk, *Theological Dictionary of the New Testament* 1: 765.
16 *Ibid.* 767.
17 Hays, *Echoes of Scripture* 150.
18 Talbert, *Reading Corinthians* 153.
19 *Ibid.* 154.
20 Käsemann, *Perspectives on Paul* 155.
21 Susan Handelman, *The Slayers of Moses: The Emergence of Rabbinic
Interpretation in Modern Literary Theory* (Albany: State University of New
York Press, 1982) 86–90.
22 Shira Wolosky, "Derrida, Jabès, Levinas: Sign-Theory as Ethical Discourse," *Prooftexts: A Journal of Jewish Literary History* 2.3 (1982): 294.
23 *Ibid.* 298.
24 Within this scheme, the Christian is not presented as a unique alternative. The same thing occurs in Handelman's *The Slayers of Moses*.
Although Handelman subtitles her opening section, "The Interpretive
Agon of Greek, Jew, and Christian," her goal is to separate Jewish
thought from "Greco-Christian" conceptuality.
25 See *WD* 29–30.
26 On this metaphor in Ezekiel, Jeremiah, and Paul, see Hays, *Echoes of
Scripture* 128.
27 Cf. also Jeremiah 17:13, "Those who turn away from you will be
written in the dust."
28 Paul Ricoeur, *The Symbolism of Evil* 125.

15 SCRIPTURE OR *ÉCRITURE*: THE LIMITATIONS OF DERRIDA'S
DECONSTRUCTION OF ONTOTHEOLOGY

1 Wolosky, "Derrida, Jabès, Levinas" 295.
2 Herbert N. Schneidau, "The Word Against the Word: Derrida on
Textuality," *Semeia* special issue on "Derrida and Biblical Studies," ed.
Robert Detweiler, 23 (1982) 14.

3 See my conclusion for further discussion of Derrida and eschatology.

4 Mark C. Taylor, "Text as Victim," *Deconstruction and Theology*, ed. Thomas J. J. Altizer, et al. (New York: Crossroad, 1982) 73.

5 See for example the contributors to *Deconstruction and Theology*. For a good review of this volume and other attempts to appropriate deconstruction into a theological discourse see G. Douglas Atkins, "Partial Stories: Hebraic and Christian Thinking in the Wake of Deconstruction," *Journal of Religion and Literature* 15.3 (Summer 1983) 7–21.

6 Carl A. Raschke, "The Deconstruction of God," *Deconstruction and Theology* 3.

CONCLUSION: ONTOTHEOLOGY, NEGATIVE THEOLOGY, AND THE THEOLOGY OF THE CROSS

1 Hart, *The Trespass of the Sign* 186.

2 See Jean-Luc Marion, *God Without Being*, trans. Thomas A. Carlson (University of Chicago Press) 1991.

3 Hart, *The Trespass of the Sign* 193.

4 *Ibid.* 269.

5 Raoul Mortley, *From Word to Silence*, 2 vols. (Bonn and Frankfurt-on-Main: Hanstein, 1986), II: 274–275 as quoted in Toby Foshay's "Introduction: Denegation and Resentments" in *Derrida and Negative Theology*, ed. Harold Coward and Toby Foshay (Albany: SUNY Press, 1992) 18.

6 Jacques Derrida, "Post-Scriptum: Aporias, Ways and Voices," in *Derrida and Negative Theology* 312.

7 *Ibid.* 311.

8 Moltmann, *Theology of Hope* 141.

9 Moltmann, *The Crucified God* 215.

10 See Ott, *Martin Heidegger* 226–227 and 273 for the historical context of these anti-Christian pronouncements by Heidegger.

11 Martin Heidegger, "Only a God Can Save Us: *Der Spiegel*'s Interview with Martin Heidegger," *Philosophy Today* 20 (Winter 1976): 267–284.

12 It seems tragically ironic that Heidegger makes this call in an interview in which he tries to explain away his avowal of Hitler as the savior of Germany: "The *Führer* himself and he alone *is* the present and future German reality and its rule" (quoted from Heidegger's speech from the Fall of 1933 by the *Der Spiegel* interviewer in Heidegger, "Only a God Can Save Us" 271). In stark contrast, those Christian thinkers, such as Karl Barth and Dietrich Bonhoeffer, who awaited a savior described in detail in the Bible, were not fooled and opposed the Nazi regime.

13 On Luther's theology of the cross, see in addition to Moltmann's *The Crucified God*, Alister E. McGrath, *Luther's Theology of the Cross* (Oxford: Basil Blackwell, 1985), and the older, and in my view more important,

work of Walter von Loewenich, *Luther's Theology of the Cross*, trans. Herbert J. A. Bouman (Minneapolis: Augusburg Publishing House, 1976).

14 John D. Caputo, "Heidegger's Gods," in his *Demythologizing Heidegger* 180.

15 Thomas Sheehan, "Derrida and Heidegger," in *Hermeneutics and Deconstruction*, ed. Hugh J. Silverman and Don Ihde (New York: SUNY Press, 1988) 217.

16 Kearney, *Dialogues* 119.

17 Herbert N. Schneidau, "The Word Against the Word" 14.

18 Herman Rapaport, *Heidegger and Derrida: Reflections on Time and Language* (Lincoln: University of Nebraska Press, 1989) 220.

19 Taylor, *Tears* 84.

20 *Ibid.* 12.

21 Mark C. Taylor, "nO nOt nO," in *Derrida and Negative Theology* 189.

22 Caputo, *Demythologizing Heidegger* 190.

23 Kearney, *Dialogues* 107.

24 *Ibid.* 109.

25 Jacques Derrida, "Letter to John P. Leavey, Jr.," (January 2, 1981), in *Semeia* special issue on "Derrida and Biblical Studies" 61.

26 Kearney, *Dialogues* 116.

27 Jacques Derrida, "*Geschlecht* II: Heidegger's Hand," trans. John P. Leavey, in *Deconstruction and Philosophy*, ed. John Sallis (The University of Chicago Press, 1987) 193–194.

28 Jacques Derrida, "Interpreting Signatures (Nietzsche/Heidegger): Two Questions," in *Dialogue and Deconstruction* 67.

29 For another analysis of this distinction between the biblical and philosophical *logos*, see René Girard's chapter "The Logos of Heraclitus and the Logos of John," in his *Things Hidden Since the Foundation of the World*, trans. Stephen Bann and Michael Metteer (Stanford University Press, 1987) 263-280.

30 Moltmann, *The Theology of Hope* 30 and 141.

31 Ricoeur, "Religion, Atheism, and Faith," *The Conflict of Interpretations* 447.

32 *Ibid.*

33 Moltmann, *The Crucified God* 215.

34 Ricoeur, "The Language of Faith," *The Philosophy of Paul Ricoeur* 224.

35 *Ibid.*, "Religion, Atheism, and Faith," *The Conflict of Interpretations* 440.

36 *Ibid.*, "The Critique of Religion," *The Philosophy of Paul Ricoeur* 234.

37 *Ibid.*, "Religion, Atheism, and Faith," *The Conflict of Interpretations* 448.

38 *Ibid.*, "Freedom in the Light of Hope," *The Conflict of Interpretations* 403.

39 *Ibid.*, "Religion, Atheism, and Faith," *The Conflict of Interpretations* 448 and 451.

40 *Ibid.*, "The Language of Faith," *The Philosophy of Paul Ricoeur* 235.

41 Kearney, *Dialogues* 119.

42 Karl Barth, *How I Changed My Mind* (Richmond, Virginia: John Knox Press, 1966) 37.
43 Moltmann, *The Crucified God* 275.
44 Ricoeur, "Religion, Atheism, and Faith," *The Conflict of Interpretations* 447.

Bibliography

Altizer, Thomas J. J. *The Gospel of Christian Atheism*. Philadelphia: The Westminster Press. 1966.

Altizer, Thomas J. J., ed. *Deconstruction and Theology*. New York: Crossroad. 1982.

History as Apocalypse. Albany: State University of New York Press. 1985.

Arendt, Hannah. *The Life of the Mind*. 2 vols. New York: Harcourt Brace Jovanovich. 1977–1978.

Atkins, G. Douglas. "Partial Stories: Hebraic and Christian Thinking in the Wake of Deconstruction." *Journal of Religion and Literature* 15.3 (Summer 1983): 7–21.

Auerbach, Eric. *Mimesis*. Trans. Willard R. Trask. Princeton University Press. 1974.

Ballard, Bruce. *The Role of Mood in Heidegger's Ontology*. New York: University Press of America. 1990.

Barth, Karl. *God, Grace and Gospel*. Trans. James McNab. London: Oliver and Boyd. 1959.

How I Changed My Mind. Richmond, Virginia: John Knox Press. 1966.

The Epistle to the Romans. Trans. Edwyn C. Hoskyns. London: Oxford University Press. 1968.

Church Dogmatics. III/2. Ed. G. W. Bromiley and T. F. Torrance. Edinburgh: T & T. Clark. 1968.

The Christian Life. Trans. Geoffrey W. Bromiley. Grand Rapids, Michigan: William B. Eerdmans Publishing Company. 1981.

Witness to the Word: A Commentary on John 1. Trans. Geoffrey W. Bromiley. Ed. Walther Furst. Grand Rapids, Michigan: William B. Eerdmans Publishing Company. 1986.

Barthes, Roland. "The Death of an Author." *Image-Music-Text*. Trans. Stephen Heath. New York: Hill and Wang. 1977.

Bauman, Zygmunt. "Postmodernity, or Living with Ambivalence." *A Postmodern Reader*. Ed. Joseph Natoli and Linda Hutcheon. New York: State University of New York Press. 1993.

Behler, Ernst. *Confrontations: Derrida/Heidegger/Nietzsche*. Trans. Steven Taubeneck. Stanford University Press. 1991.

Beker, J. Christiaan. *Paul the Apostle: The Triumph of God in Life and Thought.* Philadelphia: Fortress Press. 1984.

Biser, Eugene. "Nietzsche: Critic in the Grand Style." Trans. Timothy F. Sellner. *Studies in Nietzsche and the Judaeo-Christian Tradition.* Ed. James C. O'Flaherty, Timothy F. Sellner, and Robert M. Helm. Chapel Hill: The University of North Carolina Press. 1985.

Blumenberg, Hans. *The Legitimacy of the Modern Age.* Trans. Robert M. Wallace. Cambridge, Massachusetts: The MIT Press. 1983.

Bonhoeffer, Dietrich. *Letters and Papers from Prison.* Ed. Eberhard Bethge. 1953. New York: SCM Press. 1972.

Bruce, F. F. *Philippians.* Vol. XI of *New International Biblical Commentary.* Ed. W. Ward Gasque. Peabody, Massachusetts: Hendrickson Publishers. 1989.

Bultmann, Rudolf. *Theology of the New Testament.* 2 vols. Trans. Kendrick Grobel. New York: Charles Scribner's Sons. 1951.

Existence and Faith. Trans. Schubert M. Ogden. New York: Living Age Books. 1960.

"New Testament and Mythology." *Kerygma and Myth: A Theological Debate.* Ed. Hans Werner Bartsch. New York: Harper and Brothers. 1961.

Primitive Christianity in Its Contemporary Setting. Trans. Reverend R. H. Fuller. 1956. New York: New American Library. 1974.

New Testament and Mythology. Trans. and Ed. Schubert M. Ogden. Philadelphia: Fortress Press. 1984.

Buren, John van. "Young Heidegger, Aristotle, Ethics." *Ethics and Danger: Essays on Heidegger and Continental Thought.* Ed. Arleen B. Dallery and Charles E. Scott. Albany: State University of New York Press. 1992. 169–185.

"The Young Heidegger: Rumor of Hidden King (1919–1926)." *Philosophy Today* 33 (1989): 99–108.

Caputo, John D. *Radical Hermeneutics: Repetition, Deconstruction, and the Hermeneutic Project.* Indianapolis: Indiana University Press. 1987.

Demythologizing Heidegger. Bloomington: Indiana University Press. 1993.

Clark, Maudemarie. *Nietzsche on Truth and Philosophy.* Cambridge University Press. 1990.

Conzelmann, Hans. *An Outline of the Theology of the New Testament.* New York: Harper & Row. 1969.

Conzelmann, Hans and Andreas Lindemann. *Interpreting the New Testament: An Introduction to the Principles and Methods of New Testament Exegesis.* Trans. Siegfried S. Schatzmann. Peabody, Massachusetts: Hendrickson Pulishers. 1988.

Coward, Harold and Toby Foshay, eds. *Derrida and Negative Theology.* Albany: State University of New York Press. 1992.

Cullman, Oscar. *Christ and Time: The Primitive Christian Conception of Time and History.* Trans. Floyd V. Filson. Philadelphia: Westminster Press. 1964.

Dallery, Arleen B. and Charles E. Scott, eds. *Ethics and Danger: Essays on Heidegger and Continental Thought*. Albany: State University of New York Press. 1992.

Davies, W. D. *Jewish and Pauline Studies*. Philadelphia: Fortress Press. 1984.

Derrida, Jacques. *Positions*. Trans. Alan Bass. University of Chicago Press. 1972.

Speech and Phenomena: And Other Essays on Husserl's Theory of Signs. Trans. David B. Allison and Newton Garver. Evanston, Illinois: Northwestern University Press. 1973.

Of Grammatology. Trans. Gayatri Chakravorty Spivak. Baltimore: The Johns Hopkins University Press. 1976.

Writing and Difference. Trans. Alan Bass. University of Chicago Press. 1978.

Margins of Philosophy. Trans. Alan Bass. University of Chicago Press. 1982.

"Letter to John P. Leavey, Jr." *Derrida and Biblical Studies*. Ed. Robert Detweiler. Special issue of *Semeia* 2.3 (1982): 61–62.

Glas. Trans. John P. Leavey and Richard Rand. Lincoln: University of Nebraska Press. 1986.

"*Geschlecht* II: Heidegger's Hand." Trans. John P. Leavey, Jr. *Deconstruction and Philosophy: The Texts of Jacques Derrida*. Ed. John Sallis. Chicago: University of Chicago Press. 1987. 161–196.

Limited, Inc. Evanston, Illinois: Northwestern University Press. 1988.

Of Spirit: Heidegger and the Question. Trans. Geoffrey Bennington and Rachel Bowlby. University of Chicago Press. 1989.

"How to Avoid Speaking: Denials." Trans. Ken Frieden. *Derrida and Negative Theology*. Ed. Harold Coward and Toby Foshay. State University of New York Press. 1992. 73–142.

"Of an Apocalyptic Tone Newly Adopted in Philosophy." Trans. John P. Leavey, Jr. *Derrida and Negative Theology*. 25–71.

"Post-Scriptum: Aporias, Ways and Voices." Trans. John P. Leavey, Jr. *Derrida and Negative Theology*. 283–323.

Aporias. Trans. Thomas Dutoit. Stanford, California: Stanford University Press. 1993.

Descartes, René. *Meditations on First Philosophy*. Trans. Donald A. Cress. Indianapolis: Hackett Publishing Company. 1979.

Detweiler, Bruce. *Nietzsche and the Politics of Aristocratic Radicalism*. University of Chicago Press. 1990.

Dodd, C. H. *The Interpretation of the Fourth Gospel*. 1953. Cambridge University Press. 1978.

Dreyfus, Hubert L. and Jane Rubin. "Kierkegaard, Division II, and Later Heidegger." Appendix to Hubert L. Dreyfus. *Being-in-the-World: A Commentary on Heidegger's* Being and Time, *Division I*. Cambridge, Massachusetts: The MIT Press. 1991. 283–340.

Ellis, E. Earle. *Paul and His Recent Interpreters*. Grand Rapids, Michigan: William B. Eerdmans Publishing Company. 1961.

Evans, Joseph Claude. *Strategies of Deconstruction: Derrida and the Myth of the Voice*. Minneapolis: University of Minnesota Press. 1991.

Falck, Colin. *Myth, Truth and Literature: Towards a True Post-Modernism*. Cambridge University Press. 1994.

Farias, Victor. *Heidegger and Nazism*. Trans. Paul Burrell. Philadelphia: Temple University Press. 1989.

Feuerbach, Ludwig. *The Essence of Christianity*. Trans. George Eliot. New York: Harper & Row. 1957.

Foshay, Toby. "Introduction: Denegation and Resentment." *Derrida and Negative Theology*. Ed. Harold Coward and Toby Foshay. Albany: SUNY Press. 1992.

Foucault, Michel. "What is an Author?" *Language, Counter-Memory, Practice*. Trans. Donald F. Bouchard and Sherry Simon. Ed. Donald F. Bouchard. Ithaca, New York: Cornell University Press. 1986.

Frei, Hans. *The Eclipse of Biblical Narrative*. New Haven: Yale University Press. 1974 .

Gadamer, Hans-Georg. *Philosophical Hermeneutics*. Trans. and Ed. David E. Linge. Berkeley: University of California Press. 1977.

Heidegger Memorial Lectures. Trans. Steven W. Davis. Ed. Werner Marx. Pittsburgh: Duquesne University Press. 1982.

"The Drama of Zarathustra." Trans. Thomas Heilke. *Nietzsche's New Seas*. Ed. Michael Gillespie and Tracy Strong. University of Chicago Press. 1988. 220–231.

Heidegger's Ways. Trans. John W. Stanley. Albany: State University of New York Press. 1994.

Gasché, Rodolphe. *Inventions of Difference: On Jacques Derrida*. Cambridge, Massachusetts: Harvard University Press. 1994.

Girard, René. "Dionysus versus the Crucified." *Modern Language Notes* 99 (1984): 816–835.

Things Hidden Since the Foundation of the World. Trans. Stephen Bann and Michael Metteer. Stanford University Press. 1987.

Guthrie, Donald. *New Testament Theology*. Grand Rapids, Michigan: Intervarsity Press. 1981.

Handelman, Susan. *The Slayers of Moses: The Emergence of Rabbinic Interpretation in Modern Literary Theory*. Albany: State University of New York Press. 1982.

Hart, Kevin. *The Trespass of the Sign: Deconstruction, Theology and Philosophy*. Cambridge University Press. 1989.

Hatab, Laurence. *Nietzsche and Eternal Recurrence: The Redemption of Time and Becoming*. Washington, D.C.: University Press of America. 1978.

Hays, Richard B. *Echoes of Scripture in the Letters of Paul*. New Haven: Yale University Press. 1989.

Hegel, G. W. F. *Early Theological Writings*. Trans. T. M. Knox. Philadelphia: University of Pennsylvania Press. 1985.

Heidegger, Martin. *Existence and Being*. Ed. Werner Brock. Chicago, Illinois: Henry Regnery Company. 1949.

"The Way Back into the Ground of Metaphysics." *Existentialism from Dostoevsky to Sartre*. Ed. Walter Kaufmann. Cleveland: Meridian Books. 1956. 206–221.

The Question of Being. Trans. Jean T. Wilde and William Kluback. New Haven, Connecticut: College and University Press. 1956.

"Letter on Humanism." *Philosophy in the Twentieth Century*. III. Ed. William Barrett and Henry D. Aiken. New York: Random House. 1962. 270–302.

Being and Time. Trans. John Macquarrie and Edward Robinson. New York: Harper and Row. 1962.

Kant and the Problem of Metaphysics. Trans. James S. Churchill. Bloomington: Indiana University Press. 1965.

Identity and Difference. Trans. Joan Stambaugh. New York: Harper and Row. 1969.

The Essence of Reasons. Trans. Terrence Malick. Evanston, Illinois: Northwestern University Press. 1969.

Hegel's Concept of Experience. New York: Harper and Row. 1970.

On Time and Being. Trans. Joan Stambaugh. New York: Harper and Row. 1972.

The End of Philosophy. Trans. Joan Stambaugh. New York: Harper and Row. 1973.

Poetry, Language, Thought. Trans. Albert Hofstadter. New York: Harper and Row. 1975.

"Phenomenology and Theology." *The Piety of Thinking*. Trans. and Commentary by James G. Hart and John C. Maraldo. Bloomington: Indiana University Press. 1976. 5–21.

"Only a God Can Save Us: *Der Spiegel*'s Interview with Martin Heidegger." *Philosophy Today* 20 (1976): 267–284.

The Question Concerning Technology and Other Essays. Trans. William Lovitt. New York: Harper and Row. 1977.

Nietzsche, I: *The Will to Power as Art*. Trans. David Farrell Krell. San Francisco: Harper and Row. 1979.

On the Way to Language. Trans. Peter D. Hertz. San Francisco: Harper and Row. 1982.

Nietzsche, IV: *Nihilism*. Trans. Frank A. Capuzzi. Ed. David Farrell Krell. San Francisco: Harper and Row. 1982.

Nietzsche, II: *The Eternal Recurrence of the Same*. Trans. David Farrell Krell. San Francisco: Harper and Row. 1984.

History of the Concept of Time, Prolegomena. Trans. Theodore Kisiel. Bloomington: Indiana University Press. 1985.

Nietzsche, III: *The Will to Power as Knowledge and as Metaphysics*. Trans.

Joan Stambaugh, David Farrell Krell and Frank A. Capuzzi. Ed. David Farrell Krell. San Francisco: Harper and Row, Publishers. 1987.

The Basic Problems of Phenomenology. Trans. Albert Hofstadter. Bloomington: Indiana University Press. 1988.

Higgins, Kathleen. *Nietzsche's* Zarathustra. Philadelphia: Temple University Press. 1987.

The Holy Bible: New International Version. 1973. Grand Rapids, Michigan: Zondervan. 1984.

Husserl, Edmund. *Ideas: General Introduction to Pure Phenomenology.* Trans. W. R. Boyce Gibson. 1931. New York: Collier Books. 1962.

The Interlinear Hebrew-Greek-English Bible. 4 vols. Ed. and Trans. Jay P. Green. Peabody, Massachusetts: Hendrickson Publishers. 1985.

Jaspers, Karl. *Nietzsche and Christianity.* Trans. E. B. Ashton. 1961. Chicago, Illinois: Henry Regnery Company. 1967.

Jonas, Hans. "Heidegger and Theology." *Review of Metaphysics* 18 (1964): 203–233.

The Gnostic Religion: The Message of the Alien God and the Beginnings of Christianity. Boston, Massachusetts: Beacon Press. 1963.

Philosophical Essays: From Ancient Creed to Philosophical Man. Englewood Cliffs, New Jersey: Prentice Hall. 1974.

Kant, Immanuel. *Foundations of the Metaphysics of Morals and What is Enlightenment?* Trans. Lewis White Beck. New York: Bobbs-Merrill. 1959.

Käsemann, Ernst. *Perspectives on Paul.* Trans. Margaret Kohl. Philadelphia: Fortress Press. 1971.

Kaufmann, Walter. *Nietzsche: Philosopher, Psychologist, Antichrist.* 1950. Princeton University Press. 1968.

Preface. *The Antichrist. The Portable Nietzsche.* 1954. New York: Penguin Books. 1982. 565–569.

Kearney, Richard. *Dialogues with Contemporary Continental Thinkers: The Phenomenological Heritage.* Manchester University Press. 1984.

Kent, Homer A. "Philippians." Vol. xi of *The Expositor's Bible Commentary.* 12 vols. Ed. Frank E. Gaebelein. Grand Rapids, Michigan: Zondervan Publishing House. 1978. 93–160.

Kierkegaard, Søren. *The Concept of Anxiety.* Trans. Reidar Thomte. Princeton University Press. 1980.

Kisiel, Theodore. "Heidegger's Apology: Biography as Philosophy and Ideology." *The Heidegger Case: On Philosophy and Politics.* Ed. Tom Rockmore and Joseph Margolis. Philadelphia: Temple University Press. 1992.

The Genesis of Being and Time. Berkeley: University of California Press. 1993.

Knight, G. Wilson. *Christ and Nietzsche.* London: Staples Press. 1970.

Kockelmans, Joseph J., ed. *A Companion to Martin Heidegger's* Being and Time. Washington D.C.: University Press of America. 1986.

Hermeneutic Phenomenology: Lectures and Essays. Washington, D.C.: University Press of America. 1988.

Kovacs, George. *The Question of God in Heidegger's Phenomenology.* Evanston, Illinois: Northwestern University Press. 1990.

Krell, David Farrell. *Intimations of Mortality: Time, Truth, and Finitude in Heidegger's Thinking of Being.* University Park: The Pennsylvania State University Press. 1986.

Krieger, Murray. "Literature and *Ecriture*: Constructions and Deconstructions in Recent Literary Theory." *Studies in the Literary Imagination* 12 (Spring 1979): 1–12.

Kümmel, Werner Georg. *Promise and Fulfillment: The Eschatological Message of Jesus.* 1957. London: SCM Press. 1961.

Man in the New Testament. Trans. John J. Vincent. Philadelphia: The Westminster Press. 1963.

Küng, Hans. *Does God Exist?: An Answer for Today.* Trans. Edward Quinn. Garden City, New York: Doubleday & Company. 1980.

Ladd, George Eldon. *The Pattern of New Testament Truth.* Grand Rapids, Michigan: William B. Eerdmans Publishing Company. 1968.

The Presence of the Future: The Eschatology of Biblical Realism. Grand Rapids, Michigan: William B. Eerdmans Publishing Company. 1981.

A Theology of the New Testament. Grand Rapids, Michigan: William B. Eerdmans. 1991.

Lampert, Laurence. "Heidegger's Nietzsche Interpretation." *Man and World* 7 (1974): 353–378.

Nietzsche's Teaching: An Interpretation of Thus Spoke Zarathustra. New Haven: Yale University Press. 1986.

Lawrence, Joseph P. "Nietzsche and Heidegger." *History of European Ideas* 11 (1989): 711–717.

Lincoln, Andrew T. *Paradise Now and Not Yet: Studies in the Role of the Heavenly Dimension in Paul's Thought with Special Reference to His Eschatology.* 1981. Grand Rapids, Michigan: Baker Book House. 1991.

Loewenich, Walter von. *Luther's Theology of the Cross.* Trans. Herbert J. A. Bouman. Minneapolis: Augsburg Publishing House. 1976.

Löwith, Karl. *Meaning in History.* University of Chicago Press. 1949.

From Hegel to Nietzsche. Trans. David E. Green. New York: Holt, Rinehart and Winston. 1964.

Luft, Eric von der. "Sources of Nietzsche's 'God is Dead!' and Its Meaning for Heidegger." *Journal of the History of Ideas* 45 (1984): 263–276.

Lyotard, Jean-François. *The Postmodern Condition: A Report on Knowledge.* Trans. Geoff Bennington and Brian Massumi. Minneapolis: University of Minnesota Press. 1984.

Macquarrie, John. *An Existentialist Theology: A Comparison of Heidegger and Bultmann.* New York: Harper and Row, Publishers. 1965.

Magnus, Bernd. *Heidegger's Metahistory of Philosophy:* Amor Fati, *Being and Truth.* The Hague: Martinus Nijhoff. 1970.

Nietzsche's Existential Imperative. Bloomington: Indiana University Press. 1978.

Marcel, Gabriel. *Tragic Wisdom and Beyond*. Trans. Stephen Jolin and Peter McCormick. Evanston: Northwestern University Press. 1973.

Marion, Jean-Luc. *God Without Being*. Trans. Thomas A. Carlson. University of Chicago Press. 1991.

McGrath, Alister E. *Luther's Theology of the Cross*. Oxford: Basil Blackwell. 1985.

Mencken, Henry L. *The Philosophy of Friedrich Nietzsche*. Boston: Luce and Company. 1908.

Michelfelder, Diane P. and Richard E. Palmer, eds. *Dialogue and Deconstruction: The Gadamer–Derrida Encounter*. Albany: State University of New York Press. 1989.

Moltmann, Jürgen. *Theology Today*. Trans. John Bowden. Philadelphia: Trinity Press International. 1988.

The Crucified God: The Cross of Christ as the Foundation and Criticism of Christian Theology. Trans. R. A. Wilson and John Bowden. 1974. San Francisco: Harper San Francisco. 1991.

Theology of Hope: On the Ground and Implications of a Christian Eschatology. Trans. James W. Leitch. 1975. New York: Harper Collins Publishers. 1991.

Moule, C. F. D. *Essays in New Testament Interpretation*. Cambridge University Press. 1982.

Mueller, David L. *Karl Barth*. Peabody, Massachusetts: Hendrickson Publishers. 1972.

Nehamas, Alexander. *Nietzsche: Life as Literature*. Cambridge, Massachusetts: Harvard University Press. 1985.

Nelson, Donald F. "Nietzsche, Zarathustra, and *Jesus Redivivus*: The Unholy Trinity." *The Germanic Review* 48 (1973): 175–188.

Niebuhr, Reinhold. *Beyond Tragedy: Essays on the Christian Interpretation of History*. New York: Charles Scribner's Sons. 1937.

Nietzsche, Friedrich. *The Will to Power*. Trans. Walter Kaufmann and R. J. Hollingdale. Ed. Walter Kaufmann. New York: Vintage Books. 1968.

The Gay Science. Trans. Walter Kaufmann. New York: Vintage Books. 1974.

Thus Spoke Zarathustra: A Book for None and All. Trans. Walter Kaufmann. 1954. New York: Penguin Books. 1978.

Twilight of the Idols or, How One Philosophizes with a Hammer. The Portable Nietzsche. Ed. and Trans. Walter Kaufmann. 1954. New York: Penguin Books. 1982. 465–563.

The Antichrist. The Portable Nietzsche. Ed. and Trans. Walter Kaufmann. 1954. New York: Penguin Books. 1982. 568–656.

Beyond Good and Evil: Prelude to a Philosophy of the Future. Trans. Walter Kaufmann. 1966. New York: Vintage Books. 1989.

Daybreak: Thoughts on the Prejudices of Morality. Trans. R. J. Hollingdale. 1982. Cambridge University Press. 1989.

Ecce Homo. Trans. Walter Kaufmann. On the Genealogy of Morals *and* Ecce Homo. Ed. Walter Kaufmann. 1967. New York: Vintage Books. 1989. 215–335.

On the Genealogy of Morals: A Polemic. Trans. Walter Kaufmann and R. J. Hollingdale. On the Genealogy of Morals *and* Ecce Homo. Ed. Walter Kaufmann. 1967. New York: Vintage Books. 1989. 13–163.

Human, All Too Human: A Book for Free Spirits. Trans. R. J. Hollingdale. 1986. Cambridge University Press. 1990.

O'Flaherty, James C., Timothy F. Sellner, and Robert M. Helm. *Studies in Nietzsche and the Judaeo-Christian Tradition.* Chapel Hill: The University of North Carolina Press. 1985.

Ott, Hugo. *Martin Heidegger: A Political Life.* Trans. Allan Blunden. New York: Basic Books. 1993.

Patzia, Arthur G. *Ephesians, Colossians, Philemon.* Vol. x of *New International Biblical Commentary.* Ed. W. Ward Gasque. Peabody, Massachusetts: Hendrickson Publishers. 1990.

Perkins, Pheme. "Philippians: Theology for the Heavenly Politeuma." *Pauline Theology,* I: *Thessalonians, Philippians, Galatians, Philemon.* Ed. Jouette M. Bassler. Minneapolis: Fortress Press. 1991.

Pippin, Robert B. "Nietzsche, Heidegger and the Metaphysics of Modernity." *Nietzsche and Modern German Thought.* Ed. Keith Ansell-Pearson. New York: Routledge. 1991.

Plato. "Phaedo." Trans. R. S. Bluck. *The Dialogues of Plato.* New York: Bantam Books. 1986. 63–134.

Pöggeler, Otto. *Martin Heidegger's Path of Thinking.* Trans. Daniel Magurshak and Sigmund Barber. 1987. Atlantic Highlands, New Jersey: Humanities Press International, Inc. 1990.

Rad, Gerhard von. *Old Testament Theology.* 2 vols. Trans. D. M. G. Stalker. New York: Harper and Row. 1965.

Rapaport, Herman. *Heidegger and Derrida: Reflections on Time and Language.* Lincoln: University of Nebraska Press. 1989.

Ricoeur, Paul. *The Symbolism of Evil.* Trans. Emerson Buchanan. New York: Harper & Row. 1967.

The Conflict of Interpretations. Ed. Don Ihde. Evanston, Illinois: Northwestern University Press. 1974.

The Philosophy of Paul Ricoeur. Ed. Charles E. Reagan and David Stewart. Boston, Massachusetts: Beacon Press. 1978.

From Text to Action: Essays in Hermeneutics, II. Trans. Kathleen Blamey and John B. Thompson. Evanston, Illinois: Northwestern University Press. 1991.

Ridderbos, Herman. *Paul: An Outline of His Theology.* Trans. John Richard de Witt. Grand Rapids, Michigan: William B. Eerdmans Publishing Company. 1975.

The Ryrie Study Bible. New American Standard Version. Ed. Charles Cadwell Ryrie. Chicago: Moody Press. 1978.

Scharlemann, Robert P., ed. *Negation and Theology*. Charlottesville: University Press of Virginia. 1992.

Scheler, Max. *Ressentiment*. Trans. William W. Holdheim. Ed. Lewis A. Coser. New York: Free Press of Glencoe. 1961.

Schneidau, Herbert. "The Word Against the Word: Derrida on Textuality." *Derrida and Biblical Studies*. Ed. Robert Detweiler. Special issue of *Semeia* 2.3 (1982): 5–28.

Schopenhauer, Arthur. *The World as Will and Representation*. 2 vols. Trans. E. F. J. Payne. New York: Dover Publications, Inc. 1969.

Arthur Schopenhauer: Essays and Aphorisms. Trans. and Ed. R. J. Hollingdale. Middlesex, England: Penguin Books Ltd. 1970.

Schrag, Calvin O. *Existence and Freedom: Toward an Ontology of Human Finitude*. Evanston: Northwestern University Press. 1961.

Silverman, Hugh J. and Don Ihde, eds. *Hermeneutics and Deconstruction*. New York: State University of New York Press. 1988.

Stack, George J. *Kierkegaard's Existential Ethics*. The University of Alabama Press. 1977.

Stambaugh, Joan. "Nihilism and the End of Philosophy." *Research in Phenomenology* 15 (1985): 79–97.

Steiner, George. *Martin Heidegger*. Great Britain: Harvester Press. 1978.

Real Presences. The University of Chicago Press. 1989.

Strozier, Robert M. *Derrida, and the Metaphysics of Subjectivity*. New York: Mouton de Gruyter. 1988.

Talbert, Charles H. *Reading Corinthians: A Literary and Theological Commentary on 1 and 2 Corinthians*. New York: Crossroad. 1987.

Taminiaux, Jacques. *Heidegger and the Project of Fundamental Ontology*. Trans. Michael Gendre. New York: SUNY Press. 1991.

Taylor, Mark C. *Deconstructing Theology*. New York: The Crossroad Publishing Company. 1982.

Tears. State University of New York Press. 1990.

Tertulian, Nicolas. "The History of Being and Political Revolution," in *The Heidegger Case: On Philosophy and Politics*. Ed. Tom Rockmore and Joseph Margolis. Philadelphia: Temple University Press. 1992.

Theological Dictionary of the New Testament. 10 vols. Trans. Geoffrey W. Bromiley. Ed. Gerhard Kittel and Gerhard Friedrich. 1964. Grand Rapids, Michigan: William B. Eerdmans Publishing Company. 1983.

Theological Dictionary of the New Testament. Trans. and abridged Geoffrey W. Bromiley. Ed. Gerhard Kittel and Gerhard Friedrich. Grand Rapids, Michigan: William B. Eerdmans Publishing Company. 1985.

Vaughan, Curtis. "Colossians." Vol. XI of *The Expositor's Bible Commentary*. 12 vols. Ed. Frank E. Gaebelein. Grand Rapids, Michigan: Zondervan Publishing House. 1978. 161–226.

Vos, Geerhardus. *The Pauline Eschatology.* 1930. Grand Rapids, Michigan: Baker Book House. 1979.

Wilder, Amos. *Eschatology and Ethics in the Teaching of Jesus.* 1939. Westport, Connecticut: Greenwood Press Publishers. 1950.

Willis, Wendell, ed. *The Kingdom of God in 20th-Century Interpretation.* Peabody, Massachusetts: Hendrickson Publishers. 1987.

Wolosky, Shira. "Derrida, Jabès, Levinas: Sign-Theory as Ethical Discourse." *Prooftexts: A Journal of Jewish Literary History* 2.3 (1982): 282–302.

Wyschogrod, Michael. *Kierkegaard and Heidegger: Ontology of Existence.* New York: Humanities Press. 1969.

Zimmerman, Michael E. *Eclipse of the Self: The Development of Heidegger's Concept of Authenticity.* Athens: Ohio University Press. 1981.

Index

Printed in the United Kingdom
by Lightning Source UK Ltd.
9744400001B/199